# Combat Trauma

# Combat Trauma

*Imaginaries of War and
Citizenship in
Post-9|11 America*

## Nadia Abu El-Haj

**VERSO**
London • New York

First published by Verso 2022
© Nadia Abu El-Haj 2022

1 3 5 7 9 10 8 6 4 2

**Verso**
UK: 6 Meard Street, London W1F 0EG
US: 388 Atlantic Avenue, Brooklyn, NY 11217
versobooks.com

Verso is the imprint of New Left Books

ISBN-13: 978-1-78873-842-2
ISBN-13: 978-1-78873-844-6 (US EBK)
ISBN-13: 978-1-78873-843-9 (UK EBK)

**British Library Cataloguing in Publication Data**
A catalogue record for this book is available from the British Library

**Library of Congress Cataloging-in-Publication Data**
A catalog record for this book is available from the Library of Congress

Typeset in Sabon by MJ & N Gavan, Truro, Cornwall
Printed and bound by CPI Group (UK) Ltd, Croydon, CR0 4YY

*For Aya*

# Contents

# Introduction

Esther Schrader, writing in the *Los Angeles Times* in 2004, was one of the first journalists to report a developing mental health emergency among American military personnel returning from war. She described soldiers like Matt LaBranche who were coming home with "their bodies whole but their psyches deeply wounded" in numbers that seemed, to mental health experts, to indicate a looming crisis. "One out of six soldiers returning from Iraq is suffering the effects of post-traumatic stress," Schrader reported, "and as more come home, that number is widely expected to grow."[1] LaBranche is described as a soldier with "no history of mental illness" who returned "a different person": angry, suffering, unable to get painful images out of his head, newly violent toward his wife and children. Echoing Schrader, a growing number of articles reported on wounded and traumatized soldiers facing neglect and not receiving treatment they desperately needed.[2] To Schrader and other observers, this seemed to preface a repeat performance of what had happened decades ago after soldiers returned from the war in Vietnam. Citing mental health experts, she proposed that "if Iraq veterans can be helped sooner, they may fare better than those who fought in Vietnam."[3] As the post-9/11 wars have ground on, year after year, decade upon decade, accounts of the devastating psychological afterlives of combat became ever more ubiquitous in the public domain.

The traumatized soldier is an old and enduring figure in the American social and political imaginary. He emerges during the Civil War with concern over "soldier's heart," a disorder manifested through constricted breath and palpitations, understood to signify mental and not just physiological distress.[4] He moves through the shell-shocked soldier of World War I, the veteran suffering "combat fatigue" in World War II, and appears in deeply fraught arguments over "post–Vietnam syndrome" and post-traumatic stress disorder (PTSD) in the aftermath of the American war in Vietnam. Yet there remains something distinctive in its most recent iteration during the long "War on Terror." In contrast to earlier appearances, in the new millennium, combat trauma is recognized as a legitimate diagnosis in military medicine and widely accepted as real, painful, and debilitating by the public at large. What's more, this acceptance of combat trauma coincides with decades-long wars in Afghanistan and Iraq, during which fewer than one percent of US citizens served in the military. The result, according to a broad array of voices, is a "civil-military divide" that cleaves the nation in two. At the intersection of these two realities—two decades of war and but a fraction of citizens waging it—combat trauma has become one powerful iterative ground on which the so-called War on Terror appears on the home front, perhaps, for the public at large, the primary one. And on the terrain of this "combat-trauma imaginary," as I will call it, a particular ethics and politics of citizenship find form.

The US invasions and occupations of Iraq and Afghanistan are the first sustained, combat-intensive American wars launched in an era when both the medical profession and the American public recognize post-traumatic stress disorder as a common and real response to myriad encounters with violence, including, archetypally perhaps, combat. In newspaper and magazine articles, on radio and television newscasts, through novels, poetry, memoirs, movies, and television series, depictions of soldiers returning from the war zone with serious psychological wounds are ubiquitous.⁵ Moreover, although current discourse works with more than one image of the "traumatized vet," in contrast to the late 1970s and early 1980s, when Hollywood began its reckoning with the American war in Vietnam, the popular culture figures we are seeing now are by and large neither *Apocalypse Now* nor Rambo-type figures. They tend not to be soldiers so damaged by war that they wreak havoc and terror on the battlefield and at home. Today's image of the traumatized soldier depicts a suffering subject. The appropriate response is sympathy rather than fear or even simple hero worship.⁶

The national conversation about the post-9/11 wars, such as it is, has been mediated to a great extent through representations of the psychic life of the American soldier-cum-veteran. The starting point for this book is to ask: with what consequences? What does war appear to be when it is discussed, represented, and grasped primarily through the lens of the soldier, now home, living with PTSD, at risk of suicide, and grappling with "moral injury"—a different and purportedly novel understanding of the "invisible wounds" of war? And what might be the crucial political conversations that, simply in failing to appear, are excluded from public debate and consciousness, when so much of the focus is on the trauma suffered by American troops?

This book brings an anthropological sensibility to the post-9/11 wars and the militarism of contemporary American society, and it does so by considering the optics of a powerful and pervasive stand-in for these wars: the figure of the traumatized American soldier. It sets out to understand the ethics, politics, and attendant obligations of citizenship that are at work in and through this figure. I do not produce an account of "what it is like to go to war."⁷ A growing journalistic and scholarly literature tells the story of the wars from the soldier's point of view: by reporters embedded in the war zone or back home with veterans; by scholars who have done ethnographic fieldwork on military bases or at military and Veterans Administration (VA) hospitals, including anthropologists writing about the post-9/11 wars.⁸ By way of contrast, I choose not to crawl into "the military bed," to borrow Elliott Colla's felicitous term.⁹ Accounts from the perspective of the military bed can produce powerful insights into the experiences of war for American troops and the often devastating afterlives; some even provide critical readings of militarism, patriotism, and homecoming.[10] Nevertheless, because they are embedded in the soldier's point of view, they never escape an American national-imperial frame. Rather than achieving some measure of critical distance, accounts of the lives of soldiers and veterans told from their own points of view, whether in literature, film, television, war reporting, scholarship, or journalism, tend to reproduce the basic terms of what Americans have come to expect of a "good war story"—that is, as Viet Thanh Nguyen writes, one that keeps the soldier front and center.[11]

While no doubt offering lessons in what it is like to go to and return from war, arguably of value in a nation-state with no universal draft, such narratives nevertheless misrepresent American military violence across the globe. Critical intentions aside, a "good war story" renders the war and all the attendant suffering an almost exclusively American affair, effacing the US military's destruction of the lives of Others. Although war stories told from the soldier's point of view sometimes mention or represent in passing those on the receiving end of American military violence, sometimes even offering a fleeting moment of sympathy or recognition for the Other civilians, they quickly move on because *their* story is not the topic at hand.[12] Iraqis or Afghans appear only as backdrops, not as subjects articulating their own perspectives on and experiences of war. Frequently enough, when they do appear, it is as the cause of the trauma the American soldier suffers.[13]

Rather than trouble the foundations of American militarism, good war stories instead are a building block of the very discursive and institutional frameworks that reproduce the militarism that sustains American wars.[14] And there is far more at stake here than overlooking or misrepresenting the Other. This genre of recounting war endangers the very possibility of political critique. Readers are often addressed in terms of an American national "we" and are called upon to understand and be compassionate vis-à-vis the soldier's experience of war. A good war story is simultaneously an epistemological demand: Defer to the soldier's point of view! What it is like to go to war and what it is like to "know" war become one and the same thing. The combatant's truth becomes the truth of war.[15]

Anthropologist Kenneth MacLeish wrote in his study of soldiers at Fort Hood that he "made a deliberate decision ... to steer clear of direct engagement with the subject of killing." The decision came in part, he explains, as "an outgrowth of the ethnographic material: soldiers spoke far more about feelings of vulnerability and exposure than they did about killing."[16] Why did they speak so little about killing, one might ask? Is it that killing is so taken for granted? Is it that it is too painful to discuss? Might it matter to engage the subject of killing in a book about "making war," even if soldiers themselves rarely discussed it? Or, as Zoë Wool recounts, "At war and at home soldiers talk about what they do as 'a job' or 'work' more often than anything else," even as her informants suffer immensely this "job's" afterlives.[17] And yet, "Even when he wishes it were, a *soldier's work is not allowed to be the same as a carpenter's*; the violence that is its most fundamental characteristic is framed and reframed again and again, continually calling forth some kind of accounting or justification."[18]

Surely, even if national sacrifice and the trope of heroism are worthy targets of critique, we should not concede the point that doing the work of the military, that fighting wars, is *just another job* or simply a matter of soldier vulnerability. Such deference to the soldier's point of view sidesteps the crucial questions of what the wars are for and whether they are legitimate or just. It effaces the experiences of those on the receiving end of American military violence, combatants and civilians alike, who might well consider destruction and killing to be the central task of American soldiers and of war itself.[19] And it sidesteps the question of responsibility and culpability for the wars that is borne by *all* American citizens, soldiers and the public alike. Moreover, it echoes a pervasive sense in American society that those who have not gone off to war can never really know what war is like and as such must defer to those who do. The American public is not entitled to judge. No matter its explicit political commitments or claims, in other words, a good war story is not—and can never be—anti-war.[20]

Even as I refuse to embed myself ethnographically in the soldiers' points of view, I put the *figure* of the traumatized soldier center stage in my account. He is perhaps the paramount figure through which the post-9/11 wars appear for and are engaged by the American public. This book provides an account of this figure in terms of who he has been, who he is now, and how he came to be, and it explores the essential work he does in stifling political critique and in sustaining and suborning American militarism in the post-9/11 era in the process. Many scholars, journalists, and (ex-)soldiers have argued not simply that the American public is disengaged, but also that the War on Terror is absent from American consciousness. That is an accurate description only if one presumes that the (returned) soldier has nothing to do with the war.[21] The *figure* of the traumatized soldier and veteran is very present to the public. Perhaps one could say, from an American point of view, he *is* the war.

By exploring the figure of the traumatized soldier in public culture, I aim to destabilize received truths about America's post-9/11 wars—among liberals and conservatives alike. What if the truth is that the wars have been, in fact, ubiquitous in American consciousness but appear through the figure of the soldier, rather than the actual conduct of the war on the ground and the subjects and forms of life that he has put in harm's way? What if the ceaseless demand for public "recognition" of and improved care for the traumatized soldier is not an unequivocal ethical good, as it might seem to be when measured against the supposed neglect and warehousing of veterans in the aftermath of the American war in Vietnam? What if this incessant demand that attention be paid—that "we" must do a better job of recognizing and caring for the troops—is among the incitements to American militarism, in helping attach the American public to the virtue of the soldier and, thereby, to the project of war?

In the chapters that follow, I trace shifting institutional, disciplinary, and discursive orientations through which the science of psychiatry, in tandem with domestic political struggles and imperial hubris, created the political conditions for the American empire's self-reproduction through war. The book gives an account of PTSD and its changing meanings and referents inside the psychiatric profession over the past five decades. And it explores the ways in which different clinical theories of combat trauma emerge from within and reshape political and ethical practices as well as common-sense assumptions about war and its afterlives. The different ways in which the field of psychiatry has defined combat trauma and approached healing war's psychic wounds, I argue, have had political consequences that reach well beyond seemingly arcane disciplinary debates about etiology and clinical care. Theories of combat trauma have been taken up, reinterpreted, and harnessed by citizens in a variety of contexts through discourses and practices that frame particular public engagements, such as they are, with war.

The book unfolds along several narrative and analytic arcs. Broadly construed, this is a genealogical account of the diagnostic category of PTSD within the field of American psychiatry, as well as an anthropological and social theoretical engagement with war, militarism, and citizenship writ large. In interrogating key moments in the origins and peregrinations of PTSD as a diagnostic category, I pay attention to its movements back and forth between a focus on "military" as distinct from "civilian" trauma. I explore, in clinical and social contexts, why and how American psychiatry has framed and reframed PTSD in the ways it has from the 1970s to the present and with what clinical and political consequences. First articulated in the early-to-mid 1970s as the "post-Vietnam syndrome," it gave way by the mid-1980s to an understanding of PTSD as a "condition of victimhood," an arc through which "civilian" trauma came into focus for American psychiatry, with the result that perpetrators abroad could become victims at home.[22]

During the so-called War on Terror, the etiologies and symptomology of PTSD have been redefined once again. Efforts have been underway since the early aughts to expand the parameters of the diagnostic category and to delimit distinct and/or supplemental conditions appearing in these latest American wars, including traumatic brain injury (TBI)—an organic injury to the brain understood to be the result of blast injuries—and moral injury, sometimes referred to as an injury to the soul. While TBI has been the subject of far more extensive clinical research, moral injury is more central to my concerns in this book: Even if many of its symptoms overlap with those of PTSD, as a physiological injury, TBI operates within a very different medical and moral grammar.[23] Trauma in the sense of psychological and/or moral suffering—even if regarded as having neurological or genetic components—is a different kind of "injury" than TBI, and it circulates within and informs social and political imaginaries in distinct ways, as I elaborate in this book.

The book also traces the concept of soldier trauma as it is taken up within wider communities of practice and discourse about healing, citizenship, national obligation, and war. I revisit the political activism of anti-war psychiatrists and veterans defining and treating soldier trauma during and in the immediate aftermath of the American war in Vietnam; I likewise examine what is, for the most part, a self-avowedly moral rather than political discourse that drives the work of theologians, nonprofit organizations, and churches in the present moment to confront and respond to the psychological or, as they term it, "moral" pain resulting from these more recent wars.

In contrast to widespread talk about moral obligation, I approach the pervasive contemporary public discourse about combat trauma and the need for the American public to care for returning soldiers—or, in the parlance, to "support the troops"— as decidedly political. To grapple with the trauma experienced by American military personnel is to always raise the question of America's wars abroad and the attendant issues of imperial violence, political responsibility, moral obligation, and citizenship at home, even if only through a deafening silence. In the here and now, I argue, the discourse of soldier trauma, framed as a "moral" obligation purportedly shorn of "politics"—that is, that one must support the troops regardless of whether or not one supports the war—is a fundamental building block of American militarism.

There is a long-standing argument, reaching back in most accounts to the American war in Vietnam, regarding the political implications of framing soldiers' struggles with the wars they have fought in the language of "trauma." According to sociologist Jerry Lembcke, "Prior to 1972 ... the image of veterans marching arm-and-arm with other anti-war activists dominated the American view of their return." The figure of the returning soldier was more political than medical. Returning soldiers joined anti-war protests and lent their experience and knowledge of war to the cause. But all that was to change. By the early 1970s, Lembcke maintains, with the introduction of "post-Vietnam syndrome" to describe the mental suffering experienced by returning vets, and subsequently of PTSD as the official diagnosis, conversations about "the trauma-stricken veteran" came to dominate the public sphere. The radical behavior and influence of veterans opposed to the war was pathologized and thereby depoliticized.[24]

Scholars such as Allan Young, Ben Shephard, Wilbur Scott, and Didier Fassin and Richard Rechtman tell a similar story of depoliticization. As each of them argues in their own way, the success of the struggle by anti-war psychiatrists and veterans to convince the American Psychiatric Association of the reality of combat trauma paradoxically marked the moment when the political and ethical questions of trauma and war were set aside. Once PTSD was established as a recognized condition in 1980, the brutal behavior of American troops in Vietnam was "normalized" as but an outcome of the fog of war, albeit a pathological one. Scholars of the post-9/11 wars also question the consequences of the power of PTSD as a diagnostic category, but they do so through a different set of questions. For example, with PTSD's focus on the individual patient, and given its simple and linear understanding of the causes and lived experiences of war-zone trauma, PTSD does not account for the phenomenology of soldiers' suffering, which is "collective, chronic, generalized," and not defined by a clear, originary event. That is, PTSD cannot address the question of what it is like to "make war."[25]

The purpose of this book is not to rehearse such arguments nor to accept *a priori* their underlying assumptions. It instead begins by recuperating a specific understanding of combat trauma that emerged in response to the American war in Vietnam, an understanding that I argue the scholarly literature, when it is not misconstruing it, passes over too quickly to capture fully its radical potential.[26] The concept of post-Vietnam syndrome, as it was understood at the time, entailed both a psychodynamic theory of combat trauma and a radical political critique of that war. It did not, *pace* Lembcke, depoliticize the figure of the anti-war vet. As initially framed, the trauma of American veterans centered on perpetration, not victimhood. Psychiatric discourse and radical politics, healing and anti-war activism were cut from the same cloth: Recognizing the trauma of American troops in the late 1960s and early 1970s did not require denying or sidelining the harms they had wrought on Vietnam and its citizens, imperial harm that expanded into Laos and Cambodia as the years wore on. Rather than reading the (mis)treatment of Vietnam veterans as something that "haunts" American society today, as is often the case, in Chapter 1 I argue that the ways in which the trauma of combat was initially articulated by psychiatrists and anti-war veterans presents us with a radical model worthy of revisiting. In the spirit of developing a politically critical engagement with the post-9/11 wars, the concept of post-Vietnam Syndrome required neither denying the postwar psychological suffering with which many a veteran lives nor refusing to engage in a sustained critical analysis and conversation about US global power and hubris and the damage these unleash on the world.

I then turn to trace the shifts through which PTSD has gone over the intervening decades to mean and to do something very different: During the 1980s, PTSD was refigured as a consequence of victimhood and emerged as one building block of conservative efforts to rewrite the history of the Vietnam War and its veterans. Part of the transformation is specific to the discipline of psychiatry: American psychiatry moved ever further away from a more humanist and psychodynamic frame, embracing instead biophysiological models of mental disorder, cognitivist-behavioral therapies, and what has come to be known as "evidence-based medicine." But as Chapter 2 shows, that is only one piece of a far more complicated tale. At the moment of the Reagan "revolution" and the effort to reconstruct the meaning of the American war in Vietnam—when the narrative first emerged that American society is "haunted" by its failure there—two otherwise disparate movements converged on PTSD to seek public and legal recognition of harms suffered. A white, conservative "victims-of-crime" movement, on the one hand, and feminist activists fighting for the recognition of rape and sexual assault, on the other, together transformed PTSD into a condition of victimhood and established its ubiquity and power in the American social and political landscape. The differences between the conception of combat trauma initially articulated by critics of the war in Vietnam and that of "civilian trauma," as focused on by the discipline of psychiatry beginning in the 1980s and as understood by the American public by the turn of the millennium, were vast and consequential, both clinically and politically, as would become apparent when the United States entered into its new round of sustained counterinsurgency wars.

What happens in the post-9/11 period when large numbers of soldiers returning from war zones are diagnosed as suffering from PTSD? What do psychologists do with evidence-based treatment protocols for PTSD that were developed largely based on the experiences of victims of single, violent incidents (especially sexual assault) when treating the psychological wounds of soldiers returning from war? How do they grapple with the etiology and phenomenology of soldier trauma? Chapters 3 and 4 follow the work of military and VA-affiliated psychiatrists and psychologists researching and treating trauma in military and veteran populations. I trace shifting clinical approaches to combat trauma, including discussions of "moral injury," and I argue that those developments not only redefine trauma once again, they also trouble, if only ever so slightly, the psychiatric profession's commitment to biophysiological models of mental illness, with consequences for how one understands the psychiatric subject, and thereby what it may take for her to heal. More broadly, I situate those clinical interventions within the larger context of the military's interest in and federal funding for treating the psychological wounds of war: If in the latter years of the war in Vietnam, talk of combat trauma—a pervasive "post-Vietnam syndrome"—was understood by both the Nixon administration and the military as signaling anti-war activism, recognizing and treating combat trauma today is just one more essential component of making war. At the convergence of evidence-based medical approaches to PTSD and the increasing attention paid by the Department of Defense and VA to combat's inevitable and, presumably, treatable "invisible wounds," it is hard to find the political and ethical commitments central to the work of psychiatrists and veterans who, decades ago, grappled with the meaning and afterlives of the American war in Vietnam.

Chapters 5 and 6 turn to the broader public domain and explore various contexts in which the figure of the traumatized soldier, tethered to particular clinical understandings of soldier trauma, appears and circulates in American society writ large. This book is not simply an account of changes in the American psychological professions' categorizations and treatments of trauma. Most centrally, it provides a reading of the ways in which a broader world has taken up that language and imagery, as my attention to the work of churches, nongovernmental organizations, and a prevalent public discourse makes clear. The figure of the traumatized soldier, along with the debt and sympathy presumed to be owed that figure, saturates American public culture, making it difficult to speak—even think, perhaps—a radical critique of US empire and militarism. The book's closing chapters examine ways in which the American public—as members of charities, churches, and other nonprofit groups and projects, or simply as individuals—are working with or being called upon to respond to veterans and soldiers suffering the psychological wounds of war. I explore alternative languages of soldier trauma (as an encounter with radical evil, as sin) as well as other modalities of healing—pastoral care, rituals, theater—that both draw upon and operate in tandem and sometimes in competition with psychiatric medicine. Shared among these alternative approaches is the idea that healing can only happen through "community." Soldiers' healing is articulated as a (national and/ or religious) collective project; all citizens are duty-bound, *at least rhetorically*, to take part, while at one and the same time, political questions about the wars or concerns about those Others who have been harmed by the US military and its personnel are largely excluded from the communities of practice and conversation I describe.

Finally, in Chapter 6, I parse a discourse about the so-called civil-military divide, analyzing the ways in which soldier trauma frames public conversations about war, about what it means to know war, who *can know* war, and the American public's responsibility to care for those who "have served." As we will see, political speech is replaced in this discourse by a language of moral obligation, and a concern with the national self displaces what Hannah Arendt called for as "care for the world," the political act of collectively engaging, *thinking with and as* one another in order to build a common world.[27]

Taken together, the chapters that follow tell a story about how the PTSD diagnostic, born initially of a radical, anti-imperial, and anti-war politics articulated in psychiatric terms has emerged as one of the pillars holding up the enormous edifice of what Andrew Bacevich has named "the new American militarism."[28] Filtered through a decades-long history during which the American war in Vietnam was reconstructed as part and parcel of the nation's shift to the political right, the discourse of soldier trauma—indeed, one might say, the rhetorical obsession with it—in the post-9/11 era suborns a decidedly different politics from what we saw in the latter years of the war in Vietnam. The way it has appeared for the duration of the wars, PTSD focuses attention almost exclusively on the so-called warriors and declares it an obligation of "civilian" citizens to honor, listen to, and care for those sent off to war "in our name."

And *pace* David Kieran's argument, I insist, such public attention does not signal an anti-war politics.[29] (In August 2021, as
Afghanistan fell to the Taliban, the plight of refugees—more
specifically, of Afghan allies left behind—finally garnered public
attention, but it was very short lived and, to say the least, too
little, too late.) Moreover, the epistemological (and aesthetic)
politics associated with the diagnosis privileges the soldier as the
only citizen who can ever really know war, such that the ethical
obligation to care for the troops sidelines the very possibility of
debating the justness of the wars or acknowledging the harms
that the US military has inflicted on societies and persons so very
far away—which is to say, it erodes the possibility of politics
itself. Accordingly, some of the most central and urgent questions have been largely foreclosed: Were these wars legitimate?
What were their goals? What specifically has the American military been doing overseas? Whom has it harmed? What might
US citizens, soldiers and non-soldiers alike, owe those Others
who, for decades now, have been subjected to the onslaught of
American military violence and who have to live with its long-
term consequences as the United States cuts and runs? Even if
not entirely absent from the public domain, such questions have
been neither central to nor sustained in discussions of America's
post-9/11 wars.

To be clear, the figure of the Iraqi or Afghan killed or harmed
does appear in talk of war—civilian casualties are mentioned and
discussed, albeit often as the cause of the combat trauma from
which many an American soldier now suffers. Nevertheless, to
borrow a distinction made by philosopher Stanley Cavell, such
facts may be "known," but they are rarely "acknowledged": The
destruction of others' homes, villages, and lives has not arisen
as a matter of urgent public concern and action in the American
public domain. This is true even among progressive political
movements that emerged and became increasingly consequential
during the Trump presidency: They were far more focused on
and animated by other political crises—racist policing, migrant
detention, the Muslim ban—than by the fact that the US was
and *still is at war*.[30] Today's combat-trauma imaginary, in short,

14

has generated a deafening silence about what should be urgent and pressing political questions bearing on life, death, and the global reach of US military power. And through this silence, the American public is conscripted into the work of war. Simply put: one cannot "support the troops"—certainly not in the sense in which that slogan is understood today—and at the same time oppose the wars.

## Humanitarianism at Home, Imperial War Abroad

The "trauma imaginary," by which I mean a set of fundamental assumptions and taken-for-granted truths about the nature of trauma that are widely shared in US society, extends well beyond its more specific iteration as a consequence of combat.[31] Up until the early to mid-1980s, the traumatized subject—soldiers returning from war, women in the aftermath of rape, children in the aftermath of incest—was often an object of suspicion. Was the soldier perhaps unpatriotic, a malingerer, or a drug addict whose addiction had nothing to do with the war? Did incest or rape really precipitate long-term psychological distress? Was the girls' and women's involvement in the incident really all that innocent?[32]

By the time of the 9/11 attacks on New York and Washington, DC, a different clinical truth and cultural sensibility had taken hold in regard to the traumatized subject. The prevailing common sense was that people who are subjected to violence suffer trauma, and they require—and *deserve*—immediate attention. That commitment was evident in one of the initial steps taken following the collapse of the Twin Towers in lower Manhattan. The city mobilized thousands of mental health personnel to attend to the city's citizens—residents and first responders alike. It was widely predicted that not just the city but the nation as a whole was about to witness an increase in cases of PTSD. Millions of Americans had watched the collapse of the Twin Towers on live television, and the expectation was that they would be traumatized for days, weeks, and even years to come. As Didier Fassin and Richard Rechtman put it, "after the mourning, the trauma remains."[33] The psychological scars left by violence endure and they must be attended to.

Attending to the psychological scars left by violence would take on a different meaning and focus after the United States launched its post-9/11 wars. While it would be naive to claim that the military simply accepts PTSD as a recognized condition, that there is no longer any suspicion or stigma attached to the diagnosis, it is nevertheless the case that the military and the Veterans Administration, with its expansive network of hospitals and clinics, are paying far more sympathetic attention to the psychological wounds of combat in the post-9/11 era than during any previous American war. In July 2003, only four months after the United States invaded Iraq, the Army Surgeon General appointed a mental health advisory team (MHAT) to travel to the war theater and assess mental health issues among deployed troops.[34] The military may have underestimated how extensive psychological casualties would be, as controversies about military failures to adequately respond to PTSD and TBI have emerged and criticisms over the effectiveness of treatment protocols have proliferated.[35] Nevertheless, institutional attention to the mental health of soldiers and veterans of the post-9/11 wars has reached a level never seen before, a change that cannot be understood separately from a more general shift in how trauma and the traumatized subject have come to be recognized in social and political worlds beyond the military.[36]

Trauma's emergence as a powerful cultural idiom in the contemporary world is part and parcel of a broader reconfiguration of political sensibilities about care over the past several decades. This "new humanitarianism," as it is sometimes named, encompasses a few related phenomena that together signal a significant shift in political legibility, marking a transformation of left politics toward a focus on relieving human "suffering," rather than the fight for equality, justice, or material redistribution. The establishment of Médicins Sans Frontières (MSF) in Paris in 1971 is one event taken to mark the birth of this novel progressive sensibility.[37] Led by ex-Marxist intellectuals who had become disillusioned with both the European left and anti-colonial revolutions in the so-called Third World, a new form of activism emerged.[38] The goal was "not to improve the human condition, but to alleviate suffering wherever it occurs, in their case, in the form of emergency medical care."[39] Concerned primarily about those who "fall outside the ambit of care by nation-states" and driven by a commitment to care for "the disinherited of the world," practitioners of the new humanitarianism replaced a "politics of justice" with a "politics of compassion."[40] The famine in Ethiopia in the mid-1980s played a critical role in the organization's development, encouraging the focus of their work on bodily suffering.[41] By end of the decade, "humanitarian psychiatry" was born. Originating in the aftermath of the massive earthquake in Armenia in 1989, within ten years, "mental health specialists" were "indispensable" to the work of organizations such as MSF.[42]

The scope of the new humanitarianism involves more than just providing care, understood here, in contrast to Arendt's understanding, as a non-political act. New humanitarian workers understand themselves to be witnesses to the horrors the world chooses to ignore and they "speak in the name of those who are assumed not to have access to the public arena."[43] New humanitarian psychiatry, according to Fassin, is less a practice of "clinical evaluation" than of "moral judgment." Psychiatrists and psychologists witness and testify to the suffering of the people they encounter in the field: earthquake victims in Armenia in 1989, or Palestinian youth bearing the brunt of Israeli state violence post-2000 in Palestine. The aim of such testimony is to "evoke, in ordinary language, the experience of state brutality" and to generate sympathy "for the misfortune of one's neighbor." Such sympathy, it is presumed, will generate "the moral indignation that can prompt action to end it."[44] In the work of the new humanitarianism, in short, moral obligation— that is, an ethical turn—replaces talk of politics; the obligation to respond to emergencies, to relieve suffering—physiological and psychological alike—is understood as ideologically neutral and thus "post"-political.

A second, parallel transformation in global politics likewise signals a shift away from a language of political struggle toward one of moral duty. In the post–Cold War era, the United States and its NATO allies have launched military operations in the name of a "responsibility to protect."[45] According to Robert Meister, the end of the Cold War in 1989 gave birth to this "New Human Rights Regime." Wars are launched as humanitarian interventions. A new human rights regime imagines a future "after evil." It characterizes the twentieth century as "a century of genocide" and, taking up and generalizing the post-Holocaust sensibility of "never again," it insists on the "ethical imperative … to 'get it right' this time—to rescue the victims of a likely massacre before it is too late."[46] Within the logics of both the new human rights regime and contemporary humanitarianism, interventions are argued to be moral imperatives rather than political or self-interested acts. They aim to prevent cruelty and alleviate (imminent) suffering rather than establish political or economic justice. Who would not want to relieve the suffering of the child traumatized by war or occupation? Of the woman who has been trafficked and sexually abused?[47] The "post-1989 politics of human rights," in Meister's words, "presents itself as an *ethical* transcendence of the politics of revolution."[48]

In this book, I take arguments about the moral sensibilities that have framed humanitarianism and human rights interventions over the past several decades into a rather different field of operation, so as to examine the American political imaginary underwriting the post-9/11 wars—wars that were launched and sustained on explicitly ideological, that is, *political*—grounds. The suffering soldier, the need for compassion and the obligation to care, this discourse of humanitarian reason and its self-description as non- or post-political echoes through much of the conversation on the home front about the "costs" of the war, which is to say, the costs *to American troops*. Over the past two decades, the American public has been called upon to respond with compassion and care to the psychological suffering of those in the "all-volunteer force" (AVF) who have gone off to to support his contention. Wellman did not include Choate's examination of Wellman's doctor. Here it is:

Mr. Choate: Doctor, you said in your direct examination that you examined Mr. Sage and, if I understand you correctly, you said that you sought the first instance to locate his heart to learn how severe the shock was to him. Doctor, you realize you are under oath, and you don't mean to tell the court and jury that you went to the extent of trying to find Russell Sage's heart!

Witness: Yes.

Mr. Choate: With all your temerity in testifying, you would not be willing to state to the court and jury that you found Russell Sage's heart!

Witness: Yes.

Mr. Choate: You testified that on an occasion when an explosion like this takes place, there is an enlargement of the heart. You are not, I am sure, so reckless as to mean that you found an enlargement of Russell Sage's heart?

If you hold in your mind as you read this examination the fact that Sage was one of the richest and stingiest men in the world, you can well imagine the ironical humor skimmed off by Choate's examination.

There was another appeal, this time by Sage. The basis of the appeal was that the trial court had refused to give the following instruction tendered by Sage's counsel: "If the jury finds from the evidence that the defendant did take the plaintiff and use him as a shield, but that this action was involuntary, or such as would instinctively result from a sudden and irresistible impulse in the war "in our name."[49] Mental health practitioners in the military and the VA have been designing and refining clinical protocols in the hopes of developing more effective treatments for combat trauma. At the same time, organizations such as Volunteers of America and churches and clergy across the country have developed programs and invented rituals to help soldiers heal, evidence not merely of a particular moral sensibility but also of the neoliberal structural reality in which much of the work of "care" has been outsourced to private and, more specifically in the US, to religious organizations.[50] More generally, citizens who have not gone off to war have been called upon to recognize, listen to, and care for those who did and who are now suffering its afterlives. Theater of War, a nonprofit based in New York City, stages scenes from ancient Greek dramas not only on military bases, but also in fora that bring "civilians and veterans" together, in an effort to facilitate the expression of pain and rage on the part of soldiers and veterans and to encourage the nonmilitary public to listen to and recognize their pain, to help soldiers and the nation heal (see Chapter 5). Journalists and scholars have called on the American public to pay attention to the suffering soldiers and vets in their midst, to listen without judgment to their accounts of war, to help with the "largest reintegration" of military personnel into civilian life since the Vietnam war (Chapter 6). The general sensibility among those doing this kind of work is that support for the troops is sacrosanct, regardless of one's position on the wars. Supporting the troops is *not* a political act or choice. By and large, political debate about the virtue and conduct of the wars is extruded from this domain of care as discourse and practice. In its place, trauma—psychological pain sometimes framed as moral suffering—stands center stage. The question of violence, the violence perpetrated and suffered by American military personnel is reframed as a trauma that they suffer, and the subjective experience of the suffering soldier becomes the meaning of the war.[51]

## The Super-Citizen and the Civilian

In the War on Terror, we have an instance of humanitarian government with a rather significant twist, for it speaks in the language of the nation rather than humanity. It is also conditioned by a long arc of imperial hubris that arrogates to itself the right to invade and occupy other national territories and is sustained by an enduring belief in its own civilizational superiority, even if in its contemporary configuration it no longer has an appetite for an extended and costly civilizing mission.[52] The attacks on 9/11 occasioned a rearticulation of US power, global politics, militarism and war.[53] The so-called Global War on Terror was unleashed as retribution for the attacks on American cities, a war to defend "our way of life"—that is, Judeo-Christian civilization, secularism, and democracy—against the "barbarity" of (radical) Islam. A humanitarian emergency is no longer the name of the game. Whether in Afghanistan, where Al-Qaeda was located, or in Iraq on purely specious grounds, US ventures into those countries realized a shift in American militarism that had been long in the making. That is, despite an almost epochal break that echoes through the scholarly literature on the new international human rights regime, not all contemporary wars—and certainly not the so-called Global War on Terror—are waged on humanitarian pretenses.

As Andrew Bacevich has argued, George W. Bush's "doctrine of preventive war" was not new. With roots in the notion of "deterrence" in the post-1945 era, by the 1970s the doctrine was being rethought. "The big lesson" military theorists took from the American failure in Vietnam was not only that "soldiers needed new and better ways to fight."[54] The war also led security pundits like Albert Wohlstetter, the so-called "dean of American nuclear strategists," to develop such an expansive conception of American "vulnerability" that it muddied the waters between defensive and offensive military actions. In short, Wohlstetter believed, "Properly protecting America's safety and well-being required the ability to eliminate threats before they fully developed." From the Strategic Defense Initiative of the Reagan administration to a more general commitment to prevent future threats, Bacevich argues, the commitment to "*bringing force to bear to thwart possible aggression*" found its "clearest articulation" in the post-9/11 Bush Doctrine.[55]

The (partially) reconfigured US security state that came into being in the aftermath of 9/11, according to Joseph Masco, "constitutes a dangerous *future* as its object of concern."[56] In the invasions and occupations of Afghanistan and Iraq, in the war's reach into the so-called tribal regions of Pakistan, and as the War on Terror increasingly exceeds any territorial limits, with drone strikes and special operations forces far and wide, we see these wars being fought in categorically political terms: in defense of freedom, democracy, secularism, and "our way of life." But while a "language of hard-edged political struggle" grounds the call for war against the enemy abroad, it is a "discourse of sentimental humanitarianism"[57] that shapes discursive practices and institutional apparatuses at home, which articulate and enact a moral obligation to care for the troops who went off to war "in our name."

If there is a "responsibility to protect" in this way of thinking, it is the American soldier who needs protection from the trauma he has suffered. The pain and suffering toward which a presumptive "we" has an obligation to be compassionate is the pain and suffering of the Americans who prosecuted the war. These individuals, returning to Miriam Ticktin's words, do not "fall outside the ambit of care by nation-states," as do the subjects with whom international humanitarian organizations work.[58] They are the nation-state's iconic citizens. And yet, as Judith Herman wrote over three decades ago, "To hold traumatic reality in consciousness requires a social contract *that affirms and protects the victim.*"[59] The figure of the traumatized soldier does not fit seamlessly into this victim frame, and yet, as I argue in what follows, it feeds off of its ethical demand. The soldier is victim and iconic citizen at one and the same time, and the demand that the American public hold that citizen in high regard, that it care for and recognize its debt to this Janus-faced figure, is key to producing and sustaining a hyper-militaristic society that without a draft—without a massive military force—does not and cannot recognize itself as such.

## The Other 1 Percent

Who are these troops that the American public is supposed to support? Writing for *Time Magazine* in 2011, reporter Mark Thompson described an abyss dividing "the soldier" from "the civilian" in American society. He means by this that the vast majority of Americans who have not served in the military are on one side and soldiers are on the other. "Think of the military as the Other 1%," wrote Thompson, "some 2.4 million troops have fought in and around Afghanistan and Iraq since 9/11, exactly 1% of the 240 million Americans over 18."[60] Most of these volunteers come from the middle three quartiles of household income, which is to say, neither the very rich nor the very poor send their sons and daughters to the military in significant numbers; and, contrary to what is often assumed, the military's racial makeup adheres quite closely to the racial makeup of the society as whole, although as one moves up the ranks or into the special forces, that is far less true.[61] Being a soldier these days is largely a "middle-class" job, in an economy in which the middle class is faced with fewer and fewer avenues to economic security and social mobility.[62]

The all-volunteer force is a different military than the one that fought in Vietnam. Nevertheless, the distinctions are not quite as clear-cut as one might assume. It is definitely smaller, and yet, if today only 0.5 percent of the American population is in the military (as distinct from 1 percent of those over the age of 18), that number was 1.8 percent during the era of the war in Vietnam. Not an insignificant difference, but compare that to World War II, when 8.7 percent of American citizens were in the military.[63] In addition, even during the American war in Vietnam, only one-third of military personnel were drafted; the rest volunteered, albeit sometimes because volunteering gave them more control over which branch they would join and in what capacity. What's more, the draft was hardly equitable on either class or racial lines, and it became increasingly less so over time. In the words of *New York Times* reporter Daniel Phillips, "When the draft ended, there was a great deal of hand wringing amongst policy makers that that might cause things to become unequal ... And those hand wringers lost the argument because the draft was already really, really, unequal." Donald Trump's four deferments and exemptions were hardly an exception, notes Phillips: "If you were in college or had some connections you didn't have to serve. You could either get out of it entirely or at least get some plum assignment where you were likely not to get killed."[64]

The one thing the draft perhaps had going for it was geographic distribution. It brought citizens from across the country into the military. With the AVF, that is no longer the case.[65] As reported in the *Los Angeles Times* (in 2015), "Some 49 percent of the 1.3 million active-duty service members in the US are concentrated in just five states—California, Virginia, Texas, North Carolina and Georgia."[66] Or, as Phillips notes, The "old states of the confederacy ... totally overrepresent now in terms of the number of people per capita who enlist in the military." Geographic separation and the fact that increasing numbers of military families are living on "mega bases" concentrated "below the Mason-Dixon line" are making it less likely that average American citizens might be acquainted with any of their fellow citizens in the military.[67] Much of the data suggests that the most important factor in determining whether or not someone decides to enlist is "familiarity with the military," which, if true, means that a growing "civil-military" divide might be hard to avoid.

According to Amy Schafer, we are witnessing the development of a "military caste." As of 2015, 25 percent of new recruits had a parent who served in the military; expanding that to broader kinship networks (aunts/uncles, siblings, grandparent, cousins), the number rises to 75 percent.[68] "It's a family business," says Dave Borno, a retired Army lieutenant who was in command of all allied troops in Afghanistan in 2003–2004. With two sons in the Army, he notes, "my kids deploy around the world ...

their classmates as kids on military bases are the people they're fighting with."[69] As Schafer sees it, "for military kids you have to actively opt out from military service." For everyone else, you have to "opt in," and that may coincide with "significant societal pressure not to."[70]

The US military has been an AVF—a professional, or all-volunteer force—since President Richard Nixon ended the draft in 1973. And although the armed force that took shape post-draft was decades old by the turn of the new millennium, 9/11 marked a significant turning point in its history. The invasions of Afghanistan and Iraq are the first sustained American wars fought with the AVF. As the wars dragged on—now at its "end," the war in Afghanistan is the longest war in American history—the number of soldiers required has posed problems for the military, especially for the Army, which provides by far the largest percentage of troops deployed.[71] With no draft to increase the size of the military, soldiers and Marines have rotated repeatedly in and out of the war zones, with severe consequences for, among other things, their mental health (see Chapter 3). As Dave Phillips of the *New York Times* told the hosts of the podcast *Thank You for Your Service*, "guys who are my age have spent their entire lives fighting in Iraq and Afghanistan." He asks, "Is it fair for us to let a very small section of the population go back to Iraq and Afghanistan ten times?"[72]

## Military Exceptionalism: The Valorization and Victimization of US Soldiers

In *The Rise of the Military Welfare State*, Jennifer Mittelstadt describes how, beginning in the late 1970s, and then most decisively during the Reagan presidency, the military carved out its own space of exception in the US polity. Just as welfare programs faced precipitous declines in funding, "the military's social and economic support" expanded significantly.[73] In this way, "military service increasingly intertwined citizenship with entitlement," in contrast to most of America's allies. "From

Britain to the Netherlands to France," writes Mittelstadt, "both during the eras of conscription and volunteer forces, soldiers, like other citizens, gained most of their social welfare benefits via universal entitlements granted by the state." This exceptional "entitlement" of American military personnel, it is worth emphasizing, signified far more than material support: Throughout the 1970s and into the 1980s, the Army's officer corps and its civilian leadership "drew sharp lines differentiating military social and economic supports from civilian ones" on the grounds that the military was not just any other kind of job, and they found a staunch ally in President Reagan, who "arguably did more than anyone to advance the belief that military service constituted a special and elevated category." For Reagan, soldiers were the nation's "ideal citizens."[74] Together with his unwavering opposition to reinstituting the draft, as Andrew Bacevich argues, Reagan established "support *for* 'the troops'—as distinct from actual service *with* them—as the new standard of civic responsibility."[75] While the military and its social and economic support systems have undergone a variety of shifts over the past several decades, the soldier as ideal citizen has not only endured but become even more supercharged in the post-9/11 era.[76] With but a small fraction of the nation's citizens fighting seemingly endless wars, the "troops," as Bacevich notes, have emerged as "heroes to whom the nation owes an immense debt of gratitude."[77]

The significance and force of the so-called civil-military divide reaches far and wide. Profound questions of equity arise for a democratic state that increasingly "outsources" its fighting to an ever smaller and particular subset of the population, let alone to private contractors (aka. mercenaries), who go all but unaddressed and unacknowledged in conversations about the civil-military divide, heroism, and soldier trauma.[78] Profound political questions arise when military personnel are ideologically more conservative and Christian evangelical than the country as a whole.[79] And yet, rather than generating robust, political debates about citizenship, entitlement, and war, among other critical issues, a decline in the numbers of Americans over the age of eighteen enlisting in the US military has been accompanied by a rise in militarism: a respect for, deference to, and civic obligation towards the military and its personnel.

These two entangled phenomena—a general population with little contact with the military or its personnel, on the one hand, and a "sentimentalized version of the American military experience and an idealized image of the American soldier," on the other—have generated a distinct political reality, which I read differently than most journalists and scholars to date.[80] Many have argued that the wars are barely visible in American society, but that statement can be true only on the presumption that the constant invocation of the traumatized soldier in the public domain somehow fails to signal engagement with the wars. The military appears incessantly in public and political speech in the United States, particularly as to its personnel and the sacrifices they have made. In addition, while it is true that most American citizens are disengaged from political debates about war and peace, it may not be due just to a lack of interest but also as a consequence of a prevailing discourse insisting that citizens who have not served have neither much of a right nor much of an ability to speak about the wars, let alone criticize or question military personnel (see chapters 5 and 6). Chris Marvin, a former US helicopter pilot and platoon leader in Afghanistan as well as founder of Got Your 6, a veterans' support organization, was asked in an interview whether the valorization and glorification of the military might "contribute to a culture where it's forbidden to question or criticize the military itself."[81] His response was to state emphatically that such a culture is not a potential danger on the horizon. "That's where we are."[82]

As to how we got here, Marvin identifies two stereotypes of soldiers and veterans he sees circulating in film, television, and other media. There is the veteran-as-hero (valorization), and there is the veteran broken by the war (victimization). For Marvin, this is a study in contrasts. Yet, as the post-9/11 social and political imaginary has evolved, the two figures are neither at odds nor even all that distinct. Valorization and victimization are entangled—soldier trauma is heroic suffering—and together they shape the way the War on Terror has been engaged with and understood on the home front.

## The Soldier as Witness

It is no historical accident that one core task of humanitarian organizations over the last several decades of the twentieth century came to be witnessing the suffering of the oppressed. Noting that the practice of "recording testimonies" of war emerged earlier, historian Annette Wieviorka argues that World War II turned it into "a movement." Many of those who perished left behind personal accounts of the violence of the Nazi genocide. In the postwar period, first-person testimonies—accounts left behind and, even more centrally, testimonies of those who survived—served as evidence for the "demands for justice" that were being made. In Wieviorka's telling, the 1961 trial of Adolph Eichmann in a Jerusalem court marked "the advent of the witness." In that courtroom, survivor testimony took center stage. This was a history lesson told not just through the "cold" medium of history but via an "appeal to emotion."[83] By the end of the Eichmann trial, the "survivor" had acquired "a social identity" at the heart of which stood "a new function: to be the bearer of history." A decade later saw the founding of archival projects devoted to collecting and recording testimonies of Holocaust survivors, understood to be primary evidentiary grounds for writing the history of the genocide.[84] And over the decades to come, witnessing was transformed into a far broader phenomenon: "Politically, testimony ... acquired a visible presence in such varied contexts as truth commissions, human rights theories and humanitarian work."[85]

The witness, the survivor, the survivor as witness: as concepts and political figures, they came out of twentieth-century encounters with the extreme—the Holocaust and Hiroshima in particular.[86] Testimony would be a way of "repairing the irreparable." Testimony to such horrors also came to be understood as enacting "a duty to remember." By the end of the twentieth century, Wieviorka argues, the witness had been transformed into "an apostle and a prophet," bearing insights into evil and the depths to which humanity could sink that no one else could even fathom.[87] As the idea that encounters with the extreme generate trauma gained broad credibility,[88] so too did the assumption that survivors of traumatic experiences needed to speak their truth and be listened to and believed.[89] That is, the witness's prophetic quality was inseparable from her trauma. In the post-9/11 era in American society, one pervasive iteration of this grammar of trauma, witnessing, and truth-telling speaks of soldiers, combat, and war.[90]

The soldier as a witness to war is not new.[91] But located, as it is today, between the widespread recognition of the reality of traumatic injury, on the one hand, and the moral and political authority of the survivor as witness, on the other, the soldier-witness takes on a broad and powerful cultural significance. Yet, this particular survivor-qua-witness is complex. While prior witnesses spoke squarely as victims—survivors of the camps, survivors of the bombings of Hiroshima and Nagasaki, survivors of sexual assault—the soldier does not. Indeed, the soldier cannot occupy that political or ethical space. He is, to borrow Roy Scranton's term, a "trauma-hero."[92] Young, excited, patriotic, in search of adventure, he goes off to war only to come back in possession of insights that others cannot possibly fathom and he suffers psychological pain as a result. Combat is horror, but also invigorating; it is painful but also sublime. Upon his return, Scranton writes, the trauma-hero "struggles to turn the inassimilable reality of the traumatic event into narrative but finds himself blocked at every turn: the memories slip from his grasp, no one wants to hear about the horrors he's seen; and it is impossible for people who were not there to understand." The soldier "has learned 'momentous truths' about human existence that rend the illusory rules of modern civilization," truths that "no one wants to know."[93]

More akin to the Holocaust survivor than to the classic subject of humanitarian concern—say, the Palestinian child traumatized by Israeli state violence or the woman victim of sexual violence seeking asylum in France—the trauma-hero can and does speak for himself.[94] Soldiers have authority and credibility in the public arena; they are presumed to have not only the ability to speak but the *right to demand an audience*. The same is true of the rapidly proliferating literary canon emerging from these unfinished wars; it is "as if the truth of war experience" can be "expressed by no one other than armed combatants."[95] Whether as a writer of fiction or memoir, as a speaker to domestic audiences or merely as a soldier or veteran having an encounter at work or the university, when the soldier speaks of war it is often in speech acts that echo the grammar of identity politics. He grounds his knowledge in experiences only a soldier can lay claim to, and his subject position—as soldier, as veteran—is often framed and defined by a constitutive "injury" even as it is simultaneously tethered to the heroism of having stepped up, sacrificed, and served. The Other citizen—that is, the American "civilian"—is called upon to listen and to care.[96] In the final two chapters of the book, I examine the way such war stories are told, not as a form of literature but as rituals of healing and testimonies to soldiers' suffering. Such public narratives appear through a variety of often entangled practices and in a variety of settings. Storytelling is a therapeutic act, a way to *work through* the trauma; it is also an act of witnessing that teaches the American public what it is like to go to war.

There is a ubiquitous discourse that calls upon the American public not just to listen to but also to care for those who went to war in any number of ways. Churches and their members, non-governmental organizations (often Christian), as well as clergy and theologians have taken up the project of reintegrating veterans into the lives they left behind. As I elaborate in Chapter 5, some practitioners turn to pastoral care, which by and large replicates the post-political sensibility characterizing the work of the new humanitarians. Even as they adopt a specific, recent iteration of combat trauma as moral injury, they suggest that concepts like radical evil and sin are better descriptions of what soldiers encountered or committed in the war zone and that psychiatric medicine is not up to the task of healing these wounds of the soul. Others develop community-based rituals as supplements or alternatives to clinical care. As I discuss in Chapter 6, for those members of the American public not directly engaged in projects of veteran care and reintegration, care appears as a rhetorical and ideological command: "Civilians" have a duty to help reintegrate soldiers and veterans into everyday communities—at universities, in hometowns. With an emphasis on engaged listening and nonjudgment, I argue, the therapist's couch emerges as the felicitous form of "civilian" citizenship when faced with "those who have served."

Soldiers are the other 1 percent, the super-citizen to whom the American public both owes a debt and must defer. Such deference is a consequence not just of the soldier's valorization, however. It is difficult for Americans to question or critique the military today because of the way a soldier's valor is inseparable from his victimhood. The suffering of the trauma-hero must be attended to and the form that attention must take demands "the moralist anti-politics," to borrow Miriam Ticktin's words, of the new humanitarianism.[97] And this seemingly ethical and moral claim works in the service of a categorically nationalist, imperial, and militaristic project, society, and state.

The soldier as "super-citizen" is juxtaposed to the "civilian," a very different kind of American citizen in public discourse.[98] These civilians are not noncombatants in a war zone, not the inhabitants of territories that American soldiers invade and occupy. In everyday American parlance these days, "civilian" is most frequently meant to invoke the American citizen who never enlisted. As I discuss in Chapter 6, this civilian, with no experience of war, cannot for that very reason know anything meaningful about what it is like. This civilian is innocent, an innocence made possible by the sacrifice of soldiers who go off to war in her name. She owes soldiers an unrepayable debt for what they have sacrificed and suffered—and that means she must step up and *care*. As ubiquitous a figure the soldier is in the post-9/11 public domain, this imagined civilian powerfully condenses the depth of American militarism at home: *Citizens* have become *civilians*. Moreover, it powerfully condenses the distinct brutality of American militarism, in that only a nation with the imperial privilege of fighting its wars on someone else's soil can so commonly associate the term *civilian* with someone who is innocent of the violence and brutality of war.

The result is that difficult, uncomfortable, and yet essential political questions become hard to pose, let alone sustain. Even as some progressive lawmakers, activists, and veterans attempt to insert critiques of American militarism, imperial power, and war into national political priorities and debates, fundamental questions about the legitimacy of the wars, about their conduct, the global expansion of the US military, and about reparations for the millions of Iraqis, Afghans, and so many others who suffer US military violence remain, by and large, unacknowledged. For all the talk of a "civil-military" divide, the one point on which politicians and the public—left and right, liberal and conservative—seem for the most part to agree is on the respect owed by civilians to the military.[99] At this level of ideology, there is perhaps no civil-military divide at all. There is instead an entire nation deeply invested in the military, with citizens-turned-civilians united by both the pervasive absence of anti-militarist criticism and a commitment—even if merely a rhetorical one—to care.

# PART ONE

## FROM AGENT TO VICTIM

# 1

# Psychiatry as Radical Critique

## "Post-Vietnam Syndrome"

While the figure of the trauma-hero has deeper historical roots, I begin my account in the time of the Vietnam War because conversations in the post-9/11 era about the relationships among war, American troops, and the public at large continuously reference that earlier war. The combat-trauma imaginary of the new millennium emerges from a particular reading of the war and what is presumed to be its major lesson—that the mistreatment of US veterans by a hostile anti-war public upon their return from the battlefields of Vietnam must never be repeated. As I trace over the next two chapters, while during the war and in its immediate aftermath a pervasive political critique of the war and US military brutality on the battlefields was shared across diverse swaths of American society, a decade hence, the war had been transformed into an "American tragedy" and the critique redirected from US militarism as such onto the American public. In the words of one historian, "the deepest shame related to the Vietnam war" became "not the war itself, but America's failure to embrace its military veterans."[1]

The aftermath of American war in Vietnam is also a turning point in the development of clinical and public understandings of combat trauma. The inclusion of post-traumatic stress disorder as a category in the American Psychiatric Association's *Diagnostic and Statistical Manual* (DSM-III) in 1980 resulted from the demand to understand and treat traumatized combat veterans of the war. Initially driven by activism among anti-war veterans and their psychiatrist allies, by 1980, with the official recognition of PTSD, a fundamental shift had occurred. Trauma was legitimized as a real and painful afterlife of myriad encounters with violence.[2] As argued in much of the scholarly literature, this acknowledgement of PTSD had far broader implications. The fight to recognize the trauma of American veterans, Allan Young and Ben Shephard, among others, maintain, was the perfect remedy for the country's political divisions over the war. The focus on soldiers as traumatized "victims" allowed Americans of all stripes to set aside their political differences and focus instead on the suffering of veterans and their need to heal.

The war in Vietnam was not the moment when trauma emerged as a means of circling the wagons of care around US troops, however. Nor do stories of veterans being "spat upon" and abandoned by the public at large reflect what really happened. On the contrary, the American war in Vietnam had been singular in that veterans themselves took to the streets in significant numbers to oppose and demand an end to the war they had fought. Rather than being despised by the anti-war movement, by the 1970s anti-war veterans had become powerful and privileged voices in the struggle, in large part through the work of the organization Vietnam Veterans Against the War (VVAW). Moreover, anti-war veterans and psychiatrists working together developed the concept of "post-Vietnam syndrome," an understanding of combat trauma that refused to separate individual psychic trauma from politics—that is, from the imperial, racist, and destructive historical acts and events through which it was born. Perpetration and not victimization was seen to be the cardinal reason for postwar suffering.[3]

Over the next two chapters, I retell the genealogy of PTSD, taking another look at how combat trauma came to be absorbed within a humanitarian logic, which, in being shorn of a language of political struggle, came to speak only of victimhood, compassion, and care. While the scholarly literature tends to read the significance of post-Vietnam syndrome primarily from the perspective of its endpoint—the codification of PTSD and its incorporation into the DSM-III in 1980—I pause to unpack the concept and the problem space within which it emerged.[4] I begin by reconstructing the meaning of post-Vietnam syndrome in the early to mid-1970s and the struggle to get the American Psychiatric Association (APA) to recognize the trauma of American veterans, and then I turn to give an account of the transformation of PTSD in the decade to come. I extend the origin story of PTSD into an era of postwar conservative politics, during which the American political imaginary was being reshaped in fundamental ways.

As I show, the figure of the traumatized American veteran operated in the 1970s within a complex ethical and political field in which recognizing that many returning veterans were suffering from trauma was not taken to exempt them or the US public at large from political and moral responsibility for their actions on the battlefields of Vietnam. Neither the psychiatrists who theorized post-Vietnam syndrome nor the veterans with whom they worked sought in any simple sense to cast returning soldiers as "victims." On the contrary, in this understanding of combat trauma, moral transgression—that is, the perpetration of violence—was often the primary cause of psychological pain. And psychiatrists and veterans alike insisted that recognizing and taking responsibility for having perpetrated violence was essential to healing combat's psychic wounds. In this combat-trauma imaginary, engaging in public, political protest was integral to psychiatric care.

I recuperate this psychiatric critique of the American war in Vietnam in order to juxtapose it to the moralist anti-politics that saturates so much talk about combat trauma today. From the point of view of this earlier theory, certain dichotomies we find ourselves presented with in the post-9/11 period appear false, or at least unnecessary. For example, the distinctions between the moral (or ethical) and the political, the clinical and the political, or between the agency and responsibility of individual soldiers, on the one hand, and the political and institutional conditions of war-making and questions of collective responsibility, on the other. In sum, in contrast to how PTSD came to be understood over the decades to come, post-Vietnam syndrome was a clinical articulation of an anti-militarist politics of the moment that insisted on a reckoning with both personal and national responsibility and guilt. Rather than setting ethical and political questions aside, it was a powerful and productive ground on which a radical, anti-war politics was articulated and enacted in the public domain.

## Victims of the War?

The DSM-III, the APA's third *Diagnostic and Statistical Manual,* was not the first to recognize war trauma. Published in 1952, following the experience of World War II and while the war in Korea was underway, the first DSM introduced the category of gross stress reaction to describe a temporary condition suffered even by emotionally stable soldiers who had been exposed to "exceptional physical or mental stress."[5] The key term here was *temporary.* When symptoms persisted, the patient was to be diagnosed with a different, more established psychiatric disorder.[6] This understanding of combat trauma flew in the face of the way military conscription was practiced during World War II. Knowing how widespread psychiatric breakdown at the front had been during World War I, the military tried to address the problem by using psychological testing to exclude the "weak" or "ill" from conscription. That such testing did not work was made evident by the 300 percent increase in psychological casualties among American troops in comparison to the previous world war. Approximately 25 percent of medical casualties in combat divisions in the European theater were for "neuropsychiatric" reasons, and the rates were even higher in the South Pacific.[7] By the close of the war, psychiatrists had been forced to recognize once again that even "normal" men broke down at the front; combat produced psychological disturbances in men who were otherwise psychologically healthy.[8] Published in 1968, the same year as the Tet Offensive in Vietnam, DSM-II eliminated gross stress reaction as a diagnosis, in favor of the far less specific category, Adjustment Reaction to Adult Life.[9] Among possible causes of this disorder was "fear of combat"— which was understood to be a transient rather than chronic condition whose appearance coincided in time with the stressful experience, rather than presenting with a delayed onset.[10]

The American war in Vietnam changed the way combat trauma, and trauma more generally, was understood, and it did so in a manner with far-reaching consequences for psychiatric practice, social policies, and cultural and political imaginaries writ large. Into the 1960s and early 1970s, according to scholars Didier Fassin and Richard Rechtman, "trauma was rarely evoked outside the closed circles of psychiatry and psychology … The victim—who in fact was rarely thought of as a 'victim'—was tarred as illegitimate; trauma was a suspect condition." When feminists in the 1960s, drawing on work by psychiatrists treating concentration camp survivors, adopted a discourse of traumatic memory to agitate for public recognition of the trauma suffered by women subjected to sexual violence, their calls fell on deaf ears. This was to change during the 1970s, Fassin and Rechtman have maintained, when feminists joined forces with anti-war veterans, and together they produced a shift in public and medical consciousness.[11] Not only did a "public health crisis" among American veterans generate awareness of the reality of trauma, but it also led to a fundamental rethinking of its cause in ways that accommodated the demands of both the feminist activists and the Vietnam veterans. No longer was it thought that trauma presupposed either a prior psychiatric disorder or some form of "weakness." As worded in DSM-III in 1980, post-traumatic stress disorder is caused by "an event outside the range of normal human experience" that can "evoke significant symptoms of distress in most people."[12]

Citing an event as the sole cause of trauma was the first of two fundamental shifts in psychiatric understandings of the phenomenon as codified in the DSM-III. Second, and equally transformational, was the decision to include under a single diagnostic rubric both "the perpetrators and the victims of atrocities," the implications of which reached well beyond medical practice, Fassin and Rechtman, among others, have argued.[13] As noted previously, it has been argued that PTSD offered a solution to the political divisions tearing American society apart at the seams. For or against the war, the idiom of trauma—even if born of what American soldiers had done—allowed everyone to sympathize with Vietnam veterans destroyed by the war, all the while papering over the divisive question of who should actually bear responsibility for their (psychic) pain.[14] The importance of recognizing combat trauma was framed as a moral question, as "the failure to make a place for PTSD would be equivalent to blaming the victim for his misfortune—misfortunes inflicted on him by both his government and his enemies," in Allan Young's words.[15] The psychiatric profession had put ethical and political questions aside.[16]

In broad strokes, this widely accepted history captures how PTSD was developed as a psychiatric category along with the social fact of how it displaced political critique by collapsing the category of perpetrator into victim. At a more granular level, however, there is another story to be told. In the hands of its original architects, what was first termed post-Vietnam syndrome opened a different ethical space and, in doing so, also opened rather than closed a radical political one. Premised on a distinct understanding of combat trauma born of the counterinsurgency war in Vietnam, it offered a theory and language through which a trenchant and sustained critique of the war found voice. Far from marking the moment of the birth of a moralist anti-politics of trauma and victimhood, the American war in Vietnam, in other words, was the one US war during which the ethical and political dangers of imperial warfare were articulated in and through a psychiatric gaze.

## The Trauma of the Perpetrator

Work on the DMS-III began in 1974, around the same time that the psychological aftermath of the war was becoming evident to mental health practitioners treating young men returning from combat. Initial forecasts, going into the war, had been for "heavy psychiatric casualties," but by 1966 those "ominous" expectations had been "replaced by extremely optimistic statistical assessments."[17] Treatment protocols adopted from earlier wars—treat immediately, treat close to the front, return the men to their units as quickly as possible—seemed to be working.[18] Likewise, it seemed that earlier lessons regarding the risks of extended combat exposure were being successfully implemented in the military's "rotation system," limiting soldiers' overseas tours of duty. Peter G. Bourne, an Army captain and physician who spent one year (1965–1966) in Vietnam as chief of the Army's Psychiatric Research Team found himself able to declare that "the problem of Acute Combat Reaction had been solved."[19]

Despite the purported success in reducing psychiatric casualties, however, mental health practitioners working with veterans confronted a dramatically different reality. They were finding symptoms of traumatic distress to be widespread, not only from the number of patients being treated for it at Veterans Administration (VA) hospitals but also in self-destructive behavior they identified in ex-soldiers and Marines that seemed anything but exceptional.[20] It was argued by some, especially by the late 1960s and 1970s, that drug abuse, insubordination, and fragging (assaulting/killing officers) were unrecognized symptoms of combat stress in the war zone itself.[21]

By the early 1970s, perpetration—or more specifically, committing atrocities—had arisen as a mental health concern among psychiatrists and other mental health practitioners working with Vietnam vets. Sarah Haley, a social worker at the Boston VA, tells the story of her first patient, a veteran who came into her office falling apart.[22] He was convinced that members of his platoon were out to kill him, because they worried he would tell others about a massacre they had carried out in a Vietnamese village. Haley took the soldier's story at face value. Her colleagues at the Boston VA did not.[23] The man was "obviously delusional, obviously in full-blown psychosis," her colleagues argued.[24] Over the next three years, forty of the one hundred and thirty patients whom Haley treated recounted being responsible for atrocities in Vietnam.[25]

Haley's first patient's purported delusions turned out to be the massacre at My Lai. And as psychiatrists discovered and the US public was to learn, that massacre was far less exceptional than the US military claimed. Committing acts of excessive violence—rape, summary executions, torture, the dismemberment of "enemy" bodies—was rampant. The American military strategy seemed to be to encourage troops to "kill anything that moves."[26] Over time, mental health professionals identified much of the suffering they were seeing among veterans as the aftereffects of having witnessed—and of having carried out—atrocities during the war.

Taking as their starting point the recognition of PTSD in 1980, several scholars have pointed to the dire political and ethical consequences of framing perpetrators as suffering post-traumatic stress disorder. Anthropologist Allan Young, for example, critiques the category of the "self-traumatized perpetrator," an "ordinary" man sent off to war who, upon his return, suffers as a result of atrocities he committed and yet is understood to bear little or no moral responsibility for his actions.[27] Or as Ben Shephard, a British journalist and war historian, puts it, "Instead of forcing the men to take responsibility for their actions the psychiatrists and American society excused them. What was done in Vietnam, instead of being seen as a moral outrage, an aberration, something never to be repeated, somehow became the norm, the standard."[28]

If we put the focus instead on the motivations and political commitments of the psychiatrists and veterans who articulated post-Vietnam syndrome as an understanding of the mental anguish of veterans, we end up with a rather different reading of the politics of the self-traumatized perpetrator, however. Noting the "ordinariness" of the men who acted as they did was not intended to excuse either the men who fought the war or the nation as a whole, as I will show. Instead, in much the same way that Hannah Arendt's argument about the "banality of evil" in *Eichmann in Jerusalem* was neither an apologia for Eichmann's war crimes nor a denial of his moral and legal responsibility for his decisions and actions, as it has often been misread, this was a project to understand how it was that ordinary men could carry out extraordinary crimes.[29] Just as Arendt's radical writings on the Eichmann trial produced a reading of the Nazi regime's bureaucratic ordinariness and attempted to explain how the killing machine operated through a mentality shared by order-following bureaucrats everywhere, the concept of "post-Vietnam syndrome" was a radical critique of the US military and its actions on the killing fields in Vietnam. It showcased the ways in which atrocities were a structural outcome of the imperial hubris and indelible racism of the American war. Post-Vietnam syndrome delineated a framework through which the war's violence was understood, critiqued, spoken about, and politically opposed.

Before delving into this critique of imperial war, however, I explore in some detail the revision process for the *Diagnostic and Statistical Manual*. I elaborate the frameworks that drove understandings of what came to be known as PTSD in DSM-III, so as to set up a contrast between the deliberations that took place in the 1970s, when some of the key players responsible for defining traumatic stress were also advocating against the war, and the conversations and forms of politics that would frame discussions for revising PTSD in the decade to come, during which trauma was transformed into a condition of victimhood (see Chapter 2).

## PTSD and the DSM-III

At the end of the war in Vietnam, the APA's task force charged with revising the DSM had no intention of reintroducing stress

43

reactions associated with combat into the new edition.[30] As Chaim Shatan, a New York City–based psychoanalyst who worked with Vietnam veterans, recounted in the spring of 1975, he learned from "the public defender of Ashbury Park, New Jersey" that the task force had "no plans for reinstating" anything along the lines of the DSM-I's gross stress reaction category. That public defender, Shatan declared, "should get a medal for revealing the political significance of diagnosis."[31]

Together with Robert J. Lifton (a New York City–based psychiatrist and Yale University professor, who also worked with veterans and was a key figure in theorizing post-Vietnam syndrome), Shatan reached out to Robert Spitzer, professor of psychiatry at Columbia University and chair of the task force appointed by the APA to revise the DSM-II. Shatan and Lifton argued that the DSM-III needed a category for the diagnosis of post-combat stress because Vietnam veterans were falling through the cracks.[32] Spitzer asked for empirical evidence. In response, the American Orthopsychiatric Society commissioned a study group to draft a proposal for the DSM-III, and Shatan was put in charge.[33] The group came to be known as the Vietnam Veterans Working Group (VVWG). Spitzer instructed Nancy Andreasen, a specialist in stress responses to burn injuries, and chair of the APA's Committee on Reactive Disorders, to be in touch with Lifton, Shatan, and Jack Smith (a Vietnam vet who headed the National Veterans Resource Project, organized under auspices of National Council of Churches).[34] Together they developed etiological and symptomatic criteria for a diagnosis of traumatic stress.[35] As its membership expanded over time, the work of the VVWG became a powerful, even decisive force in the defining PTSD for the DSM-III.

By the time of the APA's annual meetings in 1976, "official thinking" had begun to consider reactions to "catastrophic phenomena, but only as acute, short-term clinical experiences," with no possibility of "delayed clinical course." Implicitly referring to Nancy Andreasen and her orientation toward stress disorders, Shatan notes, the "psychological experience of civilian burn patients was the model."[36] Shatan's own reports and memoranda lay out a very different set of parameters that the VVWG considered essential, including the kind of etiological event, duration of the disorder, and time of onset. Each of these phenomena were argued to manifest in a particular way in the aftermath of combat and, more generally, in the aftermath of other "catastrophic" and "man-made" experiences.

Much deliberation within the working group, among members of the Committee on Reactive Disorders, and in negotiations between the two focused on defining the "stressor" (or etiological event). "How severe should it be? Does the type of stressor matter?" (man-made versus natural disaster, for example). The committee, Andreasen recalls, considered "combat, death camps, industrial accidents, natural disasters, mass catastrophes, and violent acts against individuals." Regardless of the type of stressor, they found, all patients exhibited "characteristic symptoms."[37]

From the correspondence and memos housed in the APA archives, it is clear that Andreasen's frames of reference were common among psychiatrists engaged in deliberations regarding a new diagnostic category for traumatic stress. I found no evidence there that feminist concerns were influential in formulating the criteria for what came to be known as PTSD. As Robert J. Lifton told me in an interview, "I don't remember in terms of my own experience, [any] conscious influence [from the] women's movement ... I was exposed, I was aware of women's experience and [the] movement," but "I don't remember thinking of women's abuse in thinking about veterans." In contrast, his prior work on survivors of the atomic bombing of Hiroshima "was extremely important ... because it immersed me deeply with what happened to people who were exposed to an atomic bomb, and trauma [is an] understated word for it ... I brought that into my work with Vietnam veterans."

In my reading, documents in the APA archives support existing historical and genealogical accounts of PTSD as having been born of pressure that came largely from psychiatrists working with Vietnam veterans.[38] But the documents do not support the argument that feminist concerns with sexual assault also played a key role, as would be the case in the decade to come, when PTSD became tethered to the experience of victimization.[39] Rape appears at times as a topic of discussion, and it was listed in DSM-III as one possible etiological event. Sexual assault, in other words, figured to some extent in the committee's conversations about trauma as a reaction to stress, even though the body of research on which the committee and the VVWG drew focused on other kinds of events. Nevertheless, when rape makes an appearance in documents in the APA archives, it is referred to as a *relatively uncommon* event.[40]

If a review of the archival evidence shows that feminist concerns and voices played no significant role in these discussions, it also offers no evidence of a debate about the ethical consequences of merging victim and perpetrator into a single diagnostic category. In contrast, there was extensive discussion of whether combat and other kinds of war-related (or "extreme") violence merited a specific designation. "What seems to have been left slightly open," Lifton wrote in a letter to Spitzer, "was the question of whether or not there would be a special sub-category under traumatic syndrome for '*massive* psychic trauma' or the like. While it is true that there is much overlap between what might be called 'ordinary' traumatic syndrome and the massive or extraordinary variety (death camps, Hiroshima, etc.), I feel strongly that the latter experience should be recognized as a specific entity." He suggested Spitzer take a look at several books, all of them dealing with the trauma of camp survivors.[41]

From the perspective of the VVWG, two distinctions were clinically decisive. The first had to do with "the difference between ordinary traumatic syndromes and the massive variety," with the latter tending to have "greater and longer lasting impact on individuals and groups."[42] What concerned the working group was the *intensity* of the difference between "ordinary" instances and what Shatan referred to as the "preternatural" quality of the violence of war and genocide.[43] It was on those grounds that some victims and perpetrators shared a clinical space. "In counter-guerilla combat in Vietnam, terror was so total and the dehumanization of Orientals so pervasive that mass slaughter became almost as automatic as it was in Nazi death camps"; "to adapt and survive in such a setting, the soldier must deform his 'self' as radically as concentration camp inmates did in the psychotic reality of the extermination camp." Shatan, however, was not positing any *moral* equivalence here.

The second distinction on which the working group insisted was that between a "natural" catastrophe and one that was "man-made." In proposing revisions to the April 1977 draft of the DSM-III, the VVWG argued that stress disorders born of a natural disaster, such as a flood, versus ones caused by a "social catastrophe" like combat or a concentration camp, require different approaches to treatment.[44] Whereas Andreasen believed stress syndromes to be "a final *common* pathway reached by experiencing a variety of *different types of stressors*"[45] and favored a more integrated approach,[46] the VVWG held that different kinds of "catastrophic" events led to divergent clinical symptoms and outcomes.

By the time PTSD became an official category in the APA's diagnostic manual, the VVWG had achieved much of what it had set out to do. It had also conceded a lot of ground. The working group managed to get the DSM-III to incorporate "most of [the] formulations on stress disorders, for combat veterans, Holocaust survivors and victims of other brutalizations, both man-made and 'natural.'" And they pressed successfully to have the "delayed onset" of symptoms be recognized explicitly in the DSM-III.[47] But at the same time, the VVWG conceded, most importantly, the distinction between man-made and natural disasters, along with a formal recognition that stress disorders resulting from catastrophic violence are a very different order of things as compared to more quotidian crimes. Yet the working group had not been blind to the potential downsides going into these negotiations, even at the most basic of levels. Reluctant though they were "to fix and freeze what we know to be fluid and flowing, we felt we should try and give 'a name and an address' to those whose lives are being wasted."[48]

## Anti-war Psychiatry

Long before the APA got on board, psychiatrists treating veterans of the war in Vietnam had been busy formulating an understanding of combat trauma, and their conceptual work and activism, while ultimately essential to the definition and acceptance of PTSD as a recognized diagnosis, is not reducible to that end point. Post-Vietnam syndrome, as distinct from PTSD, was founded upon, and in turn facilitated, radical political commitments and practices. In Shatan's words, "Whether we like it or not, psychiatry cannot avoid being a 'morally engaged' discipline." Its "root concepts ... embody certain moral and perforce sociopolitical values," such that "our interventions ... directly affect the processes by which values are formed and transmitted in society."[49] The moral and the political are not posited as alternatives here; the former necessitates the latter.

In November 1969, Lifton was on a plane to Toronto when he read an article in the New York Times about the massacre at My Lai.[50] He reports being overcome with rage, "directed partly toward the warmakers in power, and partly toward myself for not having personally done more to confront or resist American slaughter of Vietnamese."[51] Lifton began working with the New York chapter of VVAW and over time was invited to join the anti-war veterans' "rap groups"—therapeutic encounters in which veterans and psychiatrists came together in informal settings to process the vets' wartime experiences.[52] At the same time, Lifton began researching the American war in Vietnam, focusing on the massacre at My Lai. He wanted to understand why US troops behaved as they did. Taken together, his exploration of My Lai and his work with the VVAW informed his theory of the trauma suffered by veterans in the aftermath of their participation in the war.

Lifton proposed that veterans of the war in Vietnam faced challenges quite different from those encountered by veterans of previous twentieth-century wars. This war was a counter-guerilla war, with no obvious lines of defense. There was no clear way to distinguish enemy locations or to be certain who was a guerilla and who a civilian. The killing was also relatively intimate, affording none of the "psychological protection of distance." And while, wrote Lifton, "there is little ethical difference ... between killing someone far away whom one cannot see, and looking directly into the victim's eyes from five or ten feet away while pulling the trigger, there is a considerable psychological difference between the two acts." To further compound matters, the killing occurred in the context of a war with no clear-cut purpose or significance, making it brutally apparent to American soldiers that they were engaged in nothing more than killing *tout court*.[53] And then, at the end of their tours, these young men returned home to a nation that had no more faith in the cause than did they. In short, Lifton's political critique of the war was all over his psychological analysis. These men were traumatized by *what they had done*—shoving Viet Cong suspects out of helicopters, beheading enemy combatants, massacring villagers, raping women. Nor was that experience limited to exceptional cases. My Lai was not an aberration in the context of this excessively brutal counterinsurgency war.[54]

American veterans of the war were self-traumatized perpetrators, to return to Allan Young's term. But for Lifton, as was true for Shatan, Haley, and the many other mental health practitioners working with Vietnam vets, the figure of the self-traumatized perpetrator was not an apologia for the violence American men had unleashed. It was offered as a radical political insight into the character of and reasons for the overwhelming violence unleashed on Vietnam and neighboring countries as they were dragged into the ever-expanding vortex of American military violence.

Lifton's work on trauma began in the 1960s as a study of the psychological afterlife of the US nuclear bombing of Hiroshima. He found that the bomb that killed hundreds of thousands of human beings and incinerated the city also shattered the symbolic universe of those who lived. In the throes of this "massive psychic trauma," how were people to make sense of the experience? Nothing in their lives could have prepared them to assimilate such an apocalyptic event. The *hibakusha* or "explosion-affected person(s)" suffered guilt for having survived such massive and grotesque carnage: "the *grotesqueness surrounding the death imprint* ... conveyed the psychological sense that death was not only everywhere, but was bizarre, unnatural, indecent, absurd."[55] Nuclear destruction was an experience whose meaning could not be grasped. "One of the great difficulties in all of the extreme situations I've studied," Lifton told Cathy Caruth two decades later, "is that people subjected to them had no prior images through which to connect with them, or very few. What in one's life would enable one to connect with Hiroshima?"[56]

Based on his work on Hiroshima, the "survivor" emerged as a key concept for Lifton. He used the term in reference to "one who has come into contact with death in some bodily or psychic fashion and has himself remained alive," making the point that survivors identify with the dead.[57] They suffer a form of guilt that nurtures a sense of responsibility toward those who died and find meaning by bearing witness to the suffering of those who endured abhorrent and untimely death. They "judge, and indeed judge harshly, their own behavior and that of other survivors on the basis of the degree of respect it demonstrates toward the dead."[58] "Carrying through that responsibility is a way of transforming pain and guilt into responsibility [and that] has enormous therapeutic value." It is "that survivor mission, that enables one to be an integrated human being once more."[59]

In Lifton's analysis, what he called "the atrocity-producing situation" that was the war in Vietnam also generated survivors. American soldiers were immersed in grotesque death and they carried the burden of the dead in whose name they acted in the world. But on the battlefields of Vietnam, survivorship and the form of witnessing to which it gave birth constituted a perverse inversion of post-Hiroshima survivorship. In Vietnam, there was only *"false"* witnessing—a misdirected attempt to give meaning to the lives of fellow American soldiers who had been killed by unleashing vengeance on innocent people.

My Lai appears as but one iconic instance of false witnessing in Vietnam. While perhaps exceptional "in its dimensions," it captured "some of the quality" of American troops' war experience more generally. Its "predominant emotional tone [was] of an all-encompassing absurdity and moral inversion."[60] Shatan argued that the absurdity and moral inversion of the war began with military training, rooted in a racist political imaginary that justified the war and its tactics. Counter-guerilla training involved a rather particular iteration of boot camp "brutalization": "recruits were punched and ridiculed if they failed to understand that the term 'Vietnamese' was never to be used; only the epithets 'gook,' 'dink,' 'slant' were allowed—for friend and foe alike." Once on the ground in Vietnam, that dehumanization extended to all Vietnamese—to "*any* Oriental."[61] On the killing fields of Vietnam, in other words, soldiers lived in a counterfeit moral universe.[62]

American soldiers experienced combat as endless grueling effort resulting in reversible "wins." No one really knew what he was fighting for or who the enemy was. As a consequence, according to one VA psychiatrist, combat emerged as nothing more than "'an exercise in survival.'" In the words of one veteran, quoted by Lifton, *"I don't know why I'm here. You don't know why you're here. But since we're both here, we might as well try to do a good job and do our best to stay alive."*[63] An exercise in survival in an unwinnable war with enemy combatants that merged in and out of the population at large, the American war in Vietnam was a situation all but guaranteed to produce atrocities. "To some extent," Lifton told me, "all wars have atrocity-producing situations, but … counterinsurgency wars are more prone to regularize or routinize" it.

In formulating his understanding of the overall atrocity that was the American war in Vietnam, Lifton drew on an essay by Jean-Paul Sartre. "Can we say," asks Sartre, "that the armed forces of the USA are killing the Vietnamese for the simple reason that they are Vietnamese?" Sartre's *On Genocide* (1968) provides a history of genocide that begins with colonial armies in the nineteenth century. While genocide is not an invention of the twentieth century, Sartre argues, something novel nevertheless appears in Europe during World War II. Colonial forces had long operated by terrorizing civilian populations, and they had committed "cultural genocide." But colonial rule was dependent on the expropriation of labor (and natural resources) on the cheap, and "this value as almost free manpower" generated a measure of military restraint. In Nazi Germany, Sartre maintains, Jews had no such "value." There was nothing to protect them. The Jew was killed "simply *because he was a Jew*."[64]

The structure of colonial wars shifted following World War II, however, with consequences for genocidal violence, according to Sartre. With the rise of anti-colonial independence movements, colonial powers retained their superiority in terms of arms, but they were at a distinct disadvantage in terms of numbers. "Against partisans backed by the entire population, colonial armies are helpless." The only means of winning the war, "the only anti-guerilla strategy" that might be effective "is the destruction of that people." Sartre concludes, "Total genocide ... reveals itself as the foundation of anti-guerrilla strategy." And quite specifically, following the French defeat in Vietnam, any limits to genocide as a strategy in that particular war vanished. The Americans, in contrast to the French, had no significant economic interests in the country and could easily sacrifice those they had. The US government did not select genocide per se, Sartre explains, but genocide "appears as the *only possible reaction* to the rebellion of *a whole people* against its oppressors."[65] According to Sartre, the "present example of genocide"' is "the latest result of the unequal development of societies, total war fought to the bitter end by one side only and without the slightest degree of reciprocity."[66]

In analyzing the atrocity-producing situation that was the war in Vietnam, Lifton referenced Sartre's analysis to argue that the war had that "special combination of elements" identified in *On Genocide*: a counterinsurgency war waged by a nation whose military might far outstrips that of the country it invaded and a guerilla movement that is not easy to separate from the population as a whole. The result was "a compelling internal sequence that constitutes the psychological or experiential dimension of the atrocity-producing situation," Lifton proposed. *Every* American soldier becomes capable of being a war criminal: "men of very divergent backgrounds—indeed just about *anyone*—can enter into the 'psychology of slaughter.'"[67]

At the center of Lifton's intellectual project stood the relationships among historical events, or "external circumstances," and the individual "psychology or experiential dimension." Together with Erik Erikson, the psychologist and psychoanalyst, and Bruce Mazlish, a historian who drew on psychoanalytic theory in his work, Lifton founded the Wellfleet Psychohistory Group, which, beginning in the 1960s, met annually at his house in Wellfleet, MA. Lifton explored the psychological consequences of "extreme historical situations" for those who survived[68] and examined the psychological effects of coming face to face with "evil" and "absurdity."[69] To be clear, he was not interested in Evil and Absurdity as transcendental facts or concepts. Like Arendt, Lifton was interested in evil's banality. During one Wellfleet conference, Erikson asked Lifton whether veterans "think they really have touched evil there," and Lifton responded, "I have no doubt about it," adding, "there's evil with a cap E and a small e ... This is something with a small e and all the more painful for it, because there's nowhere to put it or understand it."[70]

Vietnam veterans were suffering the psychological consequences of having confronted—and having enacted—evil in the course of an imperial war that was, to return to Sartre's understanding, genocidal in its very nature. The atrocities that American troops carried out in Vietnam, Lifton argued, were instances of false witnessing—of paying homage to their dead brothers-in-arms in a distorted moral universe in which the goal was to "kill anything that moves." As was the case with "survivors" of Hiroshima, US troops in Vietnam had to "give significant inner form—to 'formulate'—[their] war-linked death immersion," but they did so by carrying out atrocities on the killing fields they made of Vietnam.[71] In Shatan's formulation, the massacre in My Lai was an instance of "militarized mourning," that is, of pathological and unresolved grief directed outward toward the "enemy" rather than, as in Sigmund Freud's understanding of melancholia, turned inward onto the self.

Militarized mourning, Shatan explains, "*externalizes* the vast impulses of survival guilt, hatred, and aggression towards the lost relationship ... these impulses are redirected in a way which purports to honor the 'sacred' dead. This redirection is the ceremonial vengeance."[72]

The routine atrocities committed by ordinary US troops in Vietnam, in other words, were the manifestations of traumatic grief. The very quotidian character of the soldiers' brutality formed the ground, among psychiatrists such as Lifton and Shatan, for a radical political critique of imperial war and power, including its inherent racism and excessive violence. As was the case for Frantz Fanon, who, as a psychiatrist at a French-run hospital in Blida-Joinville during the Algerian War of Independence, treated French military and police personnel who tortured Algerian suspects, colonial violence was fundamental to their theorizations of politics and trauma alike.[73] Like their French counterparts in Algeria, American perpetrators were understood as being self-traumatized in the context of an imperial war that depended on naked, excessive, and racialized violence. No more than Fanon was pardoning French torturers in analyzing the trauma of perpetrators in Algeria were Lifton and Shatan seeking to normalize the violence carried out by American troops in Vietnam. The banality of American military violence—its very ordinariness—was precisely what made it so dangerous. Only a radical transformation of American power across the globe could make it stop.

## Vietnam Veterans Against the War

The war produced not just war criminals but also radical critics of the war they had fought. Some US soldiers, upon returning home, transformed themselves into authentic witnesses to the horrors perpetrated on the killing fields of Vietnam. As noted above, this was especially true of the particular subset of veterans associated with the Vietnam Veterans Against the War (VVAW), with whom Lifton, Shatan, Haley, and others collaborated in developing the concept of post-Vietnam syndrome. While small in absolute numbers, the VVAW was the most public of veteran voices at the time, as members frequently spoke, testified, and demonstrated against the American war in Vietnam. Andrew E. Hunt, a historian who has written an account of veteran opposition to the war, documents the central role the VVAW played in the anti-war movement following its founding in 1967. Veterans in the VVAW came mostly from working-class backgrounds, and almost none of them went to Vietnam as radicals. Instead, they were transformed by the war. "Officers and GIs, desk clerks, combat veterans and bomber pilots," they all joined the VVAW. While initially "either hostile or indifferent to the vets," by the early 1970s the anti-war movement had accepted anti-war veterans, who now stood at the "forefront of the nationwide struggle to end the Vietnam war."[74]

As one of its first large-scale actions, in January 1971, the VVAW staged a Winter Soldier Investigation in Detroit. Veterans came from across the country to testify to the war crimes they had witnessed and committed, arguing that such crimes were "the inevitable outcome of American military policies in Southeast Asia." Testifying was as much therapy as it was an act of politics, and veterans put their combat trauma squarely on display. Speaking of how basic training had conditioned soldiers to commit atrocities, one veteran recalled what he described as "the last lesson you catch in the United States before you leave for Vietnam," imparted, in his case, by an officer at Camp Pendleton. "'He has this rabbit,'" the veteran said, referring to the officer, "'and then in a couple of seconds after just about everyone falls in love with it ... he cracks the neck, skins it, disembowels it.'" Former soldiers told story after story of summary executions and rape. In the words of one reporter, as "the accounts slogged on, the very commonness, the quotidian character of atrocity, identified itself as the core of dehumanization that accounts for war crimes."[75]

Over the next few months, members of the VVAW testified before the Senate, and at the end of weeklong demonstrations in Washington, DC, hundreds of combat veterans threw their medals on the congressional steps. Their experiences—the horrors they recounted and suffered—bestowed legitimacy on their opposition to the war. These were men "who had served their nation in Vietnam, they could not be dismissed as hippies or radicals. Nor could they be accused of wishing to avoid service." When addressing the public at large, they spoke of the "criminality of the US war effort," seeking to end the war "by undermining its moral basis," and they did so while revealing and acknowledging their own psychological pain.[76]

These anti-war veterans took on a "survivor mission," analogous if never morally equivalent to the *hibakusha* in Lifton's analysis. They provided insight and public testimony into a specific crisis of the historical moment, the brutality of American imperial power, and the destruction of Vietnam that was increasingly spilling over the borders into Laos and Cambodia. As Lifton told me in an interview, "The quest for meaning was an overarching quest that encompasses all the other themes" dealt with in the rap groups. This need for meaning "enters into feelings about the justified or unjustified nature of the war one was fighting. That was very central for anti-Vietnam veterans … I can't say if I would have been able to hold to that same structure of a quest for meaning had I worked with a different group of veterans."

Lifton was always clear that the trauma afflicting Vietnam veterans was radically different from what survivors of the atomic bomb experienced. "I wouldn't include Vietnam veterans as having the kind of massive psychic trauma of Hiroshima or the Holocaust; they are of a different order," he said. "The trauma of veterans is more complicated because they were perpetrators as well, they killed a lot of civilians … They were put structurally in that position, and were told false things or misleading things about the war [that they were] either drafted into or volunteered into. In that sense they were victimized, but…" his voice trailed off. The subtitle of Lifton's *Home from the War* references this complexity: In a phrase he borrowed from a series of articles Albert Camus wrote in 1946, Vietnam veterans were "neither victims nor executioners.[77]

American soldiers were victims of the society that sent them off to war. But in the context of Vietnam, *they were executioners* and they bore responsibility—albeit not sole responsibility—for their actions in the war. At the same time, neither Lifton nor others involved in the VVAW supported holding Lieutenant William Calley, the only American soldier convicted for the massacre at My Lai, legally responsible for war crimes, wanting instead to use the example of My Lai to expose the structural violence of the war as a whole, the fact that "the indiscriminate or deliberate killing of civilians was the US forces 'standard operating procedure.'"[78] This position has been criticized by Patrick Hagopian, who argues that individual soldiers who engaged in egregious acts of violence should not have been allowed to hide their "personal guilt among the mass"; they should have been held legally accountable. While I agree with Hagopian on the question of legal culpability, to argue that Lifton and the VVAW's position on Calley was morally flawed because it "tainted all veterans, including those *innocent* of any crime," as Hagopian argues,[79] is to misunderstand the political message at the heart of their work. For them no American veteran was innocent. The war itself was a crime.

In the rap groups with whom Lifton, Shatan, and other mental health practitioners worked, the therapeutic, the ethical, and the political were entangled from the start. And in an era in which feminists and black activists were participating in consciousness-raising projects, this "experimental" psychiatric endeavor was very much a phenomenon of its time. The fundamental idea was that healing was inseparable from "political expression," a claim that attracted a great deal of attention in pro-war circles.[80] The very idea that veterans were being traumatized by the war, let alone being traumatized by what they had personally done fighting for the US military in Vietnam, was seen as inherently subversive. The Nixon administration, for its part, had no difficulty at all understanding the implications and proceeded to harass and spy on Lifton and Shatan, on other psychiatrists, and on prominent anti-war veterans and the VVAW as a whole.[81] Among psychiatrists and politicians, this discourse of veteran trauma was seen for what it almost always was: a radical political critique of the American war in Vietnam.[82]

Lifton's analysis of the war in Vietnam was as historically specific as it was politically trenchant, even as he was seeking at the same time to reach beyond the particulars of the specific war to reflect on psychic trauma and "the survivor" as a more generalized phenomenon.[83] And in this he was not alone. For Shatan, Arthur Egendorf, Sarah Haley, Jack Smith, and other psychiatrists and veterans who worked together to elaborate post-Vietnam syndrome—and who brought their understanding of combat trauma to the attention of those developing the DSM-III—psychological analysis, historical specificity, and political critique were inseparable.

## Of Guilt and Responsibility

The concept of survivor guilt was central to clinical understandings of trauma during the 1950s and 1960s. Developed by psychiatrists working with former Nazi concentration and death camp inmates, survivor guilt was defined as "a form of unresolved grief and mourning." It was a manifestation of guilt as the key element in a complex of symptoms that William Niederland named "the survivor syndrome."[84] For psychoanalysts such as Niederland, Henry Krystal, and Bruno Bettelheim, survivor guilt came about as a "result of an *unconscious imitation of, or identification with, the aggressor.*"[85] The survivor feels guilty for what she "did" in order to survive—but that "doing" was born of a psychic economy, a fantasy; it did not necessarily imply any actual act of collusion in the real world—that is, in the case of Holocaust survivors, they had not, in reality, colluded in Nazi crimes.[86]

Psychiatrists for whom this notion of survivor guilt structured their engagement with veterans of the war in Vietnam generally adhered to certain fundamental (post-)Freudian concepts: identification with the aggressor, reversion to infantile fantasies, and the cultivation of desires that produce such forms of identification.[87] But Lifton's reformulation of the concept was also influential. As elaborated previously, survivor guilt did not index identification with the aggressor, but instead with the dead.[88] And in the context of working with Vietnam veterans, rather than with survivors of the atomic bomb, Lifton's understanding of survivor guilt was to take yet another turn. Working with anti-war veterans, he developed a far more mundane concept of guilt— "*real guilt*." There is "Realistic guilt … as contrasted with 'neurotic guilt,' e.g., Oedipal." In Shatan's summary of the responses of vets to a questionnaire, there was "an important distinction. THERE IS A REASON TO FEEL GUILTY."[89]

In his discussion of "real guilt" and "existential guilt" in reference to veterans of the American war in Vietnam, Lifton drew on Austrian theologian Martin Buber. For Buber, real guilt "occurs when someone injures an order of the human world whose foundations he knows and recognizes as those of his own existence and of all common human existence."[90] As Mardi Horowitz (a student of Bettelheim) and George Solomon put it, "Unlike guilt from childhood neuroses, revolving around the fantasies of oedipal and preoedipal configurations, realistic shame and guilt cannot be relieved simply by clear expression and working through."[91]

In referring to real guilt—to having injured an order of the human world—veterans of the American war were not cast simply as victims. The therapeutic goal was not to absolve them of responsibility for what they had done. Coming to terms with their actions—with their *real* guilt—was essential to the therapeutic process. Sarah Haley, for one, argued that the standard treatment protocols for combat-related guilt and depression, which were designed to "alleviate the guilt and thereby aid repression by taking the responsibility from the individual and placing it on a higher authority (one was following orders)," are "inappropriate" for "the veteran whose chief complaint involves responsibility for war atrocities." She recounts the story of an ex-combatant sobbing in her office: "I am a killer," he said, "and no one can forgive me. I—we should be shot. There should be a Nuremberg trial for us."[92] He believed deflecting responsibility up the chain of command was a "copout." Likewise, in rap groups, veterans described all sorts of "sins"—of commission and of omission, and as Egendorf stresses, "there is nothing in this process to suggest that what we do absolves or cures guilt. As one veteran put it, 'If you accept that you did it and you accept that it's wrong, then you've got to accept some guilt too.'"[93]

Egendorf, Haley, and other anti-war psychiatrists all insisted on the need for a different clinical approach to guilt. Drawing on a distinction Lifton developed between "static" and "animating" guilt, Horowitz and Solomon, for example, argued that the therapeutic encounter required transforming the former into the latter.[94] Whereas static guilt is experienced as a "self-punitive or self-lacerating *mea culpa*, a closed circle of guilt that goes nowhere," animating guilt "connects with an image beyond the guilt and beyond the atrocity and moves toward change and transformation." Among anti-war veterans "who, in some degree, confront their guilt in terms of responsibility, the guilt becomes energizing."[95] As Ruth Leys has put it, animating guilt "belongs less to the domain of the unconscious and the conflictual than to the domain of the individual's moral and legal culpability for the murder of others, including innocent civilians."[96]

Collaborating together in rap groups, anti-war veterans and the psychiatrists who worked with them developed a novel approach to treatment. As Shatan put it, "To men who have been steeped in death and evil beyond imagination, a 'talking cure' alone is worthless. And merely sharing their grief and outrage with comrades in the same dilemma is similarly unsatisfying. Active participation in the public arena, active opposition to the very war policies they helped carry out, was essential."[97] Nevertheless, neither therapy nor activism, and not even the combination of the two, was understood to offer straightforward salutary effects. A "cure" was not being promised. A distinguishing feature of combat trauma is that there is no "getting over" it. "Man-made catastrophic traumata tend to become 'permanent psychological implants,'" and they become "the combat veteran's or survivor's special vulnerability, a predisposition produced by the man-made stressful situation."[98]

These clinicians and anti-war veterans all echoed something of Buber's understanding of guilt. *Real* guilt—"ontic guilt"— is born of "acting or failing to act," of acts or omissions that violate "the relation between the human person and the world entrusted to him in his life."[99] And facing real guilt, they all believed, demanded that the guilty party also recognize his obligation to the world. Horowitz and Solomon insisted that healing must incorporate some form of "symbolic restitution," some "life-affirming strategies."[100] The rap groups likewise frequently insisted that culpability was not to be severed from political obligation: Healing the self required repairing the world.

Formal recognition of PTSD in the DSM-III was an achievement, albeit only partial, for the VVWG and the wider anti-war group of veterans and psychiatrists advocating on behalf of people suffering the psychological afterlives of combat in Vietnam. But it was not the only one. In addition, as Shatan noted in his final report to the VVWG,

> The most important outcome of this whole undertaking is the establishment of a Veterans Administration funded, but not VA administered, project "Operation Outreach" consisting of one hundred storefronts for the treatment of Vietnam veterans. Over fifty percent of the staff are Vietnam veterans and a high proportion represent minority groups. The staff are remarkably dedicated and have even gone so far as to undertake draft counselling and other work related to the prospect of a draft in the wake of President Carter's speech proposing a return to the draft. I need not mention what the attitude of the vast majority of those I encountered is to that proposal.[101]

Modeled on the rap groups founded by the VVWG, the VA outreach programs did not operate as clinical spaces shorn of politics, at least not until after Reagan won the presidency in 1980.

The VVAW forged a radical approach to psychiatric practice, as committed to changing the institutional sites and structures of clinical practice as it was to reconceptualizing combat trauma as inseparable from the real-world events and actions of which it was born. In bringing those two pieces together, *this particular iteration of psychiatric practice* emerged, if only for a moment, as a productive site for developing and articulating a radical critique of the war—of American imperial power and hubris, of the nation's militarism and the genocidal violence it unleashed in Vietnam.

## Coda: The Beginning of the End?

In 1980, PTSD was formally incorporated into the DSM-III as a diagnostic category. As we have seen, the diagnosis merged a far broader set of experiences than either combat or other forms of massive psychic trauma, and the specific political commitments that drove the initial iterations of post-Vietnam syndrome were erased by formal diagnostic terms. Nevertheless, traces of the moral and political commitments of key figures such as Lifton, Shatan, Haley, Egendorf, and of the VVWG and the activists who initiated the rap groups remained. It is true that, in the manual's description of PTSD, what had been addressed in terms of atrocity and perpetration now appeared under the rubric of "behaviors required for survival"; the language of perpetration and atrocities was now translated into that of "necessity." But in including this form of "behavior," the DSM-III did not cast the psychiatric subject suffering from PTSD as a mere victim, a subject shorn of agency. Guilt, moreover, was identified as a central symptom, however underspecified its terms may have been and especially in relation to conversations about the "real" guilt with which American veterans of the war in Vietnam struggled.

More generally, the publication of the DSM-III was a significant moment in the history of American psychiatry for reasons not primarily stemming from to its introduction of PTSD into psychiatric nomenclature. The broader set of changes leading to the DSM-III signaled a radical paradigm shift for the field. In the decades that followed World War II, psychiatry had come into its own in US society. Congress passed the National Mental Health Act in 1946, allocating substantial funding for training and research in psychiatry. The National Institutes of Mental Health (NIMH) was founded, and it established sixty-nine new VA hospitals, mostly to deal with psychiatric casualties from the most recent world war. Psychiatric treatment at these VA hospitals initially had a psychoanalytic bent.[102] But while it dominated the field in the first decades following the war, that "golden age of American psychoanalysis" was not to last.[103] By the 1970s, psychiatry in the United States had begun to shift away from psychoanalysis in the direction of a biomedical model.

In contrast to their psychoanalytically inclined colleagues, for whom clear and distinct diagnostic categories (let alone any sharp distinction between mental health and mental illness) were not of primary concern, the new psychiatry fashioned itself in biomedical terms. Its architects insisted it be modeled on "the rest of medicine, in which patients were understood to have diseases and in which doctors identified the diseases and then targeted them by treating the body, just as medicine identified and treated cardiac illness, thyroiditis, and diabetes."[104] While what drove the shift is too complex a story to detail here, it is possible to note a few of the critical reasons and motivations for the change. Medications to treat certain psychiatric syndromes had existed since the 1950s, but by the seventies they had become more available and were more specifically targeted; insurance companies were eliminating coverage for psychiatric treatment because they considered existing diagnoses to be too inexact; and there was pressure on the profession from Congress to come up with a clear diagnostic system.[105] Combined with additional pressure coming from certain branches of the feminist movement—pushing back against Freud's view that accounts of childhood experiences of incest and rape were seduction fantasies—and the gay movement—fighting to de-pathologize homosexuality—psychoanalysis became increasingly marginalized in psychiatric theory and practice alike.[106]

When the American Psychiatric Association appointed a committee to revise the DSM-II, the mandate was clear. Robert Spitzer was put in charge of the project because he was a strong advocate for a more "scientific" approach to psychiatry. Under Spitzer's leadership, the committee turned to a model of psychiatric illness developed in the late nineteenth and early twentieth centuries by German psychiatrist Emil Kraepelin. In contrast to Freud, Kraepelin created a taxonomy of psychiatric illnesses, and he did so by classifying according to symptoms instead of etiology or cause. Spitzer and his colleagues brought a neo-Kraepelian approach to the design of the DSM-III, in which the goal was to produce an "atheoretical description and classification" of mental illnesses.[107] With a new manual to refer to, the profession would be able to adopt a common nomenclature, or what Allan Young calls a "diagnostic metalanguage," making psychiatric diagnoses reliable in the sense of being replicable from one clinician to the next.[108] They would be able to identify precise psychiatric disorders on the basis of symptom clusters, which, the committee maintained, were the only things that could be "observed." PTSD emerged as the one exception to that rule, in that it continued to be determined with reference to its etiology: an "event outside the range of normal human experience" was essential to the diagnosis.

# 2

# The Politics of
# Victimization

## Feminism, the Victims of Crime
## Movement, and Reconstructing
## the War in Vietnam

The inclusion of PTSD as a diagnostic category in 1980 did not render it a stable object of either clinical practice or public attention in the decades that followed. Leading up to the DSM-IIIR, a revised version of the DSM-III issued in 1987, psychiatrists debated yet again both the etiology and symptomology of trauma. The result was to shift the diagnosis yet further away from the complex moral and political commitments that were essential to the understanding of post-Vietnam syndrome a decade before, and that would have powerful consequences in the post-9/11 era. Not pretending to produce a wide-reaching historical account, this chapter sketches a particular constellation of actors and political movements that, together, brought about a significant shift in how PTSD was understood—a change situated, most broadly, in a rightward shift in the American political landscape during the 1980s. The commitment on the part of conservatives to rewriting the war in Vietnam, on the one hand, and its obsession with "law and order" on the domestic front, on the other, immediate priorities for the Reagan administration when it came to power in January 1981, were fundamental to transforming the meaning—clinical and public—of PTSD.

Complex political entanglements in the United States in the early to mid-1980s occasioned an expanded public concern with the issue of victimhood in a variety of forms, along with the appearance of the figure of the "innocent" traumatized subject to which the victim label was attached. That this latest development took place during a moment when American politics was shifting sharply to the right is ultimately no accident, as conservative activists and their supporters in the Reagan administration and Congress played a central role in this reframing of trauma as victimhood. At the same time, coming from a more left-leaning political angle, the decade witnessed the rising influence of (feminist) clinicians and activists, whose work on the psychological consequences of rape and incest became central to debates over what revisions would be made to the DSM-III.

Psychiatrists engaged in extensive debates regarding how best to revise PTSD for the DSM-IIIR. But the work of experts forms only part of a far more byzantine tale. In addition to feminist activists who pressed for recognition of the traumatic aftereffects of sexual violence, the victims of crime movement loomed large over the broader transformation of what "trauma" would come to mean in an American political and cultural imaginary. Originating in the late 1960s and then, with Ronald Reagan's election to the US presidency, empowered by the federal government, the movement was instrumental in the emergence of the "victim" as the representative figure of trauma. Feminist activists, on the one hand, and activists in the crime victims' movement, on the other, each had their own particular reasons for stressing the innocence of individuals subjected to violent assaults. Nevertheless, given the broader conservative revolution and its support for victims of crime, if not specifically feminist concerns, the combined effect of the two separate movements was to cause trauma discourse to converge on a new and distinct subject: the nonmilitary, innocent victim of violent crime.

In an effort to gain recognition of rape and incest as crimes that can result in enduring psychological harm, left-leaning feminist mental health practitioners and their activist allies insisted, as they had since at least the late 1960s, on the innocence of girls and women subjected to (pervasive) male violence, largely *in the intimate sphere*. The victims of crime movement, for its part, was born of a white backlash against the civil rights movement of the 1960s, and it focused on a presumed epidemic of violent street crime, cultivating an image of a deteriorating and ever more dangerous public space with all the racist under- and overtones implied by that imaginary. These two movements (albeit feminist activists were operating without the powerful federal support showered on the victims of crime movement) together helped transform the judicial system, making it more attentive to the legal rights and emotional needs of what were called civilian victims, as distinct from the already familiar figure of the traumatized Vietnam veteran. In so doing, they redefined the concept of trauma, removing it from the intricate articulation of violence, agency, moral responsibility, politics and guilt that had been central to an understanding of the suffering of veterans of the war in Vietnam.

The 1980s also marked the moment when the effort to "move beyond" the war in Vietnam was a central project, taken up by the Reagan presidency, the US military, and an expanding chorus of conservative policymakers and pundits. In this revised telling, the story was no longer that the war had been lost on the battlefield, but that the war effort had been undermined by anti-war activists at home. Reconstructing the narrative of American defeat was accompanied by remaking the image and the suffering of its veterans, with the etiology of veteran trauma now traced to the home front. Veterans' suffering came not so much in consequence of their experiences and actions on the killing fields in Vietnam, but from the treatment they received upon returning home. Drawing on the redefinition of trauma as a condition of victimhood, Vietnam veterans were now cast as having been victimized by fellow citizens who opposed the war. In this transformed trauma imaginary, the nation would heal only if all Americans came together in support of veterans. The "warrior" deserved to be honored even if not everyone believed that to be true of the war.

## "Discovering" Rape

In 1974, Ann Burgess and Lynda Holmstrom published a landmark article in the pages of the *American Journal of Psychiatry*. "Rape affects the lives of thousands of women each year," they wrote, pointing to FBI data showing a 121 percent increase in cases of rape reported between 1960 and 1970. A Washington, DC, task force assigned to study the problem concluded that "rape was the fastest growing crime of violence" in the city. Yet, even in the face of such alarming statistics, very little was known about the psychological consequences of rape: "the literature on sexual offenses, including rape," while "voluminous," has "overlooked the victim." In an effort to remedy this neglect, the Boston College School of Nursing, together with the Boston City Hospital, founded the Victim Counseling Program, offering a twenty-four-hour crisis intervention center that was also devoted to studying victims' experiences in the aftermath of sexual assault.[1]

In their article, Burgess and Holmstrom designated a new clinical entity, rape trauma syndrome, echoing the initial name for the trauma born of combat in Vietnam—that is, post-Vietnam syndrome—albeit as we shall see, redefining its meaning in fundamental ways. Rape trauma syndrome is "the acute phase and long-term reorganization process that occurs as a result of forcible rape or attempted forcible rape," they wrote. It is "an acute stress reaction to a *life-threatening situation*." The article reports a "wide gamut of feelings" in the aftermath of rape, ranging from "fear, humiliation, and embarrassment to anger, revenge, and self-blame." But "fear of physical violence and death was the primary feeling described."[2] The experience of life-threat and the associated experience of overwhelming fear were, in short, central to the etiology and symptomology of this newly defined syndrome.[3]

Nearly a decade later, Burgess published a follow-up article in which she compared the symptoms of rape trauma syndrome to the DSM-III criteria for PTSD. She made the case for a significant overlap between the diagnostic categories, and she recounted shifts in clinical understandings of rape's psychological aftermath that had taken place since her earlier publication with Holmstrom. Up to the 1970s, rape "thrived on prudery, misunderstanding and silence," and accounts of victims' experiences were "anecdotal in nature, written primarily by feminists."[4] Over the past decade, however, things had changed: "Rather than discussing rape so exclusively in terms of intrapsychic concepts, the contemporary view began to portray rape as an event imposed upon the victim from the outside: *that is, as an external event.*"[5] In other words, the DSM-III's definition of PTSD provided Burgess with a way of framing rape that did not require engaging in questions about whether the subject's suffering was rooted in a prior psychiatric neurosis or psychosis, or, for that matter, whether she was somehow responsible for what had happened to her. Rape is an "external event" *imposed* upon the "victim from the outside." It is something *done to* her.

Burgess and Holmstrom's claim that the victim was overlooked in the scientific literature on rape up until the 1970s is not quite true. The victim had long appeared in discussions of rape, but the most common view was that she had done something to invite the assault. In other words, she was not squarely a "victim." That assumption was widespread among the public, it was shared by the police and members of the judiciary tasked with responding to sexual assaults. It was also fundamental to psychiatric and criminological understandings of rape, including an academic discipline known as "victimology," which was devoted to the study of the role of victims in eliciting criminal behavior on the part of perpetrators, including the role that rape victims played in their own victimization.[6]

In making the case for rape as a violent, criminal act, feminist psychiatrists, social workers, and their activist allies insisted on the victim's innocence. But this innocence was circumscribed: Victims of rape are innocent of any responsibility *for the particular act of violence to which they were subjected.* The innocence of the rape victim did not depend on what Miriam Ticktin has named "epistemic or experiential purity"—the "absence of knowledge or experience."[7] Specifically, it did not depend on epistemic purity in the sexual realm. On the contrary, the more radical of the 1970s feminists were adamant that women should not have to be innocent subjects in order to be recognized as victims of sexual assault. They fought for the right for women to have had a sexual past, to have a sexual present, to be able to go out at night on their own, to live alone and be independent, and to have those facts have no bearing on their status as victims of the crime of rape.

Such political demands did not go unchallenged, of course. As recounted by scholar and activist Jackie Wang, in a backlash against the women's liberation movement, there was "a surge in public campaigns targeted at women in urban areas warning of the dangers of appearing in public places alone." In New York City, the rape squad advised women to "'avoid being alone in any part of the city, at any time.'"[8] Manuals appeared that laid out rules for women to follow in (urban) public space. Women were "cautioned against defending themselves physically" if faced with an assault, and they were instructed in a variety of behaviors and routines that would enable them to avoid becoming a victim of crime. In short, historian Georgina Hickey argues, "In the 1970s and 1980s, women were told again and again by the media, by men who watched them or directed comments at them on the street, by judges, by the press, by police officers, and even by self-defense instructors that individual women [who did not self-police their own behavior] were ultimately responsible for what happened to them in public space."[9]

Feminists who demanded legal innocence for sexual assault victims resisted such "lessons" and their attendant judgments. Women organized Take Back the Night marches and self-defense workshops; they wrote articles and books taking aim at conservative manuals that advised women to retreat into safety as the way to avoid attack.[10] Second-wave feminism cast women as active subjects, not passive bystanders. These feminist activists did not embrace a condition of *victimhood*. This was not a politics of injury that characterized either the victims' rights movement, as I will show, or feminist and other forms of identity politics that would become pervasive in the decades to come.[11] Moreover, as key feminist figures—psychiatrists and activists alike—pointed out again and again, more often than not, sexual assault was committed by men the women knew, men with whom they were in intimate or familial relationships. The image of the evil and anonymous (black) predator, the aberrant male trolling for his victim in the public domain, was a wild misrepresentation of the sexual violence most women and girls face.

In her book *Against Our Will: Men, Women, and Rape*, Susan Brownmiller developed one of the more trenchant critiques of rape published in the 1970s. Rape, she wrote, is the "deployment of the penis as weapon." She argued that sexual assault was so endemic to patriarchal societies that it occurs as often in the intimate sphere as it does in war. Brownmiller savaged police practices, the legal system's evidentiary rules, and the basic assumptions that, she argued, made it nearly impossible to prosecute men for rape, especially in the majority of cases in which the rapist is no stranger to the woman.[12] Brownmiller and other radical feminists argued that women were always at risk of becoming victims of rape, because that was the very nature of patriarchal violence. In its most radical forms, this was a feminism that embraced the right to "be bad."[13] Nevertheless, during this same decade, a female victim as an innocent *subject*—as epistemically pure, to return to Ticktin's formulation—did emerge as a significant site of psychiatric and public consciousness, but it was the girl, the *child* more so than the woman, who was to be its iconic figure.

## The Innocent Child

In her landmark book *Father-Daughter Incest*, Judith Herman points out that there has long been evidence of the prevalence of adult-child sexual encounters. Referring to work by Alfred

Kinsey in the 1950s, she writes, "The Kinsey study became a household word in America," and many of its findings— for example, about extramarital sex and masturbation—had "received an enormous amount of attention and became part of common knowledge and folklore." One of his conclusions, however, had largely been ignored: that "grown men frequently permit themselves sexual liberties with children, while grown women do not." Father-daughter incest, the form of incest "most frequently reported," is paradigmatic of "female sexual victimization," Herman avowed. And insofar as the "father-daughter relationship is one of the most unequal relationships imaginable," it best represents the power relationship between women and men in general.[14]

During the 1970s and well into the 1980s, psychiatrists and feminist activists focused on the problems of incest and the sexual assault of children had to wage battle on multiple fronts. They had to convince a dubious public that incest, far from being an extremely rare event, was relatively common. They had to persuade medical professionals, the police, and judges that girls who reported sexual encounters with fathers or other male relatives or family friends were not making it up.[15] And they had to alter the widespread assumption that in those presumably rare cases when adult-child sexual encounters did occur, the girl—like the victimologists' adult rape victim—bore at least some responsibility for the crime. In short, feminist psychiatrists and activists fought to establish the figure of the innocent child, and they struggled to convince a dubious public that victims of incest—including daughters assaulted by their fathers—suffered psychological harm, even if it manifested only later in life.

The stories being told by girls and women at rape crisis centers, at hospitals, and elsewhere were key to the psychiatric and activist accounts of child sexual abuse during the 1970s and 1980s. They fought to recast women who spoke about having been sexual assaulted as reliable witnesses to their own experiences, with those experiences holding a truth previously hidden from public view.[16] Inverting the long-standing skepticism about sexual abuse stories told by children, Herman was straightforward about the implications for therapists, who "must assume that the child's complaint of sexual abuse is valid and should not be confused by initial denial by the parents."[17] Over time, believing the stories of sexual abuse that children— among others—told became an ethical, rather than just a clinical, imperative; like survivors of political catastrophes before them, victims of rape and incest were also witnesses to horrors, to what were often public secrets, and they needed to be heard and believed.[18]

Clinicians and rape crisis counselors faced an additional complication where incest was concerned. Many women told of abuses that took place in the distant past; they were recall- ing childhood events.[19] Understandings of the trauma of both Holocaust survivors and Vietnam veterans had established the possibility of delayed onset, but in both instances the temporal lag was relatively short. Some survivors of childhood sexual abuse, in contrast, were experiencing traumatic aftereffects decades hence. Even as advocates for victims of incest and child sexual assault drew on the increasing medical validation of the possibil- ity of delayed onset PTSD, they still needed to convince a dubious psychiatric community, police force, judiciary, and public of the truth-status of memories of events so long in the past.

The struggle to establish the truth-status of such long-repressed memories had profound consequences for how traumatic memory was to be understood. In *Trauma: A Genealogy,* scholar Ruth Leys traces the gradual abandonment, beginning in the 1960s, of psychoanalytic understandings of traumatic memory, along with the attendant concepts of motivated forgetting, censorship, and repression.[20] During the 1980s, trauma psychiatrists who rose to prominence—Bessel van der Kolk, Onno van der Hart, and Judith Herman, to name but a few key figures—insisted on the "literality" of memory. Theorists and clinicians framed traumatic memories as literal replays of the etiological event —as "flashbacks," as scenes from one's past that reappear and are re-experienced in the present.

This insistence on the literality of traumatic memory is conceptually inseparable from a commitment to trauma as victimhood. If victims were to be believed, if they were to be reliable witnesses to the causes of their own traumatic suffering, their memories had to be understood as dependable and credible accounts of past experiences. Holocaust survivors played a constitutive, if early, role in the transformation of traumatic memory into a literal replay of events past. Jewish survivors seeking compensation in German courts after World War II were required to prove that their camp experiences were the cause of their psychological distress. To satisfy that legal condition, a theory of trauma and of traumatic memory that did not rely on traditional psychoanalytic explanations was required. Psychiatrists such as Henry Krystal and William Niederland, who treated Holocaust survivors and fought for them to receive compensation from the German state in the 1960s, rethought classic Freudian approaches to trauma. If psychoanalysts in the United States and elsewhere had traditionally "left the real world outside the consulting room," in caring for former camp inmates, they took seriously the consequences for psychic life of "real world events." That recognition was crucial not only for substantive, clinical reasons, but also for forensic purposes: the case had to be made, in German courts, that survivors' experiences of persecution and imprisonment were the source of their current psychological suffering. And that forensic requirement "contributed to the reaction against concepts of altering the past."[21] The world outside the consulting room, in other words, informed theories of trauma in myriad ways.

For those advocating on behalf of victims of sexual assault, rendering traumatic *memory* literal likewise served crucial forensic purposes. Sexual assault victims' memories needed to be accurate, not just credible if fathers, boyfriends, acquaintances, and even strangers were going to be prosecuted for the crimes of incest and rape. This battle was waged not only against existing psychiatric practice, or even just against a particular social and political imaginary, but also against a judicial environment in which refusing to believe and/or blaming the victim was the norm. The "balance of power in the justice system" must shift "away from the father in order that he is held criminally accountable," Herman wrote.[22] For feminist psychiatrists and activists of the 1970s and 1980s, reforming the judicial system—police departments, prosecutors, judges, the courts—was a central goal. As has been true ever since struggles over the truth of traumatic neuroses first began in the late nineteenth century, forensic questions stood center stage.[23]

In addition to convincing doctors, police, judges, and ordinary citizens to credit the accounts and memories of childhood sexual assault, there remained the question of whether the reported events were psychologically harmful. Did the sexual assault of children really have long-term consequences? On this additional front in the battle, psychiatrists and activists ran up against the oldest and largest study of the sexual lives of American men and women ever published. *Sexual Behavior in the Human Female* by Alfred C. Kinsey was a landmark book in the study of sexuality, as noted earlier, and not merely for its presumed scientific rigor, but also for the impact it had on the way sex and sexuality were being talked about in American society.[24] Drawing on a huge trough of data, Kinsey reported that "24 percent of his female informants had experienced the sexual attentions of adults while they were still girls."[25] He did not find the statistic worrisome, however. Granted, 80 percent of the women reporting such encounters also recounted experiencing fear during the assault, but Kinsey held that was about social norms rather than the sexual encounter itself: "the emotional reactions of the parents, police and other adults ... may disturb the child more seriously than the contacts themselves." In his view, the "current hysteria" over the sexual abuse of children, not the acts themselves, was the cause of sexual problems later in life.[26] In short, Kinsey never denied the relative prevalence of sexual encounters between girls and men; he denied that what we call sexual abuse is abuse, that it does any harm. Two decades hence, Herman noted, it was still possible to find clinicians who held the same view. And a variety of male activists emerged advocating in favor of sexual encounters between adults—men—and (female) children in the name of "children's rights" to sexual freedom.[27]

Herman had no time for such arguments. Sexual liberation conceived in this manner rendered girls more vulnerable to sexual abuse by men. The so-called liberated position ignored the data on how girls experience sexual encounters with adults, and on how women surveyed later in life report such childhood experiences as traumatic. At stake was not just establishing the "fact of child sexual abuse," but the definition of such sexual encounters as *abuse*. For that to be accomplished feminist mental health practitioners needed to prove that sexual encounters between adults and children caused long-term psychological pain. Herman reported compelling evidence that, while harm was perhaps not inevitable, later in life child victims exhibited major depressive symptoms, attempted suicide, struggled with addiction to alcohol or drug, and reported sexual problems, promiscuity, and low self-esteem at alarming rates. Not quite a decade later, Herman would describe the psychological effects of incest in far more specific clinical terms: "Clinical studies of adult patients with a history of incestuous abuse report consistent findings of symptoms consistent with chronic or delayed post-traumatic stress disorders, as well as persistent impairments in self-esteem, self-protection, identity formation, and intimate relationships."[28] What is crucial here is that, up against prevailing misconceptions with regard to both the reality of child sexual abuse and its damaging psychological consequences, Herman, among others, turned to PTSD, a diagnostic category initially established to respond to the needs and specific manifestations of psychological pain among combat veterans, and she did so in the name of a very different kind of subject: the innocent victim of a sexual crime.

## Sexual Trauma and the DSM-IIIR

By the early 1980s, sexual assault had become central to the American Psychiatric Association's discussions of PTSD. More generally, there was increasing attention at the time being paid to "acute civilian PTSD," about which, according to psychiatrist

Allan Burstein in a memo to colleagues at the APA, "very little work has been done in the past few years."[29] Richard Kluft, a key figure in defining diagnostic criteria for multiple personality disorder (MPD), cautioned Robert Spitzer, head of the project revising the DSM-III, about "the risk that in our intense contemporary study of the tragic consequences suffered by the Viet Nam era veterans we may lose sight of the numerous and diverse antecedents and sources of PTSD." In focusing on the war, many other causes of PTSD had been relegated to the sidelines. Kluft had his own agenda in making the argument: Calling attention to the "close association between dissociation and post-traumatic syndromes," he wanted to put child abuse squarely on the table.[30] This was the moment in American society during which diagnoses of multiple personality disorder were mushrooming and advocates for patients with MPD identified child sexual abuse as its cause and insisted on its close relationship with PTSD.[31] By the mid-1980s, discussions of the relationships among these two diagnoses, PTSD and MPD, representing two very different psychiatric milieu and political projects, framed much of the conversation about how trauma might best be understood.[32] As a consequence, in the DSM-IIIR (published in 1987), a diagnosis of "PTSD" would be founded not only on a very different definition of the etiological event from that which appeared in the DSM-III, but it also offered a substantially different understanding and image of the traumatized subject herself.

A detailed analysis of the debates concerning the reclassification of PTSD as a dissociative disorder and its relationship to MPD is beyond the scope of this chapter. Suffice it to say that, as had been true while drafting a definition of PTSD for the DSM-III, a lot of time and ink was spent discussing and redefining the "stressors" responsible for traumatic injury, even as discussions about the trauma of women who had suffered sexual abuse as children drove much of the discussion on how to define the etiological event. Mental health practitioners treating soldier trauma questioned the shift. As part of a survey collecting data for the National Vietnam Veterans Readjustment Study (NVVRS), for example, William E. Schlenger asked mental health practitioners with experience treating Vietnam veterans how the etiological event should be defined. One VA clinician responded:

> The department of Veterans Benefits has tended to instruct its field personnel to require that the stressor be equated with a literal, clear-cut threat to the life of the serviceman. This is somewhat at odds with the DSM-III definition, which focuses, quite properly I believe, on the threat to the psychological integrity of the individual, certainly implying circumstances that literally threaten the life of the individual but also psychologically traumatic circumstances.

Vietnam veterans who had been assigned to graves registration, for example, often exhibit PTSD symptoms.[33] Other VA clinicians responded to other questions, including specific questions about etiology: "What specific types of trauma are likely to result in PTSD? Are there traumatic events which seem to rarely result in PTSD?"[34] In contrast to the DSM-III, which defined the etiological event more parsimoniously as involving something "outside the normal range of human experience," by the mid-1980s the specification of (perceived) life threat (to self or others) emerged as the central criterion. Despite often contentious debate, in short, a consensus was arrived at that eliminated the possibility of a traumatized person being an active agent in the traumatic event. The self-traumatized perpetrator, key to the understanding of combat trauma that emerged from psychiatrists' early work with Vietnam veterans, disappeared from the DSM-IIIR, and with it the psychiatric basis informing a radical critique of American militarism and war.

Recall that in the previous chapter, clinicians who had worked with and advocated on behalf of Vietnam veterans during the 1970s did not view life-threat as the defining feature of combat trauma. Moreover, many VA psychiatrists and psychologists consulting on the DSM-IIIR fought to maintain key aspects of that original understanding in the revised edition. One VA psychologist, for example, responded to the aforementioned questions about "types of trauma" with the following explanation: "The usual forms of trauma [that] result in PTSD are those which are life endangering (such as combat and rape), or which are perceived as life threatening." But there is more. There are actually three subtypes of the disorder: "trauma from natural causes"; trauma "from human caused events with the individual solely passive"; and "trauma from human caused events *with the individual an active agent*."[35] The "last two subtypes tend to persist longer" and they "tend to produce different levels of personal guilt."[36] The distinction between trauma caused by events in which the patient was a "passive" versus an "active" participant, the latter being traumas that produce different levels of personal *guilt*, harkens back to the possibility of the self-traumatized perpetrator who suffers from what Robert J. Lifton described as "real" or "ontic" guilt," as I discussed in Chapter 1. And this VA clinician was no outlier: Another psychologist at the VA insisted that the revised DSM criteria distinguish between a "core disorder" and a "post-traumatic disorder with survivor guilt," describing the latter subtype in relation to "persistent guilt about surviving or about behavior necessary to survive," to give but one more example.[37] Contra their recommendations, not only was the "individual as active agent" eliminated from the revised criteria for PTSD in the DSM-IIIR, so too was guilt as a core symptom.[38]

The disappearance of guilt as a possible manifestation of PTSD marks the move of the clinical definition of PTSD away from combat as its core concern. As was true of many others who worked with veterans of the war, Arthur Blank, an Army psychiatrist who later became national director of the Vet Centers of the VA, pointed to guilt as an essential feature. Criterion B, which specifies the ways in which the traumatic event is re-experienced, "should be amplified to include 'persistent guilty thoughts about behavior before or during the event,'" he wrote. Guilt signaled the psychiatric commitment that soldiers could be traumatized *by what they had done*. For clinicians who worked with veterans of combat in Vietnam, well aware of the violence for which they were responsible, the reality of trauma born of moral transgression was never in doubt.

Clinicians working with victims of sexual assault, including child sexual abuse, by contrast, were skeptical of the concept of guilt. Ruth Leys has traced the clinical and social theoretical arguments in which (survivor) guilt came to be cast as an ethically fraught concept, arguing on that basis that the marginalization of guilt as a significant manifestation of trauma was born of arguments regarding the traumatic suffering of Holocaust survivors.[39] I want to suggest that it may have been psychiatrists and activists working on behalf of rape and incest victims who sealed the deal. From their perspective, guilt appeared more often than not as "misplaced" or "irrational," and this understanding of guilt—well represented in the annals of official psychiatry, if not always in clinical practice—began to be extended to the diagnosis and treatment of traumatized Vietnam veterans. David Spiegel wrote in a letter to Robert Spitzer that the proposed criteria for PTSD had left one element "underrepresented," which he described as "the domain of control versus helplessness":

My experience is that people suffering with PTSD have an exaggerated fantasy of their ability to control the traumatic event or its consequences, which serves as a framework for repetitive unconscious fantasies of undoing the event. The rape victim repetitively thinks, "If only I had not decided to go out to the store…"; the combat veteran thinks, "If only I had not taken my buddy with me on patrol, he would not have been killed," etc. The therapeutic work is to enable them to experience their helplessness in the face of the trauma and the limits of their ability to control events … [I] would, therefore, like to see included an item related to fantasies of exaggerated control over the traumatic episode.[40]

It may not have seemed so at the time, but placing therapeutic focus on enabling survivors to recognize their own "helplessness" and accepting the reality that they had no control is part of a momentous shift. It signals an increasingly prevalent understanding of PTSD as a condition of victimhood and the beginnings of a new trauma imaginary that would recast Vietnam veterans as victims *tout court*.

Thus, by the mid-1980s, there were two iconic figures of the traumatized subject: the soldier and the female victim of rape and incest. These two figures had rather distinct experiences of violence, and yet they both came to occupy the subject position of the victim, if in radically different ways and for decidedly different political reasons. Clinically speaking, life-threat, described by Burgess and Holmstrom as "an acute stress reaction to a life-threatening situation," had become fundamental to an emerging consensus on the etiology of post-traumatic stress disorder and PTSD had become widely associated with victims of sexual abuse, among other kinds of assaults or tragedies of everyday life.[41] In turn, the political imaginary and psychiatric definition of PTSD that focused on victims and victimhood came increasingly to inform not only clinical descriptions of PTSD as suffered by American veterans of the war in Vietnam but also public understandings of combat trauma. The revised definition of PTSD that reimagines the traumatized subject as the helpless victim circles back and reframes the trauma of veterans of the war in Vietnam, completely stripping the understanding associated with post-Vietnam syndrome of its initial critical political force. In the new combat-trauma imaginary, the combatant is recast as a passive rather than active subject, by implication not so different from the child victim of incest. As summarized by one clinician at the Los Angeles VA, writing in 1984, the qualifying experiences of "war trauma" include exposure to death, observation of death and injury, threat of personal death, and torture. His categories are all life-threat situations—experienced or observed—that the traumatized subject has no particular role in producing.[42] There is no talk of perpetration here or even of "behavior required for survival." There is no place in this discourse for moral transgression, that is, for the atrocities that so many mental health workers and veterans of the American war in Vietnam had understood but a decade earlier to be the source of their postwar trauma and guilt.

In the debates over how to define PTSD for the DSM-IIIR, we see a steady march toward the convergence of trauma and victimhood. By 1994, when the DSM-IV appeared, the transformation of PTSD was complete. PTSD is caused by a life-threating event, and it is manifested through affective responses typical of experiences of fear and helplessness—that is, of victimization.

## Victimization, Redux

The 1980s not only witnessed the revision of the DSM-III, the recalibration of rape victims' agency, and the emergence of the innocent girl as an icon of abuse, it was also the decade of the President's Task Force on Victims of Crime, and during which states began enacting laws to protect the rights of victims and a federal Victims of Crime Act was passed. So, when Frank Ochberg, in the introduction to his edited volume *Post-Traumatic Therapy and Victims of Violence* (1988) announced "a new science of victimization," his novel iteration of clinical victimology was not some arcane and isolated medical specialty. It emerged in tandem with a significant political development in the victims' rights movement and the support it received from state legislatures and the federal government alike. Nor was this an exclusively government-level project. "Major mental health organizations," according to Ochberg, "have sponsored studies of victimization, and the mental health community is responding to the recommendation of the President's Task Force."[43] As I will show, this movement—whose demands converged with those of anti-rape activists, even as its understanding and depiction of violent crime diverged in fundamental ways—was a key player in the shift in public understandings of PTSD. The movement, in tandem with the anti-crime ideology of the Reagan presidency, framed trauma squarely as a condition of victimhood, a common response in the aftermath of being subjected to a violent crime. Trauma and innocence, in short, were brought together in a tight, symbiotic embrace.

Ronald Reagan's election to the US presidency in 1980 is a pivotal moment in this story, as it is in the story of the conservative reconstruction of the American loss in Vietnam, as we will see in what follows. With the Republican takeover of the federal government, the so-called victims of crime movement flourished, garnering ever increasing institutional, political, and financial support. Upon assuming the presidency, Reagan quickly launched a Task Force on Violent Crime (1981) and then a year later a Task Force on Victims of Crime (1982). The tenor of Reagan's enterprise is clear from the Letter to the President that opens the *Final Report* of the latter task force, "When you established [the Task Force] on April 23, 1982, you led the nation into a new era in the treatment of victims of crime. Never before has any President recognized the plight of those forgotten by the criminal justice system—the innocent victims of crime."[44]

In 2004, the Office for Victims of Crime History Project at the Department of Justice produced an official historical account of the victim rights movement. In this narrative, the crime-victims' movement was "an outgrowth of the rising social consciousness of the 1960s that unleashed the energies of the idealistic, twenty-something generation of the 1970s."[45] The authors, Marlene Young and John Stein, identify a variety of factors in accounting for the rise of the movement, but most generally, they argue that it was driven by the elevated levels of crime during the 1960s. By the mid-1970s a grassroots movement was gaining steam. Families and Friends of Missing Persons was founded in 1974, Parents of Murdered Children in 1978, and Protect the Innocent in 1977. The National Organization for Victim Assistance (NOVA) followed in 1975. The latter held annual conferences and provided training and educational opportunities for people working with victims. Federal funding for like-minded community groups and educational materials was on the rise during the same period, only to fall off by later in the decade. Then, when Reagan took office in early 1981, the movement gained solid support at the highest levels of the federal government.[46]

As this official history would have it, the public's concern with crime was a straightforward result of people's increasing likelihood of becoming a victim of street crime.[47] The opening words the *Final Report* of the President's Task Force on Victims of Crime sound like the lead-in to a bad 1950s crime drama:

"Something insidious has happened in America: Crime has made victims of us all ... The specter of violent crime ... lurks at the fringes of consciousness."[48] Or, as the FBI's *Uniform Crime Report* would declare just over a decade later, "Every American now has a realistic chance of murder victimization in view of the random nature that crime has assumed."[49]

Statements like these conceal a radically different truth. As Loïc Wacquant has shown, the FBI's assertion about the danger faced by "every American" is contradicted by its own evidence. The latter, Wacquant writes, betrays "the obdurate social and geographic patterning of serious offenses against persons." Class, race, sex, and not unrelatedly, where one lived—all of these factors determined how likely one was to be a victim of crime. Crime was not all that random in the 1980s, all the public discourse about a crime wave notwithstanding—nor was it all that random in the 1970s or the 1960s, or at any time since. For all the public concern about crime and an increasing support for the "war" being waged on it, crime rates from the 1960s through the 1990s generally stagnated and then declined.[50]

Understanding the rise in the public concern with violent crime in the US in the latter part of the twentieth century requires placing it in the context of the civil rights movement and the challenge to white dominance that movement posed. The rhetoric of "law and order," as Michelle Alexander argues, first emerged in the 1950s, as part of a project by southern governors and law enforcement officials to mobilize anti-civil rights sentiment and tether it to demands for law and order, and that project continued through the 1960s and in the decades to come.[51] At the same time, assuming that the backlash to progressive gains in civil rights came exclusively from white southern conservatives is too facile; as Elizabeth Hinton has documented, the implementation of punitive federal anti-crime policies and the rise of the carceral state was a "thoroughly bipartisan" affair. President Lyndon B. Johnson was as committed to law and order as he was to his anti-poverty programs. In 1964, the same year he launched the War on Poverty, Johnson also submitted to Congress the Law Enforcement Assistance Act

(LEAA), which established a role for the federal government in state-level law enforcement institutions and practices. The rationale for the legislation was the "fact" of rising crime rates, despite the reality that violent crime was pretty consistently on the decline, continuing a decades-long trend.[52] Throughout the 1960s, political protests against the racial state were cast as criminal acts, and the courts were accused of overlooking the problem by issuing lenient sentences.[53] In the words of Richard Nixon leading up to his successful campaign for the presidency, the increasing rate of crime "can be traced directly to the spread of the corrosive doctrine that every citizen possesses an inherent right to decide for himself which laws to obey and when to disobey them."[54]

The 1960s did witness a brief increase in the national crime rate, Alexander notes, or at least so it appears.[55] Yet, following Wacquant's argument, the increase would have been *localized* in time and space. But instead of focusing on structural causes for this apparent rise, such as unemployment and sustained poverty, the media "sensationalized" crime and framed the problem as evidence of "the breakdown in lawfulness, morality, and social stability in the wake of the Civil Rights Movement." Along with the so-called riots in Harlem and Rochester in 1964, and the uprisings that rocked the country following Martin Luther King's assassination in 1968, those who were so inclined had plenty of sensational news footage to point to, blaming the civil rights movement as the leading cause of "rampant crime." During his 1964 presidential campaign Barry Goldwater warned voters, "Choose the way of [the Johnson] Administration and you have the way of mobs in the street."[56] After the so-called Watts riots in 1965, Hinton argues, an emerging political consensus cast "crime as specific to black urban youth"; the only solution imagined was to increase the presence of "law enforcement in vulnerable neighborhoods."[57] A Gallup Poll in 1968 reported 81 percent of respondents agreeing with the statement that "law and order has broken down in this country"; and a majority blamed "Negroes who start riots and 'Communists'" for the breakdown.[58] During the 1968 presidential campaign, Nixon, the Republican candidate, and George Wallace, an independent and segregationist former governor of Alabama, both took pains to incite (white) fear of crime in their calls for law and order. Together, Nixon and Wallace received 57 percent of the vote.[59] Law and order had become the idiom for talking about race without naming it as such—that is, it grounded a new racial imaginary that would structure policing and the carceral state for decades to come.

Jill Lepore traces the roots of the victims' rights movement back to the Warren Court and a series of decisions that protected defendants' rights against overly invasive policing and prosecutorial practices.[60] Between 1961 and 1966, the Supreme Court ruled, for example, that evidence obtained without a search warrant was inadmissible in a court of law and that suspects must be informed of their rights upon being arrested, which included the right to have an attorney. A liberal court purportedly "soft on crime" became the rallying cry among proponents of "re-balancing" the way the police and judiciary operated: the rights of criminals should not be allowed to trump those of victims, they argued. Beginning in earnest in the 1970s and increasing in power through the early 1980s, the pro-victim movement fought to make the police and the judiciary more attentive to the experiences and needs of victims, including their psychological needs.

When Reagan was elected to the presidency in 1980, he inherited nearly two decades of successful efforts to expand federal law enforcement capabilities and promote increasingly punitive strategies for approaching crime. While continuing that tradition, however, the Reagan administration also marked a crucial turning point. Using thinly veiled racist language to portray social welfare and poverty alleviation programs as part of the problem rather than the solution, programs designed and implemented to provide assistance to people who needed it, in the words of the new president, actually encouraged "laziness, dependency, and single motherhood."[61] Invoking images of "welfare queens" and criminal "predators" throughout his campaign, Reagan was elected with strong support from white voters, including an alienated and largely poor white working class.[62] Upon taking office, he declared the continuing war against urban street crime his top domestic priority,[63] shifting the FBI's focus away from white collar crime. The Reagan administration also launched the War on Drugs,[64] and it increased exponentially the budgets of federal law enforcement agencies.[65] Reagan charged his Presidential Task Force on Victims of Crime with addressing "the needs of millions of Americans and their families who are victimized by crime every year and who often carry the scars into the years to come."[66]

As the flip side of law and order, the "get tough on crime" campaign elevated the status of victims of crime, who over time would be granted a larger and larger role in the operation of the judicial system. In the movement's pro-victim discourse, the victim is a citizen-subject worthy of and entitled to rights that she was being denied. But more than a mere victim (of crime), this citizen-subject is also traumatized, suffering psychological harm that required—indeed, deserved—both institutional recognition and therapeutic care. With this, race politics in the post-civil rights era—in the form of "law-and-order" campaigns and the victims of crime movement—become key pieces in the story of how PTSD came to be defined as a condition of victimhood.

### The Worthy Citizen

[The] essential reality [is] that almost all Americans, at some time in their lives, will be touched by crime. Among the most difficult obstacles are the myths that if people are wise, virtuous, and cautious, they will escape, and that those who are victimized are somehow responsible for their fate. These are pernicious falsehoods ... To adopt the attitude of victim culpability is to accept that citizens have lost the right to walk their streets safely regardless of the hour or locale; it is to abandon these times and places to be claimed as the hunting preserves of the lawless.[67]

The rejection of "victim culpability" echoes the language of feminist mental health practitioners and activists who fought for incest and rape to be recognized as the serious and wide-spread crimes that they were, and in this sense feminist activist projects were there to be appropriated as a model for the victims of crime movement. Nevertheless, in other ways the two movements could not have diverged more fundamentally. Feminist psychiatrists, social workers, and activists such as Herman and Brownmiller, and, for that matter, psychiatrists such as Richard Kluft recognized—more precisely, they *insisted* on it being recognized—that most women and girls who suffered sexual assault did so at the hands of men they knew. The victims of crime movement, in contrast, along with the presidential task force, was obsessed with what they called "street crime," the anonymous criminal, the random attack: a college student murdered during her first afternoon at college; a pharmacist robbed at gunpoint; a child molested by the driver of his school bus; the mother who looks away for a moment and her child is kidnapped; a woman raped and tortured for five hours after being carjacked from a shopping center parking lot.[68] The more lurid, the better, seemed to be the motto, which meant, of course, that the movement dealt in sensational exceptions to the patterns of actual criminal activity.

In its defense of victims' rights, the task force proposed a series of changes to federal and state laws, among them the protection of victims' privacy, the admission of hearsay, an amendment to bail law making evidence that the accused is a danger to the community a reason to deny bail, and a public registry of people who have been arrested for committing sexual assault or child molestation. The most sweeping recommendation from the task force, however, was a proposed amendment to the Constitution, on the argument that the "fundamental rights of innocent citizens cannot be adequately preserved by any less decisive action." More to the point of PTSD, the task force believed the criminal justice system needed to attend to victims' mental health needs. To this end, police officers required training in administering "psychological first-aid." They had to be taught that victims "may experience depression, dependence, anger, a feeling of loss or control, guilt, uncontrollable fear, either alone or in combination, and the response by the police must be both appropriate and sensitive."[69]

Attending to the psychological needs of victims of crime had been fundamental to the organized feminist response to rape and sexual assault a decade earlier. The first three victims' assistance programs in the United States were founded in 1972, and two of them were rape crisis centers, based on the principle that the emotional aspect of victimhood "be recognized as a critical part of the injury inflicted."[70] At the same time, another category of "invisible" victims was becoming increasingly vocal in the public domain: the survivors of homicide victims, and they built a movement of their own, looking to the work of feminist activists responding to the emotional crisis of rape survivors as a model for their own projects.[71] In the late 1970s, two former police officers published books on the psychological needs of victims of crime, and over time their recommendations were used to train police assigned to victims of crime units to come.[72] More generally, as Young wrote in 1988, "flowing directly from the understanding of post-traumatic stress and crisis are a set of tools to aid in the diagnosis, intervention, and treatment of the distress precipitated by crime and other traumas." Taken together with the development of a "network of service programs" designed for their care, victims of crime "today" are far more likely to recover from "the psychological wounds of victimization" than were their "counterparts" but a mere decade ago.[73]

The foundations for psychological crisis intervention may have been laid in the 1970s by feminist activists, but psychological first-aid for victims of crime would truly flourish only in the decades to come. It did so largely because of the power and reach of the National Organization for Victim Assistance (NOVA), which fielded its first crisis response team in 1986 in response to a mass murder committed in the Edmond, Oklahoma, post office. NOVA "initiated a practical model for community crisis intervention in the aftermath of tragedy that affects large groups of people," the success of which "engendered the National Crisis Response Project, which made trained volunteer crisis intervention available to address the emotional impact of crime and other disasters." Funding for such projects would continue to expand through the 1990s, under the leadership of President Clinton and his embrace of a punitive anti-crime agenda.[74] By September 2001, psychiatric crisis intervention in the aftermath of tragedy had become such the norm that, as I mentioned in the introduction, one of the first responses to the attacks on the Twin Towers in Manhattan was to mobilize mental health practitioners for city residents and first responders who had survived.

By the mid-1990s, the campaign to transform the judicial system to be more responsive to the so-called rights of victims had come into its own. Victims now had their own set of legal rights, including the right to be heard in sentencing and parole hearings via "victim impact statements." In Jill Lepore's words, these statements combine the "therapeutic, speak-your-truth commitment of a trauma centered feminism and the punitive, lock-them-up-imperative of law-and-order conservatism."[75] Yet perhaps one effect of the victim impact statement was to expose the false binary between the "feminist" and the "conservative." The victims' rights movement did not focus on "the issue of criminal violence against women," despite the rhetoric of the task force reports—no surprise, given that the conservative politics of the Reagan revolution, within which it gained national recognition and power, had organized against feminism and its critique of the patriarchal, nuclear family. It is also no surprise then that over time, the National Coalition Against Sexual Assault and the National Coalition Against Domestic Violence broke from NOVA. These feminist organizations were not aligned with the Reagan administration, and they did not want to be "criminal justice institutions." Instead, they understood their work to be building a grassroots movement.[76] Nevertheless, it was *in tandem* that a progressive, if largely white, feminist movement, on the one hand, and a conservative, anti-racial justice victims-of-crime movement, on the other, were behind the reform of key aspects of the criminal justice system as they concern us here. In so doing, they also helped to transform the meaning of PTSD in an American social imaginary.

By the 1990s, paralleling developments in France, albeit here in response to a presumed epidemic of crime rather than "terror," psychiatric first-aid had become an established part of crisis response, with trauma understood to be a common response to the experience of violence that required immediate attention.[77] The traumatized subject had become increasingly synonymous with the nonmilitary and presumptively white citizen *qua* innocent victim of sexual assault and other violent crimes.

## (Post-)Vietnam Syndrome Reimagined

The trauma of Vietnam veterans was also incorporated into the new clinical victimology, moving an acknowledgment of the role of perpetration and guilt ever further off center stage. One example is the volume edited by Frank Ochberg, *Post-Traumatic Therapy and Victims of Violence,* in which he lists the VA among places where victims can be found. Under the rubric the Victim of War and Atrocity, the volume discusses three populations: American veterans of the war in Vietnam; survivors of Nazi concentration camps and their children; and refugees from Southeast Asia displaced by the American war.[78] Holocaust survivors clearly occupy the position of the victim, Ochberg writes, but even if counterintuitive, the Vietnam veteran may not be as radically different as might be assumed. Key to post-traumatic therapy for Holocaust survivors was the "restoration of personal integrity and Jewish identity." By "analogy," Ochberg states, "the adolescent American soldier in Vietnam endured state-sanctioned carnage and upon returning home was treated as a pariah by fellow Americans, causing a loss of a sense of homeland, family, and culture."[79]

John P. Wilson, one of the authors in the volume, offers a particularly telling example of the ways in which the Vietnam veteran's trauma was reframed in the 1980s. Delving into the character of their "victimization," he writes, "By victimized, we do not wish to convey the impression that all Vietnam veterans were victims in the traditional sense of being coerced and helpless victims of circumstances." Wilson concedes the difference between obvious victims and men returning from combat routinely waged against a civilian population. Nevertheless, veterans *are* victims; they are victims of humiliation suffered by being met with a critical homecoming. Vietnam veterans were "rejected, exploited, and pushed down by government and society both during and after the war," Wilson declared; they were denied adequate benefits and psychological care.[80] In Wilson's hands, the etiology of veteran trauma is no longer rooted in the war itself—in what American troops experienced and did on the battlefields of Vietnam. It is a consequence of the soldier's own society's callous disregard for the sacrifices he made in Vietnam. Reframing the veteran as victim was so pervasive by 1992 that even Judith Herman would fall prey to such depictions. In *Trauma and Recovery,* she notes "commonalities" among Vietnam veterans and incest and rape survivors without ever explicitly acknowledging their distinct subject positions in relation to violence, an elision that is quite extraordinary given how prominent rape was in veteran testimonies in the early to mid-1970s about atrocities committed by American troops during the war.[81]

Wilson's psychiatric analysis resonates with a much more general reframing of the war and its veterans that came to prominence in the 1980s. Casting the Vietnam veteran as victim was rooted less in an improved clinical understanding of veterans' trauma than in a political climate in which the United States was grappling with the legacy of the failed war. The war in Vietnam and the position of its veterans in American society emerged as fraught objects of public debate, ever more so as the 1970s gave way to the 1980s. With a pervasive narrative of both a crisis among Vietnam veterans (unemployment, trauma, addiction) and their supposed neglect and rejection by Americans upon their return home, presidents from Richard Nixon through Jimmy Carter sought to honor and recognize veterans of a war that had so divided the nation. Nixon proclaimed Vietnam Veteran Day on March 29, 1974. And on July 1, 1980, President Carter, following his declaration of Vietnam Veterans Week to coincide with Memorial Day in 1979,[82] signed a congressional resolution authorizing the creation of a Vietnam War memorial in Washington, DC.[83]

By the mid-1970s, thinkers on the political right, such as Norman Podhoretz, Walter Laqueur, and others associated with the magazine *Commentary*, had begun self-consciously to reframe the story of the war as part of rebuilding American "power, prestige, and patriotism."[84] As this group of conservative cold warriors saw things, the ability of the United States to exercise its military power abroad depended on the war in Vietnam being rehabilitated at home.[85] With the conservative takeover of the political arena following the 1980 presidential election, their commitment to rewriting the history and meaning of the war would have powerful allies inside the White House.

During Reagan's presidency, realizing the dreams of the conservative movement that accompanied it to power, reinvesting the war with dignity and honor became a national political mission. "Several years [ago]," Reagan declared, "we brought home a group of American fighting men who obeyed their country's call and fought as bravely and well as any Americans in our history. They came home without a victory not because they had been defeated but because they had been denied permission to win."[86] Far from a misadventure, in this rendition, the war in Vietnam was a "noble cause."[87] According to Andrew Bacevich, Reagan and his allies were "determined to reverse Vietnam War–induced disillusionment so that the public, Congress, and military officers would overcome their reluctance to use force abroad," and "refurbishing the image of the war" by rewriting the reasons for military defeat was essential to that ambition.[88] Moreover, refurbishing the image of the war necessitated remaking the image of its veterans as well—and reconstructing the public's purported negative attitude toward them.

The 1980s were witness to many a public ritual designed to recognize and honor Vietnam veterans. On May 7, 1985, for example, a quarter of a million vets marched in a ticker-tape parade in New York City; nearly a million people lined the streets in support. Demonstrations large and small continued in the years to come—in Houston, Chicago, and smaller cities across the nation. Meanwhile, in November 1982, the dedication ceremony for the Vietnam Veterans Memorial was attended by as many as 150,000 individuals. As part of a four-day tribute, "the names of all 57,939 servicemen who died in Vietnam were read at the Washington Cathedral."[89]

As the American political imaginary continued its shift rightward, so too did psychiatric theorizations of trauma suffered by American veterans transform. That is not to say that mental health practitioners working with veterans necessarily abandoned the understanding that veterans were traumatized by the violence they experienced and enacted in Vietnam, even if they did also increasingly reframe their trauma as also born of their mistreatment upon returning home. Nevertheless, theories and explanations of Vietnam War–era combat trauma traveled ever further away from the radical politics of its original architects. In the words of the *National Vietnam Veterans Readjustment Study*, submitted to the Senate Committee on Veterans Affairs on July 14, 1988,

> During the 13 years since the Ford proclamation [formally ending the American war in Vietnam], the Nation has hotly debated the nature and extent of the problem faced by these Vietnam era veterans in readjusting to civilian life. Hundreds of articles and dozens of books concerning Vietnam veterans' readjustment to civilian life have been published, and the plight of these veterans has been a popular theme in the news media, television, and motion pictures. In part, the resurgence of public interest in the Vietnam War and its veterans reflects some dramatic and precedent-setting changes in the country's socioemotional climate in recent years, changes that have gradually depoliticized somewhat the debate over the mental health of Vietnam veterans.[90]

Depoliticization was, of course, a decidedly political move. It became part of professional practice and official policy alike. Therapists at VA clinics and Veterans Outreach Centers—the latter initially established as an alternative to the VA, which was a suspect institution to many a veteran, who often refused to go—increasingly "depoliticized the veteran patients' moral questioning" by moving to a "more professional model" to replace earlier models of peer counseling and rap groups.[91] This shift in therapeutic approach was already in the making by the late 1970s, but it took official, institutional form only with the appointment of Arthur Blank as director of the Veterans' Outreach program in 1982. Highly cognizant of the Reagan administration's suspicion of the program and the risk it posed to funding, Blank, himself a former a military psychiatrist in Vietnam and subsequently an anti-war activist—a member of the VVAW and a founder of its Connecticut chapter—pushed for the centers' "professionalization" and purged them of anti-war activists. That is what it took to save the centers from the budget cuts proposed by the Reagan administration.[92]

The call for depoliticization reached well beyond the halls of clinical care, however. Even as the Reagan administration and conservative pundits fought in explicitly ideological terms against a reading of the Vietnam War as both imperial over-reach and a loss on the battlefield, so, too, did they partake in a national project—and growing sentiment—that the nation needed to "heal" from the war—that is, it needed to set aside political divisions and support the veterans who had returned from Vietnam. The project to build the Vietnam War memorial was framed from its beginning as just such an effort. As described by Hagopian, "the memorial's sponsors espoused a depoliticized version of the discourse of healing and reconciliation that emerged in discussions of Vietnam vets and the 'post-Vietnam Syndrome' in the 1970s." By being "apolitical" —by refusing to make any "statement about the war"—the memorial would unite Americans regardless of their political opinions on the war itself. The struggle to build the memorial would not escape politics altogether, as Maya Lin's design was argued by many a conservative politician and veteran to be a mark of shame. Ideological conflicts over how best to memorialize American veterans ultimately led to a compromise in which a more heroic-looking statue was added to the site, and it was only at that point that Reagan agreed to speak at the memorial. Nevertheless, it was in presenting a discourse of healing from the war as *apolitical,* as a call to citizens of any ideological stripe to welcome the veterans home, that the project was launched and realized, and that a "resolution" for those who opposed Maya Lin's design was achieved. And such talk of national healing was inseparable from rereading the war in Vietnam and recasting the psychological trauma suffered by Vietnam vets. Also part of this purported step beyond politics in the 1980s was a backlash against veterans who had been vocal critics of the war. Veterans who felt that their war and their sacrifices had been sorely maligned denied that atrocities were "standard operating procedure." They rejected "the stigma that ... attached to service in Vietnam."[93] They resented the pervasive image of the traumatized and psychotic vet that dominated films, television series, and newspaper accounts.

Tellingly, by the end of the 1970s, the focus of anti-war veteran activism itself had changed. Even among the radicals of the VVAW, attention had turned inward. With the war behind them, veterans were demanding benefits, treatment, and recognition from the US government. In Patrick Hagopian's words, they "were said to merely crave recognition and acceptance by their fellow Americans."[94] And with that narrative as frame, the war itself was recast as an "*American* tragedy." The war had "badly wounded and divided the nation," and now it was necessary that attention be paid to "those Americans who seemed most obviously wounded by the war—Vietnam veterans."[95] Two decades later, by the late 1990s, as noted by Jerry Lembcke, a veteran of the war and a sociologist at the College of Holy Cross, "the 'remembered' Vietnam war was not the war itself but the homecoming experience of the Vietnam Veterans," a memory of "Vietnam" that casts its long shadow over public discourse about the post-9/11 wars to this day.[96]

Emerging together with this backlash against anti-war politics and its representation of former American soldiers was a shift in where to locate the source of the psychological struggles (many) veterans faced, as discussed previously. If the experience of combat, and having committed or witnessed the commission of atrocities, dominated understandings of post-Vietnam syndrome in the mid-1970s—if, in other words, its focus was on the character of imperial violence abroad—by later in the decade and even more so through the 1980s, an alternative narrative began to congeal among mental health practitioners and in the public domain. American society was to blame for the Vietnam debacle. Even the seemingly settled issue of delayed onset—whether it was possible for symptoms of trauma to first begin to appear long after the traumatizing event—was brought back into question. Why assume that to be the only possible explanation for PTSD symptoms appearing years after veterans returned from the battlefield? Was it not possible, mental health practitioners were beginning to ask, that "the rate of psychiatric illness might also have been worsened by changing societal attitudes toward the war?" Tensions between "civilians" and soldiers were argued to have "augmented the difficulties of readjustment to civilian life."[97] As was true of Wilson's understanding of Vietnam veterans and their relationship to the new science of victimization, the US government and American society were to blame for veteran "readjustment" problems, that is, for their trauma. Seymour Leventman, a sociologist at Boston University, declared: "one can only reiterate that the negative legacy of Vietnam lies more in civilian society than on the psyches of Veterans."[98] In 1985, Arthur Egendorf would proclaim, "Sympathy for the Vietnam veteran has now joined motherhood and apple pie as a hallmark of true Americanism."[99]

By the mid-1980s, post-Vietnam syndrome, a diagnosis born of the early collaboration between radical psychiatrists and anti-war veterans, had given way to "the Vietnam syndrome." The psychological pain initially conceived as resulting from being an agent and instrument of American military violence in Southeast Asia had faded into near oblivion. As Robert J. Lifton lamented in an interview, the term they invented as a political critique of an imperial war was converted "into a symptom of a regime reluctant to get into Vietnam-like situations." The Vietnam syndrome now referred to the anti-war public sentiments which, according to conservatives like Podhoretz, were standing in the way of the United States fulfilling its historic mission through the free exercise of military power in a dangerous and divided world. The 1980s project of rewriting the war and transforming the figure of the veteran occurred alongside the rebuilding of the military as a professional force made up entirely of volunteers. Together the two projects would ensure, or so the thinking went, that this defeatist Vietnam syndrome would be set aside once and for all.[100]

# PART TWO

## 9/11 AND ITS AFTERMATH

# 3

# Soldier's Trauma, Revisited

As we have seen in the concept's development over nearly a half century, PTSD is anything but a stable object. Nevertheless, when the United States invaded Afghanistan on October 7, 2001, and subsequently Iraq on March 20, 2003, and as it became embroiled in sustained conflicts with neither a clear definition of victory nor an exit strategy, it did so in a psychiatric milieu quite different from those of previous American wars. Post-traumatic stress disorder was now widely recognized as a very real affliction and a relatively common combat injury. And as the wars dragged on, medical studies, federal documents, newspaper and magazine articles, television and radio newscasts, and talk programs declared over and over that PTSD was "one of the signature injuries of the US conflicts in Afghanistan and Iraq."[1] Federal funding for research on PTSD in military and veteran populations has mushroomed since 2001, and with a steady stream of war casualties reviving the 1970s-era focus on combat trauma, clinical understandings of PTSD—its etiology, phenomenology, and treatment protocols—have begun to shift yet again. In the context of decades-long wars, cardinal assumptions that grounded definitions of PTSD in the DSM-III and subsequent editions have begun to fray.

Albeit reframed within the demands and evidentiary protocols of what is known as "evidence-based medicine," the medical paradigm that took over the field of psychiatry during the 1990s, many of the questions being posed in the new millennium sound familiar. Does the etiology of PTSD require a "life-threatening" event? Can exposure to other, less immediately imperiling forms of trauma also cause the condition? Is "fear" its definitive affective response? Other questions that have arisen over the past two decades, however, fly in the face of one of the DSM-III's central commitments: that the specific character of the traumatic event does not matter. Clinical researchers are asking whether acts of perpetration produce different kinds of traumatic afterlives than do experiences of life-threat, as well as whether all precipitating events are necessarily sudden, dramatic, severe. In responding to such questions, clinical researchers in the military and the VA in the post-9/11 period have developed specific treatment protocols for different kinds of war-zone traumas. Some have proposed "moral injury" as a distinct traumatic experience, a concept that harkens back to the post-Vietnam syndrome's focus on moral transgression, albeit, as I will show, stripped of the radical anti-war political commitments that informed that earlier understanding of combat trauma and of what it would take to heal.

Over the next two chapters, I map contemporary psychiatric debates about the character of combat trauma and the most effective treatment protocols for dealing with it that have emerged in very different disciplinary and political milieus than existed during the war in Vietnam. I discuss disciplinary and institutional demands that frame how war trauma must be tracked and treated, tracing ongoing shifts in clinical research on combat trauma as precipitated by a return to military as distinct from "civilian" PTSD. And I pay attention to the concept of "moral injury," not primarily as a potentially new diagnostic category but more because some of its assumptions about combat, troops, war zones, and trauma are being incorporated into research on and discussions of combat-related PTSD. While these may seem to be arcane, internal disciplinary debates, they arise in the context of powerful political and fiscal concerns, and they iterate and inform the combat-trauma imaginary under-girding contemporary militarism, as I will continue to track in chapters 5 and 6.

Anticipating and attempting to deal with soldier trauma has now been incorporated into the defense establishment itself, and as such, in stark contrast to its earlier framing as political cri-tique, recognizing and treating combat trauma is essential to the business of war. Trauma is but one casualty of war, both inevitable and, presumably, treatable. Effective and *short-term* treatment protocols are required for active-duty troops who need to be able to redeploy to the killing fields. It is also key vis-à-vis veteran populations, given that the costs of veterans' mental health care are projected to skyrocket for decades to come. In sum, within the context of a discipline that defines itself as "evidence-based," the military's need to sustain combat readiness in the absence of a draft and within the reality of fiscal constraints, a space and language of political critique disap-pears. Diagnosing and treating PTSD has become but one more chink in the armor of prosecuting war.

As I elaborate in Chapter 5, some clinicians have laid claim to moral injury as a "novel" (potential) diagnosis. It is a form of combat trauma, they argue, and requires a specific clinical response. We see in these debates the emergence of a psychi-atric subject reminiscent of the one imagined by the architects of post-Vietnam syndrome: she is haunted by her conscience, suffers guilt, and must embrace responsibility for what she has done if she is to heal. And yet, as I illustrate, in the context of a "culture of war"[2] that insists on the professionalism and moral-ity of both the individual American soldier and the US military as an institution, and enjoins the public to "support the troops," discussions of combat trauma as moral injury are framed by a moral relativism and political neutrality that makes it possible for clinicians, and perhaps the soldiers and veterans in their care, to sidestep the complex ethical and political questions that the architects of post-Vietnam syndrome always kept in sight. As "moral pain" meets evidence-based medicine, on the one hand, and humanitarian reason, on the other, medical science does the work of depoliticizing war.

## The State of Mental Health

Terri Tanielian, a PTSD researcher at RAND, spoke with people from the Pentagon early on in the post-9/11 wars. As she recounted before an audience at the 2018 Strong Star Combat PTSD Conference, there was a lot of "denial" about the mental health crises about to unfold. Military leaders with whom she spoke were all insisting that there was nothing to worry about. As paraphrased by Tanielian: "We don't have to worry about PTSD, because we aren't going to be there that long."[3] Less than two years later, the Pentagon was already less sanguine in their predictions. In July 2003, a mere four months into the invasion and occupation of Iraq, the US Army Surgeon General appointed a mental health advisory team (MHAT) to go into the field to evaluate mental health issues among deployed troops.[4] As summed up in a 2008 RAND report: "Early evidence suggests that the psychological toll of these deployments—many involving prolonged exposure to combat-related stress over multiple rotations—may be disproportionately high compared with the physical injuries of combat."[5]

Coming into the post-9/11 wars, historian David Kieran has argued, the Army was not prepared for the psychological fallout of the sustained, counterinsurgency wars it was about to fight. Shifting away from the war in Vietnam, by the 1980s the US military was imagining and planning for a very different kind of war: a quick, albeit devastatingly destructive confrontation with the Soviet Union, most likely on the European front.[6] That kind of war, the Army Medical Department presumed, would generate "combat fatigue," which, in contrast to PTSD, was understood to be "both short-lived and easily treatable." According to Kieran, the Army assumed that "effectively treating combat stress would prevent long-term psychological problems." The Army Medical Department's advice also cautioned that "making too much of battle fatigue might precipitate permanent disability."[7]

The fact that the Army Medical Department carried out clinical studies of combat fatigue did not translate into the implementation of sound policies on the ground, however. In none of the American invasions of the 1980s and 1990s was "combat stress control" practiced effectively, and it was not until 1994 that the Army issued its first *Leaders' Manual for Combat Stress*. More generally, according to Kieran, "If the Army entered the twenty-first century with knowledge, capacity, and an awareness of the methodological, theoretical, and institutional challenges that affected mental health care, it did not imagine the wars that it would fight after the September 11 attacks." That is not to say that previous research into the mental health of soldiers had no impact in the post-9/11 era: When the first MHAT arrived in Iraq in August 2003, it drew on expertise developed during the previous decade. Throughout the 1990s, the Walter Reed Army Institute of Research had dispatched Human Dimensions Research Teams to the places where US soldiers were deployed to conduct soldier well-being surveys. In so doing, they "developed a methodology for real-time research," which guided mental health research when the twenty-first century wars in Iraq and Afghanistan began.[8]

Focused on PTSD, major depression, and traumatic brain injury (TBI), Tanielian and Jaycox's RAND report assessed the prevalence of mental health problems among deployed troops, evaluated the availability of appropriate medical and psychiatric care, and summarized existing research on these diagnoses and on "evidence-based" treatment options.[9] Estimating that "upward of 26 percent of returning troops may have mental health conditions," the report ascribes the startling number to "advances in both medical technology and body armor" that has meant many more troops survive wounds that would have killed them during previous wars.[10] As a consequence, casualties of a different sort were proliferating, particularly the "invisible wounds" of PTSD and TBI.[11]

Whether in the RAND study or the various MHAT reports, mental health challenges presumed to be "unique" to the post-9/11 wars loom large. Even if one explanation for the high incidence of PTSD is the higher survival rates of grievously wounded soldiers, that is not the only "signal difference" between these and previous wars. The wars in Iraq and Afghanistan are the first extended conflicts the US has fought in the absence of a draft. As of October 31, 2007, 1,638,817 military personnel had deployed to Iraq or Afghanistan.[12] Seventeen years into the war, that number had risen to 2.77 million.[13] With no draft—that is, "no easily accessible personnel pool to draw on"[14] to keep up with the wars' force demands—the military has sent soldiers on longer deployments and rotated troops in and out of Iraq and Afghanistan on multiple tours. And it is the psychiatric consensus that multiple combat tours increase the chances that military personnel will experience mental health problems. The first year in which significant numbers of soldiers deployed for their third or fourth times was 2007, when data compiled by the MHAT reported that, on average, 17.9 percent of those surveyed screened positive for mental health problems (acute stress,[15] depression, or anxiety); those on their third and fourth deployments were at significantly higher risk. Rates of mental health problems rose to 27.2 percent by the third and fourth tours.[16] With numbers rising year after year, mental health issues became a "tactical dilemma" for Army leaders.[17] How was the military supposed to sustain a combat-ready force in the face of the proliferation of so-called invisible wounds?

Research teams looking for the causes of such widespread mental health problems identified a number of possible factors. "Chronic concerns" are significant precipitators, with separation from family, lack of privacy, sleep deprivation—in addition to long deployments—all correlating with increased risk to mental health. Also noted is a direct link between deployment lengths and rates of depression, anxiety, and acute stress disorder, with the highest risk for mental health problems peaking at months eight, nine, and ten in the field. The primary risk to mental health, however, is combat exposure, with the rise in psychiatric problems over the course of soldiers' deployments understood as "a function of increases in combat experiences."[18] Based on a soldier well-being survey listing thirty-three kinds of "events" soldiers might experience while deployed, RAND concludes, "regardless of the sample, measurement tool, or time of assessment, combat duty and being wounded were consistently associated with positive screens for PTSD."[19]

The "quality" and accessibility of mental health care for military personnel in the war zone and back home was another concern for the military. And the situation did not look good. The ratio of mental health professionals to total Army personnel was 1:734 in 2007, with mental health personnel in the war zones reporting staff shortages and high burnout rates.[20] As Charles W. Hoge, former director of the Division of Psychiatry and Neuroscience at the Walter Reed Army Institute of Research, pointed out along with co-authors in an article in the *American Journal of Psychiatry*, the Army had identified "deficiencies in in-theater mental health services" in 2005–2006 as a problem.[21] And beyond problems in the field, a RAND survey from 2008 found that just over half of military and ex-military personnel with diagnosable mental health problems had received treatment in the past year.[22] The reasons for the shortfall in services are complex, including not having enough mental health personnel in war zones (especially on forward operating bases) and the sheer volume of need. In addition, stigma and fear of consequences for one's military career play major roles in making military personnel wary of seeking out mental health care. What's more, RAND cautions, those who have access to care often do not have access to *effective* care. An "increase [in] the cadre of providers who are trained and certified to deliver proven (evidence-based) care, in all sectors, military and civilian, serving previously deployed personnel" is needed.[23] As medical anthropologist Erin Finley characterized the anticipated change in course, "treatment modalities ... judged on ... their ability to consistently produce positive health outcomes in clinical trials" should be preferred over treatment protocols validated on the basis of the "accumulated experience of individual providers or the theoretical orientation of professional schools of thought."[24]

## In Search of Evidence

The key concept here is *evidenced-based*. Calls to establish new measures of effectiveness for the psychiatric treatment of combat trauma, as well as for other psychiatric diagnoses, predated the post-9/11 wars, resulting from a broad shift in the discipline of psychiatry, beginning with Robert Spitzer's commitment to bringing the field in line with the rest of medicine in the DSM-III. Over time, this effort has marginalized psychodynamic approaches to clinical care in favor of biomedical models and pharmacological interventions. And that shift, as argued by Tanya Luhrmann, has been propelled as much by the shifting economy of American healthcare as by "ideology"—that is, a commitment to a "biomedical model"—or what I would call, following Thomas Kuhn, a paradigm shift within the discipline itself.[25] With the rise of managed care in the 1990s, therapeutic protocols with no time limits and no explicitly defined goals or criteria for success would no longer be covered by insurance companies. As of the 1990s, as recounted in a report by the American Psychological Association, "the evidence-based practice movement has become a key feature of health care systems and health care policy," and henceforth, "clinical practice guidelines should be based on careful systematic weighing of its data and clinical expertise."[26] Following the insistence on evidence-based practice in broader medical fields, in other words, treatment based on "intuition" or "unsystematic clinical experience" was no longer acceptable. Psychiatric practice was to be guided by "scientific, clinically relevant research."[27] As one expert in a novel field called "quality of care" told Luhrmann, therapy had to have "an identifiable role " framed "in terms of a defined population, a clear therapeutic process, and specified outcomes of with a credible time course."[28]

Neither the Department of Defense nor the Veterans Administration were shielded from this shift to evidence-based care. As early as 1999, they formed the Joint VA/DoD Evidence-Based Practice Work Group to make "decisions about which clinical practice guidelines (CPG) for specific conditions will be developed and [to oversee] their development."[29] With the rise of an interest in PTSD following the onslaught of cases from the post-9/11 wars, the working group issued its first CPG for treating PTSD in 2004.[30] Awarding four different psychotherapy interventions an A rating, *Clinical Practice Guideline for the Management of Post-Traumatic Stress* (2004) recommended cognitive therapy and exposure therapy. Six years later, the VA/DoD proudly recalled their 2004 report as having been "the first effort to bring evidence-based practice to clinicians providing care to trauma survivors and patients with stress disorders in the VA and DoD."[31]

This push for evidence-based treatment protocols was but one piece of a larger effort to standardize and centralize psychiatric treatment across the VA and DoD and to reduce its long-term costs. By 2010, the VA was no longer merely putting its official imprimatur on particular treatment protocols. Declaring prolonged exposure (PE) and cognitive processing therapy (CPT) the "gold standard" of treatments, it *required* that they "be made available to veterans throughout the system."[32] To quote Charles Hoge and his colleagues, increasing "the degree to which research has guided programmatic changes and the willingness to study these challenges to optimize clinical and public health care strategies" is among the most significant differences between post-9/11 and previous wars.[33]

Prolonged exposure therapy is based on a specific model of PTSD. In Erin Finley's description, "When a trauma occurs, the circumstances surrounding that trauma are imprinted on the memory in such a way that they become associated with high levels of physiological arousal and anxiety—an evolutionary mechanism intended to help the individual identify and elude similar dangers in future." The traumatized individual develops avoidance behaviors, a way of living that works to isolate her from possible "triggers" in the world.[34] PE interrupts the triggering process by "habituating" the patient to the triggers. As described by David J. Morris, a Marine veteran and Iraq war correspondent who wrote a memoir about his experience of PTSD, the first part of treatment involved "me closing my eyes and retelling the story of a traumatic event of my choice a number of times. This would continue until I was no longer afraid of it, and it no longer activated a fear response in my body, until … it became 'habituated.'" An "in vivo" experience followed:

> I would be asked to do things in the real world that in some way resembled the traumatic event in question. The theory is that by "reactivating" the fearful memories in the safety of a therapist's office and in the relative safety of the real non-Iraq world, I would unlearn bad trauma-related behaviors and learn to incorporate new information about the world. I would unlearn the trauma in a way not unlike the way that Pavlov trained his dogs to associate food with other, unrelated stimuli.[35]

Comprised of eight to fifteen weekly sessions, PE was designed to help patients unlearn their physiological response to the original trauma, to attenuate the affect—that is, the intense fear tied to a specific memory. In technical terms, it is an "extinction learning" model.[36]

For its part, cognitive processing therapy (CPT) is an adaptation of cognitive behavioral techniques (CBT) initially developed to treat phobias. According to Aaron Beck, one of the architects of cognitive therapy, "Therapist and patient work together to identify the patient's distorted cognitions, which are derived from his dysfunctional beliefs. These cognitions and beliefs are subjected to empirical testing."[37] Cognitive processing therapy for PTSD involves having the patient confront the traumatic event, generally over the course of twelve weekly therapy sessions, by doing a lot of "contextualizing." Therapists help patients to "learn to identify and challenge unhelpful thoughts"[38] and come to understand, for example, that their behavior or experience was the result of circumstances (the fog of war); that they were nineteen years old and had been put in an impossible situation; that they are not responsible for the death of their friend. Working together, patient and therapist compile a "stuck point" log, a list of presumed false beliefs about the trauma-inducing event that hinder recovery—for example, that "losing Nate near Sangin [in Afghanistan] was my fault. My patrol took a bad route back to base and walked into that IED. As assistant patrol leader, I should have said something."[39] One VA therapist related the story of a Vietnam veteran who had been struggling for decades with his responsibility for the death of a soldier under his command. The veteran said he let the soldier run reconnaissance at the front, even though he was still pretty "green." The therapist posed some questions. *How* responsible are you for his death? Was it you who decided on the mission? How much of the responsibility resides with officers who outranked you? How much with commanders removed from the battlefield altogether?

As it happens, however, the evidence for the effectiveness of CPT and PE in military populations is rather thin, a consequence of the fact that in the 1980s and 1990s, as I discussed in Chapter 2, clinical research on PTSD focused on "civilian" victims of violent crimes. In developing prolonged exposure and cognitive processing therapies for PTSD in the 1980s and 1990s, the main target population was victims of rape. Over time, the protocols were extended to other kinds of "civilian," single-incident traumas (an accident, a fire, an assault). By the early aughts, little evidence of their efficacy with combat trauma existed.[40] According to the VA's 2004 clinical guidelines for PTSD, randomized clinical trials of cognitive therapies demonstrated "a substantial treatment effect for civilian men and women with PTSD from a variety of non–combat-related traumas," but no trials had been conducted to specifically "evaluate the use of CT in military or veteran patients."

For its part, there had been a few randomized clinical trials of PE for "male combat-related trauma," and they concluded that the treatment is "less consistent and the degree of improvement

**Table 3.1** Evidence. (From *VA/DoD Clinical Practice Guideline for the Management of Post-Traumatic Stress*, 2004: I-21.)

| Recommendation | Sources | QE | Overall Quality | R |
|---|---|---|---|---|
| 1 CT is effective with civilian men and women exposed to combat and non-combat trauma. | Lovell, et al., 2001 Marks et al., 1998 | I | Good | A |
| 2 CT is effective with military and veterans with combat- and non-combat-related PTSD. | Working Group Consensus | III | Poor | I |
| 3 CT is effective for women with PTSD associated with sexual assualt. | Resick et al., 2002 | I | Good | A |

*QE = Equality of Evidence; R = Recommendation (see Appendix A)*

of PTSD symptoms appears to be less pronounced" than for those suffering (non–war-related) civilian traumas.[41]

In the decades following the war in Vietnam, the VA—unlike the military itself—continued to confront and treat persistent PTSD. Prior to the paradigm shift in favor of cognitive therapies, it relied on a combination of psychodynamic approaches and medications. As described by Erin Finley, who wrote about psychologists and social workers at a VA mental health clinic in San Antonio, Texas, up until about 2006 they offered individual and group-based psychotherapy, combined with medications prescribed by the psychiatrists on staff. PTSD patients were considered enrollees in the clinic's "long-term care plan." Therapy was understood to take time; PTSD was framed as an enduring disorder that could be "managed rather than cured."[42] When Finley began her ethnographic research at this Texas VA, the "standard of care," as had been true for decades at VA clinics across the country, involved drug protocols combined with a diverse array of psychodynamically inclined therapies with no preset time limits.

About the VA clinic in San Antonio, Finley writes that a "revolution was brewing" when she began her fieldwork in 2006. It marked a generational shift in how mental health personnel were being trained in the profession at large. And with more and more veterans of the post-9/11 wars coming in for treatment, younger and newer staff regarded the system in place as "unsustainable … in the absence of a continually expanding staff," which they were all too aware would not be forthcoming. The VA was coming under increasing political pressure to ensure that veterans of the American wars in Iraq and Afghanistan received what was termed "prompt and effective care," which the current system, with its policy of largely untested long-term therapy, seemed ill equipped to deliver. When hiring new staff, the San Antonio VA hospital looked for clinicians trained in cognitive behavioral therapies, particularly those "conversant with the relatively new and comparatively short-term evidence-supported treatments." The shift away from what were expected to be extended courses of treatment, writes Finley, "cut to the heart of how clinicians understood psychological trauma itself."[43] It also spoke to what kinds of funds for what kinds of treatments were likely to be available going forward.

Insofar as VA clinics across the nation did implement this transformation in standards of care for PTSD, the decision was not driven by robust clinical evidence. The VA, the DoD, and the Institute of Medicine (of the National Academy of Sciences) all recommended—and, in the case of the VA, required—CPT and PE as "first-line" treatments for PTSD despite the underwhelming results of the very few clinical trials that existed. In 2005 and 2006, the VA allocated substantial funds to pay for "the national cognitive processing therapy and prolonged exposure therapy training programs until the costs of the programs could be integrated into VAs congressional budget submission."[44] As already noted, there was immense political pressure on the VA to demonstrate that veterans were being successfully cared for. There was also a recognition that the costs of long-term psychodynamic treatments offered by the VA were unsustainable in the face of the numbers of traumatized veterans projected for the years and decades to come.[45] And, as we saw in Chapter 1, compared to the way psychiatrists understood combat trauma in the aftermath of the war in Vietnam, there was now a very different notion of the traumatized veteran himself, as a professional soldier injured on a job he signed up for rather than a traumatized subject and citizen—a draftee—coming to terms with brutal actions he witnessed and executed on behalf of the US government on foreign soil.

In their efforts to revamp clinical approaches to combat PTSD, the VA and DoD set about compiling data in real time. Officials declared that, for the first time, combat PTSD would not be studied only retrospectively; epidemiological studies "are being conducted throughout the course of the deployment cycle—i.e., a week before being deployed, while troops are in theater, and immediately upon their return."[46] In the words of the new *Practice Guidelines for the Management of Post-Traumatic Stress*, "our perspective must become prospective: building on the lessons of the past and serving those in the present but also aiming at the future in order to maximize preparedness *and, if possible, prevention*."[47] Clinical research was also to focus on trauma prevention: Are there drugs or training programs (for example, resilience training) that can prevent the onset of PTSD? Are there ways to forfend, psychologically, against combat trauma?[48] At bottom, the concern here is with force protection, that is, ensuring an adequate supply of "healthy" military personnel to carry out decades-long wars in an era in which a military draft is out of the question. There are also echoes here of a particular technoscientific fantasy: that one might find a way to conduct war while averting, in advance, its damaging psychological consequences.

In 2007, six years after the start of the post-9/11 wars, Congress allocated substantial federal funding for PTSD treatment and research. Studies were reporting a brewing mental health crisis, and they predicted astronomical increases in the costs of treatment in the years to come. With estimates of 17 percent of troops suffering from PTSD and 25 percent from psychological diagnoses of some variety, the threat of huge and ongoing disability payments to veterans well into the distant future attracted congressional attention. (By 2004, that cost had already reached $4.3 billion annually.)[49] Congress passed a $900 million budget supplement to address PTSD, two-thirds of which went to treatment and the remaining third to research. Between

2005 and 2009, VA funding for intramural PTSD research rose from $9.9 to $24.5 million, increasing the number of studies of PTSD from 47 to 96.[50] PTSD research received another federal boost on August 31, 2012, when President Obama issued Executive Order 13625, directing the DoD, VA, Department of Health and Human Services, and the Department of Homeland Security to "take steps to meet the current and future demand for mental health and substance abuse treatment services for veterans, service members, and their families."[51] An era of sub-stantial clinical research into military PTSD had begun.

## Effective Care

In response to the first funding call, Alan Peterson, a retired Army psychologist who had previously deployed to Iraq, gath-ered a team of researchers to apply for money from the DoD. Now known as Strong Star (an acronym for the South Texas Research Network Organization Guiding Studies on Trauma and Resilience), Peterson's group was awarded a $35 million grant in 2008. In 2013, they received another $45 million in federal funding. Over the first five years, Strong Star focused on evaluating existing PTSD treatment protocols. "One of the things we've found," Peterson said in an interview in 2013, "is that standard evidence-based therapies for civilian populations need some tailoring to allow them to work in a military setting. They are not 'plug and play.'"[52] Buoyed by the federal funding, beginning in 2008 Strong Star researchers began to investigate how best to adapt existing cognitive therapies to the needs of military personnel.

While the number of randomized clinical trials assessing ver-sions of cognitive processing and prolonged exposure clinical protocols in military populations has increased substantially, evidence of their effectiveness for military personnel remains equivocal at best. For example, Edna Foa, a psychologist at the University of Pennsylvania who is widely credited with having developed prolonged exposure therapy for sexual assault victims, led a study under the auspices of Strong Star. She tested different versions of PE with active-duty military personnel diagnosed with PTSD.[53] Relying on 366 participants who had deployed to Iraq and/or Afghanistan, the study focused on two questions: When delivered according to the standard protocol, is PE effective in a military population as compared to a psycho-therapy control group? And is PE delivered in a shorter, more intense format as effective as treatment according to a standard PE protocol?[54]

The good news for the military was that PE delivered over a shorter period was as effective as it was with the longer proto-col. And it lowered dropout rates.[55] The study's most striking result, however, was a rather different one: prolonged exposure delivered over eight weeks showed only "modest" reductions in PTSD symptoms when compared to *the control group*.[56] Compared to victims of sexual assault, PE for combat vet-erans did not hold up all that well, either. According to the PTSD Symptom Scale Interview (PSS-I), an instrument used to measure the presence and severity of PTSD, prolonged exposure produced a seven-point drop.[57] In contrast, a previous study of female sexual assault victims by Foa and her colleagues reported a sixteen-point drop.[58] At the six-month follow-up, Foa reports that 60 percent of those surveyed qualified for a PTSD diagno-sis. Nor are Foa's findings outliers. Randomized clinical trials of cognitive processing therapy for PTSD among military person-nel also found the protocol significantly less effective for them than for their nonmilitary counterparts.[59] What's more, looking at numbers other than the drop on the PSS-I scale, the results are even bleaker.

Dropout rates are high among soldiers and veterans, so how to keep them in treatment is a sustained focus of those doing clinical research. Speaking at the 2018 conference in San Antonio, one psychiatrist suggested that the dropout problem with evidence-based PTSD treatments "may be more related to treatment delivery modality than individual patient or treat-ment type." In a similar vein, a VA psychologist at the same conference argued that failure is *a consequence of* high dropout rates—that is, "patients not getting the 'right dose'" of CPT. We "know it works," she said, "if they get the right dose." But how was that to be achieved? The answer might be telehealth or home-based protocol deliveries, which certainly showed an improvement according to a study she carried out: dropout rates fell from 54.2 percent for office-based treatments to 20.7 percent for in home protocols. Nevertheless, one-fifth of the patient population dropping out remains rather high. What's more, calculations of "success" rates in these studies are not entirely straightforward, as the reduction in PTSD symptoms is often assessed with reference to the patient population that has completed the protocol. For example, Foa's conclusion that 60 percent of those who had completed her massed PE protocol still qualified for a PTSD diagnosis six months hence did not take into account the 48.2 percent of massed PE participants who had dropped out of the study by that point.[60]

The already disappointing success rates, in other words, are often serious overstatements, a fact that generated palpable tension at a panel on combat trauma at the annual meetings of the International Society for the Study of Traumatic Stress in the fall of 2013. While insisting on the efficacy of cognitive therapies, one panelist, a psychologist at the VA, reported that dropout rates for evidence-based treatments among veterans of the wars in Iraq and Afghanistan are about 50 percent. Someone in the audience noted how "sobering" that statistic is. Clearly frustrated by the speaker's continued commitment to the efficacy of these therapeutic protocols, the questioner continued: "Fifty percent don't come in the first place, [and] another fifty percent drop out. You end up treating fifteen percent!" A VA psychologist in the audience piled on: "At the end of the day, approximately 10 percent of [Iraq and Afghanistan] vets are engaging in PE and CBT therapies. *Ten percent* ... The uncomfortable truth is that there is all this VA effort into CBT and PE and yet they are dropping out ... Are we trying to put a round peg into a square hole?" He then suggested other options, like mindfulness, yoga, and meditation. While they may not count as the gold standard, he said, they are "harm reduction therapies [so why] don't we start there?"⁶¹ A third psychologist, visibly furious, went after the panelists: "Look at your data," she said to audience applause. "If I had a 35 to 40 percent dropout rate, I would quit … It doesn't take twelve sessions. It takes three to four years, thirty, forty, fifty, sixty sessions."⁶²

Randomized control studies demonstrate modest improvements in PTSD symptoms, at best. Dropout rates are high. Many patients fail to show up for treatment in the first place. And yet, rather than fundamentally reassessing CPT and PE—that is, rather than considering whether they might be ineffective for *substantive* reasons—recent combat PTSD research tends to tinker around the edges. Decades into a disciplinary commitment to short-term cognitive processing models for the treatment of PTSD, and faced with both an all-volunteer force that needs to be able to redeploy soldiers to the war theaters and a fiscal reality in which long-term therapeutic care is going to cost considerably more than the federal government is likely to allocate, the short-term treatment paradigm is just too powerful to be shaken to its core.

Some psychoanalytically and psychodynamically oriented practitioners do raise substantive concerns with regard to these so-called gold-standard evidence-based therapies, even as their reservations and critiques often fall on deaf ears. According to Finley, some worry that prolonged exposure is "at best unproven for use with combat PTSD and at worst unethical." Psychiatrists told her that it risks retraumatizing already vulnerable patients, who can "decompensate" from having to confront the traumatic memory too directly, possibly causing them to lose control temporarily or even to experience "a complete psychotic break."⁶³ Several psychiatrists, members of a working group on veterans' affairs of the International Psychoanalytical Association, told me that for PE to be safe and effective, the therapeutic relationship is key, in that it takes quite a bit of time and therapeutic work *before one can even begin* the exposure component. Establishing the therapeutic relationship—establishing trust—cannot be achieved during these very short-term clinical protocols.⁶⁴ Speaking to the audience in San Antonio, even a strong advocate for PE therapy among combat veterans struck a cautious note. In his experience of working with veterans of the war in Vietnam, he said, there were "keystone events that were so horrific that these men couldn't even tell us in therapy." It wasn't until session nine or ten that they would even mention the event. "Disclosure is really important," he continued, "and how to help people disclose" is complex. Remember, he cautioned, "combat PTSD is an interpersonal PTSD," the results of a "man-made" rather than "natural" disaster, to return to a distinction discussed in defining PTSD for the DSM-III.[65] And it is "also something that has many, many components to it. It is not a discrete event." He told of a Vietnam veteran he had treated who, "had three tours of duty in Vietnam [and] could describe to me years later forty-four different events that were arguably very traumatic."

In 2018, Charles W. Hoge and Kathleen M. Chard published a scathing editorial in the *Journal of the American Medical Association* on the state of treatment for combat PTSD. There is "a growing body of literature," they wrote, "showing that the margins of difference between trauma-focused and high-quality non–trauma-focused therapy conditions are negligible." Hoge and Chard do not call for the removal of cognitive processing and prolonged exposure as recommended therapies, even as they admit that could be the logical extension of their findings. Enough support in the broader medical literature remained, they thought, for the two protocols to continue to be plausibly recommended as first-line therapies. Even so, they suggest that the designation of what counts as "evidence-based" needs to be "reconsidered" and that a more substantive "evolution in PTSD treatments is required." Novel approaches, they insisted, must be pursued.[66]

Even when the VA "kicked off a rollout of PE" in 2008, requiring training for VA personnel in its techniques, they were already in search of other treatment options.[67] According to its 2014 report, the Institute of Medicine's congressional mandate included exploring "complementary and alternative therapies for PTSD, most especially, animal-assisted therapy."[68]

Yoga, meditation, therapy animals—such practices are becoming increasingly ubiquitous in efforts to care for soldiers and veterans diagnosed with PTSD. As one advocate for "mind-body" alternatives put it at the San Antonio conference, such approaches "may be more appealing for some people and associated with less stigma than 'talk therapy.'" Moreover, while a mind-body approach may not reduce PTSD symptoms, he said, it fosters a "different *relation to* those symptoms," offering a very different way of thinking about how to live with PTSD. "Rather than think I want to get rid of these intrusive thoughts," one can sit with them and learn that "they aren't going to upset me in the same way."

Given the bureaucratic and institutional commitments to evidence-based medicine, however, alternative practices are not going to be accepted on their own terms. As Tanielian of RAND told the audience at Strong Star's San Antonio conference, there has been a "rapid proliferation of nongovernmental community-based mental health support," but critical questions remain unanswered. "Most of these programs will produce data, but they don't have a comparison group, they don't know what an RCT [randomized control trial] is." Nevertheless, practitioners of alternative treatment protocols are lobbying Congress to fund their mind-body focused programs—"equine therapy, fly fishing, woodworking"—Tanielian listed them off rather dismissively. "How can we use our skills to intervene in [this] landscape?" she asked. "We know there is unmet need, so maybe we do need to be open to [alternative] interventions." But, she said, "we need evidence." In other words, the treatment of combat PTSD could not go back to the old days, during which, purportedly, there was no way to assess the success of therapeutic interventions. The hands-on experience or tacit knowledge among clinicians or alternative care practitioners who work with traumatized soldiers and veterans has no epistemological standing in the field, as randomized clinical trials are accepted as the only scientifically sound way to proceed. In this epistemological climate, one suborned by federal funding requirements, the VA, DoD, and National Institute of Mental Health are designing studies to evaluate alternative therapies for the treatment of combat trauma according to the protocols of evidence-based medicine.[69]

All of the aforementioned clinical research projects used DSM-IV criteria for diagnosing PTSD and other combat-induced mental health problems.[70] And yet a lot more seems to be going on here than can be reduced to its criteria. Reviewing the contemporary medical literature on combat PTSD and clinical guidelines for its treatment, the so-called gold-standard protocols just do not seem up to the task of grappling with the complexity, depth, and multifarious phenomenology of combat trauma. What if such approaches fundamentally misconstrue the very character of combat trauma? Brett Litz and Susan M. Orsillo, psychologists working at the VA hospital in Boston, address such questions by adumbrating a far larger and more diverse phenomenological field of traumatic experiences. In their contribution to the *Iraq War Clinician Guide* in 2004, they wrote: "It is safe to assume that all soldiers are impacted by their experiences in war. For many, surviving the challenges of war can be rewarding, maturing, and growth-promoting," thereby reproducing the rhetoric of the military and the war, as but one more possible and potentially very satisfying career.[71] Nevertheless, "the demands, stressors, and conflicts of participation in war can also be traumatizing, spiritually and morally devastating, and transformative in potentially damaging ways." After going through a clinical description of acute stress disorder, they continue, "Generally, the psychological risks from exposure to trauma are proportional to the magnitude or severity of exposure and the degree of life-threat and *perceived life-threat*."[72] The magnitude and severity of life-threat or perceived life-threat, however, is but the tip of the phenomenological iceberg. "Traumatic events," Litz and Orsillo insist, "need to be seen in the context of the totality of roles and experiences in the war-zone":

> perceived threat, low-magnitude stressors, exposures to ... civilian suffering, and exposure to death and destruction have each been found to contribute to risk for chronic PTSD. It should also

be emphasized that the trauma of war is colored by a variety of emotional experiences, not just horror, terror, and fear. Candidate emotions are sadness about losses, or frustrations about bearing witness to suffering, guilt about personal actions or emotions, and anger or rage about any number of facets of the war (e.g., command decisions, the behavior of the enemy).[73]

The consequences of combat can be experienced as "intensely demoralizing for some. It is also likely that memories of the aftermath of war (e.g., civilians dead or suffering) are particularly disturbing and salient." Litz and Orsillo elaborate: "specific terrorizing or grotesque war-zone experiences" can be traumatic, but so too can "dashed or painfully shattered expectations and beliefs about perceived coping capacities, military identity, and so forth." The clinician's job is thereby complex. She must understand "the veteran's prior schema about their role in the military (and society) and the trouble the person is having assimilating (incorporating) war-zone experiences into that existing belief system."[74] In short, they echo an understanding of PTSD that pre-dated its subsumption under the current therapeutic models; the *meaning* of the event needs to be taken into account.

Shattered expectations and beliefs, disillusionment, crises of military identity—these are not the kinds of traumatic afterlives that either prolonged exposure or cognitive processing therapies were designed to address. Nor were the gold-standard clinical protocols constructed with an awareness of the cumulative effects of complex and ongoing traumas, the cumulative assault on the psyche that both soldiers and civilians experience in war zones.[75] The architects of prolonged exposure and cognitive processing therapies for patients diagnosed with PTSD sought to alleviate the suffering of victims of a one-time, seemingly life-threatening event. And given that the development of these protocols focused on female victims of rape, as I mentioned previously, they were attentive to very particular affective states: fear, horror, anxiety, panic, modeled on and as a *physiological* response.

What about non–fear-based traumas? What about traumatic grief, the "grief of soldiers," or "militarized melancholia" about which Chaim Shatan wrote, a grief that led soldiers to seek meaning for the death of their comrades-in-arms by turning their anger outward toward any Vietnamese person they encountered on the ground?[76] For that matter, can the diagnostic criteria for PTSD recognize the "morally" or "spiritually devastating" experiences that are ubiquitous in combat? Take the following account, written by former Marine Corps veteran Tyler Boudreau, who deployed to Iraq:

> What about the orders I gave, from time to time, to use a heavy hand? What about the patrols I dispatched that returned to base with young marines in body bags? What about the approval I issued to snipers over the radio one night to shoot a man armed only with a shovel? (He was suspected of digging a hole for a roadside bomb.) Could any of these scenarios be called traumatic for me? In each case, there was violence felt and inflicted by somebody, absolutely, but my role was indirect; I was too far off to even hear the shot that felled that man with a shovel. Would any clinician in good conscience diagnose me with PTSD for those experiences alone?[77]

Or, as Lieutenant Colonel Douglas A. Pryer recounts, "I had sent [out] a platoon … Six soldiers from that platoon struck a bomb while driving two Humvees. No one was killed, but five were physically hurt. Two had leg injuries severe enough to cause them to be evacuated back to Germany. When I think about what happened to these soldiers, I feel some anger. They shouldn't have been in Iraq … But I also feel something else— feelings of personal responsibility, guilt and shame."[78]

Then there are the traumas born of the seemingly "banal" acts of carrying out an occupation: stories of coercion and humiliation inflicted upon those whose lands and homes one invades and occupies, as captured in Boudreau's account of his reaction to a documentary film about the Iraq War that he watched with a friend a few years after his return from the war zone:

> Midway through the piece, a short video clip was shown of two soldiers searching an Iraqi home. The footage was uneventful ... capturing nothing but a bit of walking around and some chitchat between the Americans and the family. Then one of the soldiers, clad in body armor, sunglasses, and an automatic rifle ... leaned toward a young Iraqi man in the living room and gave him a hug. The Iraqi submitted with limp arms and an unenthusiastic smile. The soldier ... laughed ... I felt my face get hot with rage.[79]

His friend didn't understand, Boudreau tells us. "Where's the harm in a hug?" he asked.

> The trouble is that no matter how the Iraqi man felt about the hug, there's nothing he could have done to stop it. He couldn't say no to the hug. And there was no one who could help him. Nobody at all could stop that American soldier from hugging that Iraqi man—and you could see it in their faces, they both knew it. That's what an occupation looks like. And that's the harm in a hug.[80]

As currently defined, post-traumatic stress disorder has no capacity to recognize the trauma of such experiences and actions, some of which are described, as in Boudreau's words, in unavoidably political terms, and many of which do not even plausibly qualify as an "event." The DSM-5, published in 2013, twelve years into these latest American wars, seems to have reabsorbed some aspects of the forgotten phenomenology of combat trauma recognized during the American war in Vietnam: The precipitating event continues to be defined as "exposure to actual or threatened death," but the previously key criteria that "the person's response to a traumatic event involved intense fear, helplessness, or horror" has been eliminated.[81] More broadly, some of the realities of combat trauma are beginning to creep back into larger clinical conversations about the etiological event. For example, as delineated in an Institute of Medicine report commissioned under a provision of the National Defense Authorization Act of 2010,[82] "Exposure to any potentially traumatic event—such as physical or sexual abuse, natural disaster, being threatened with death, observing death, or *taking someone else's* life—may trigger the symptoms that characterize PTSD."[83] The possibility of the self-traumatized perpetrator has returned, even if that perpetrator is now understood to be "doing his job" rather than fighting an imperial war or committing an atrocity, as I will elaborate in Chapter 4. And yet despite such (ever so slight) shifts, many assumptions remain intact. The DSM-5 continues to reduce the traumatic experience to a life-threatening event, even though the actual phenomenology of combat trauma, in particular (but no doubt, not exclusively), cannot be contained within its bounds.[84] What's more, it cannot be contained within either the requirement that there is an "event" per se, or an understanding of that event as life threatening or perceived as such. And for some patients and clinicians, the consequence is that fundamental questions about the character of combat trauma cannot be addressed. In David Morris' words,

> I wonder if by treating [PTSD] with the punitive reconditioning of Prolonged Exposure and the Yankee optimism of cognitive therapy, clinicians haven't reduced the moral questions at the heart of PTSD—the proper use of military force, the safety of women in society, the efficacy of torture—to distant also-rans, asterisks in the clinician's handbook. I wonder if in the process they haven't served to reduce one of the most powerful humanistic concepts in history to a strictly technical matter. And, coincidentally, if they haven't served to realize one of the worst fears of the founders of PTSD, people like Robert Lifton and Arthur Egendorf, who worried that the diagnosis would be morally neutered by psychiatry.[85]

Clinicians advocating for the recognition of another type of "invisible wound" of war are asking similar questions: Even as they continue to recognize PTSD as a distinct disorder, they insist that it fails to recognize many of the most traumatizing combat experiences among military personnel. Different kinds of combat experiences, Litz, Orsillo, and others argue, lead to different kinds of traumatic afterlives. In response, some clinicians are developing a different theory of combat trauma and adapting gold-standard protocols for its proper treatment. In so doing, they talk of moral and spiritual damage, sometimes even of damage to "the soul." Nevertheless, as I illustrate in the next chapter, for all of their efforts to pose a substantive challenge to the causes and meaning of combat PTSD, these clinicians never escape the reigning psychiatric paradigm and its iteration as military medicine. Their commitment to evidence-based and short-term treatment protocols endures; they approach the military as a "culture" in its own right, with clearly defined virtues and moral standards, and they demand that clinicians learn about and defer to that culture as they seek to treat soldiers who have returned from war suffering its invisible wounds. As I will show, clinicians may be talking about moral transgression and wounds to the soul, but such talk has very little to do with substantive ethical and political judgment. A commitment to cultural relativism—and an unexamined belief in the virtue of the US military—silences the very possibility of critique that such talk, prima facie, seems to imply.

# 4

# The Politics of
# Moral Injury

Since the early aughts, clinicians and researchers working with soldiers and veterans have been developing the concept of moral injury. Initially posited as a potentially novel diagnosis, over time, rather than emerging as a new official disorder, its assumptions about the myriad kinds of traumatic experiences soldiers confront in combat, and the need for a more capacious understanding of the etiology of combat trauma, have seeped back into understandings of combat PTSD. What kinds of "events" count as among its causes? Is it necessarily the case that trauma stems from particular, discrete *events* in the first place? Combat trauma is discussed now not just in terms of fear, but also in relation to guilt, shame, and grief. It can be a *moral* injury, an injury to the "soul." In this vein, clinicians have developed treatment protocols that incorporate a patient's need to "confess" their transgressions and sometimes to engage with the community and to "make amends." As a concept, moral injury harkens back to understandings of combat trauma as formulated in response to the war in Vietnam, albeit with none of the political edge of that earlier iteration. Nevertheless, framing trauma as moral destruction, as damage to the soul, iterates a different model of mental anguish. Moral injury theory presupposes a different kind of psychiatric subject and a different understanding of personhood. This subject has a conscience. Her pain is lived as grief, guilt, and shame, and, the argument is, it cannot be rationalized away. Nor is her pain attenuated or de-habituated by reliving the event over and over. She is a subject for whom questions of agency, intention, and responsibility are important and pressing; the experience of being traumatized strikes at the core of her being.

Despite its disruptive potential, however, the concept of moral injury is not positioned to pose a fundamental challenge to contemporary mainstream psychiatry, with its overriding emphasis on the fundamentally physio-biological underpinnings and manifestations of mental disorders and its insistence on evidence-based protocols. Nor does it generate a political critique of imperialism and war, as was the case with post-Vietnam syndrome. It emerges, instead, within the problem space of the "moralist anti-politics," to return to Miriam Ticktin's term, that structures civil-military relations in the United States in the post-9/11 era.[1] Nevertheless, the opening that appears here, be it ever so slight, is worth attending to. What appears through the cracks is a different kind of psychiatric conversation—clinical, ethical, and *potentially* political—about trauma, personhood, and war.

In this chapter, I pry open those cracks by considering moral injury and other emerging (re)definitions of combat trauma, and I analyze the insights and changing conceptualizations they bring in tow. At the same time, I demonstrate the almost immediate closure of their critical political potential. Although in some ways reminiscent of the radical politics that found form in and through post-Vietnam syndrome, the latter's reemergence is impossible in a clinical context in which force protection stands center stage—in which treating combat trauma is integral to the business of war. And it is impossible within a political environment in which the military and its personnel are held in such high esteem. In short, for all the talk of moral transgression, agency, guilt, and responsibility to be observed in recent discussions of combat trauma, the trauma suffered by soldiers remains radically severed from questions of the politics and ethics of the post-9/11 wars.

## A New Diagnosis?

Opening the first peer-reviewed publication on the phenomenon of "moral injury," Brett Litz, Shira Maguen, and colleagues wrote that "service members are confronted with numerous moral and ethical challenges in war." They "may act in ways that transgress deeply held moral beliefs or they may experience conflict about the unethical behaviors of others. Warriors may also bear witness to intense human suffering and cruelty that shakes their core beliefs about humanity."[2] In the face of moral challenges, in this view, soldiers may find themselves unable to "contextualize or justify" their own or others' actions; they may not be able to "accommodate" the "morally challenging experiences" of war. PTSD, a disorder defined by fear and victimhood, Litz et al. argue, cannot account for these kinds of military traumas.

> An overemphasis on danger-based harms has constrained research questions, negatively impacted the efficacy and effectiveness of extant clinical approaches and thwarted the development of novel treatments to help service members and veterans ... Focusing on danger-based harms is insufficient because, unlike civilian traumatic event contexts, there is good reason to assume that most threat-based stress reactions are mitigated by military pre-selection and tough and realistic training and preparation, and, when present, healed by indigenous military rituals and assets.[3]

There is a pressing need for systematic research on "the lasting impact of perpetrating, failing to prevent, or bearing witness to war-zone acts that produce inner conflict because of moral compromise."[4] According to the Litz and his colleagues, moral injury—"a syndrome of shame, self-handicapping, and demoralization that occurs when deeply held beliefs and expectations about moral and ethical conduct are transgressed"—needs to be better understood.[5]

By the close of first decade of the post-9/11 wars, moral injury had caught the interest of a growing number of military- and VA-affiliated mental health practitioners. Clinical research was being funded, measurement scales and treatment protocols developed and tested, and the concept of moral injury was named and defined in blogs and articles posted on official websites of the VA and DoD.[6] For all the talk at the time about moral injury being a recent discovery, however, it wasn't new. Based on years as a VA psychologist treating veterans of the American war in Vietnam, Jonathan Shay published a book about the moral hazards of combat in 1994. Upon beginning work in 1987 at the Boston VA, Shay recounts, he reread Homer's *Iliad*, curious about what might be gleaned about combat stress from the ancient Greek text. Homer begins the *Iliad* "in the moral world of the soldier," Shay writes.[7]

> The first five chapters track Homer's story of Achilles very closely: Agamemnon, Achilles' commander, betrays "what's right" by wrongfully seizing his prize of honor; indignant rage shrinks Achilles' social and moral horizon until he cares about no one but a small group of combat proven comrades; his closest friend in that circle, his second-in-command and foster brother, Patroklos dies in battle; profound grief and suicidal longing take hold of Achilles; he feels that he is already dead; he is tortured by guilt and the conviction that he should have died rather than his friend; he renounces all desire to return home alive; he goes berserk and commits atrocities against the living and the dead. This is the story of Achilles in the Iliad, not some metaphoric translation of it.[8]

Via a reading of the soldier's moral world, Shay wrote *Achilles in Vietnam* to "put before the public an understanding of the specific nature of catastrophic war experiences that not only cause lifelong disabling psychiatric symptoms but can ruin good character."[9]

Betrayal of the moral order by a commander and the destruction of good character are the two poles that ground Shay's theory of moral injury (referred to as "complex PTSD" in his second book, *Odysseus in America*).[10] Translating *thémis* as "what's right," Shay states, "When a leader destroys the legitimacy of the army's moral order by betraying 'what's right,' he inflicts manifold injuries on his men."[11]

Shay offers examples of violations of "what's right" that were pervasive in Vietnam. For example, the sense among soldiers of a lack of fairness: Risk was distributed unjustly among American troops, with enlisted men often sent out on patrols on the basis of whether or not their commanders liked them. Career officers remained far from the front, leaving enlisted men to shoulder all the risk. Soldiers also had to deal with equipment —M-16 rifles, for example—that just didn't work.[12] As it was for Achilles, Shay reasons, the repeated experience of such failures of command filled Vietnam veterans "with indignant rage." To boot, the career structure in the officer corps flew in the face of beliefs about "what's right" and destroyed the very fabric of social trust. As a rule, officers were rotated out of combat following six-month command tours, with anyone opting to stay longer out of loyalty to "their men," regarded as having "gone native"—to the severe detriment of their military careers. Perhaps most obscenely, "the *presence* of American casualties was rated as positive evidence of the commander's 'aggressiveness' and 'balls.'"[13] And then there were instances upon instances of "leadership malpractice." As recounted by one former Marine, he

and his three-man Marine fire team were left in charge of seventeen disarmed and nonresisting Vietnamese prisoners. As the sergeant was leaving the scene he said over his shoulder, "We don't need no prisoners," which my patient understood to be an instruction to kill them. My patient discovered that the other

marines were reluctant to murder the prisoners. My patient egged
them on and was the first to open fire.[14]

"I led them into sin," the former Marine told Shay.

Those are the kinds of experiences that lead to moral injuries, according to Shay. Officers betray soldiers under their
command; military codes are violated; the "berserking effects"
of the war led soldiers in Vietnam to commit (or, if not, to
witness) one atrocity after another.[15] And American veterans
would suffer their choices and actions on the killing fields of
Vietnam for the rest of their lives. As he elaborates further in
his second book, moral injury (or complex PTSD) is caused
by a "persistent human betrayal and rupture of community in
mortal-stakes situations of captivity—[which] destroys ... and
undoes character."[16]

In this discussion of betrayal and the undoing of character,
Shay poses a broad challenge to the psychiatric community in
the 1990s. In its definition of PTSD, he charges the American
Psychiatric Association with failing to capture the severity of the
disorder. The psychological consequences of combat in Vietnam
were far more devastating and persistent than its diagnosis
allowed: "When the injury invades character, and the capacity for social trust is destroyed, all possibility of a flourishing
human life is lost ... When social trust is destroyed, it is not
replaced by a vacuum, but rather by a perpetual mobilization to
fend off attack, humiliation, or exploitation, and to figure out
other people's trickery."[17]

Shay struggled with how to help these men heal, and his
answer generated a fundamental critique of the APA's hyper-
medicalization of trauma and of the psychiatric community's
approach to treatment. Healing "depends on communalization
of the trauma—being able safely to tell the story to someone
who is listening and who can be trusted to retell it truthfully
to others in the community." He called on psychiatrists to step
back from their obsession with categorizing and classifying and
instead to first *listen* to their patients. Mental health professionals need to listen to the "sacred stuff."[18]

A commitment to community, to working together, to listening guided Shay's clinical work at the Boston VA's Veteran's Independence Plus (VIP) program. He appears to echo the structure and ethical commitments of rap groups during the 1970s when he describes as the "heart of our program" the "understanding that veterans heal each other. Because we move mental health professionals off center stage, veterans can bypass many of the obstacles blocking those with complex PTSD from getting help."[19] In contrast to those earlier Vietnam War–era practitioners and veterans, however, Shay and his colleagues designed their trauma recovery program by drawing on Judith Herman's work with victims of incest and rape, following her "three-stage" recovery program.[20] Stage one: the "establishment of safety, sobriety, and self-care; Stage two, trauma-centered work of constructing a personal narrative and of grieving; Stage three, reconnecting with people, communities, ideals, and ambitions." Beginning in the mid-1980s, clinicians working according to the program accompanied groups of patients to the Vietnam War Memorial "to grieve for and commune with dead comrades in a safe and sober fellowship." The VIP program also encouraged patients to turn to other authority figures and moral frameworks in their struggles to heal. Working in the Boston area, Shay notes, the vast majority of patients were Roman Catholics and the "clinical team has encouraged many … to avail themselves of the sacrament of penance."[21]

In advancing a theory of moral injury, Shay understood the stakes and obligations of his work to be far more encompassing than a simple and straightforward medical intervention. Recounting his work at the Boston VA many years later, his writings still resonate with the psychiatric common sense of the late 1960s and early to mid-1970s:

What we do is political in the richest senses of the word. Our patients all took part in the exercise of state military power in and around Vietnam between 1965 and 1972, and their injuries trace to this participation and to how power was used in military institutions. The dominating element of power makes the *cause of injury* political; the *forms of injury* are in part political; and you have seen how the *treatment of injury* we provide is political —we foster an empowered community among the veterans we work with. The task is to create *trust*. In a fundamental sense, our treatment is a form of democratic persuasion. We are in this together and are parts of each other's future as fellow citizens.[22]

At the Boston VA, clinicians encouraged veterans "to participate in the democratic political life of the country that they fought for." As Shay understands it, "For any mental health professional to work with American combat veterans injured in the service of their country, and *not* to find incapacity for democratic participation to be a meaningful clinical issue, strikes me as odd, to say the least."[23] The ways in which moral injury has been developed and treated in the context of the post-9/11 wars must strike Shay as very odd indeed. Participation in the democratic life of the country—or, for that matter, any reference to politics at all—has no apparent place in clinical care.

## Moral Injury for the New Millennium

Shay's self-avowedly political description of the Boston VA program's therapeutic work stands in stark contrast to the narrowly clinical approach to research and treatment that characterizes the resurgence of his concept in the time of the counterterror state.[24] In a series on moral injury broadcast by the Boston public radio station WBUR in 2013, Shay described the crux of the issue as follows: "Imagine someone you trust telling you to do something you feel is deeply wrong, in a possible life-and-death situation. And you do it."[25] He shared an incident that took place in Fallujah, Iraq. A Marine sniper was "supporting an engaged infantry unit, which had losses to a very effective, well-concealed enemy sniper." After some time, the Marine identified the Iraqi sniper shooting at his unit; he also saw "a baby strapped to his front ... The marine interpreted this as use of the baby as a 'human shield.' Regardless of whether that was true, the marine understood the Law of Land Warfare and Rules of Engagement permitted him to fire on the enemy sniper ... He did fire and saw the rounds strike."[26] The Marine's "view of his duty to his brother Marines and his job description was to take the shot ... He took the shot and it did its work and he's going to live with that for the rest of his life."[27]

Shay relates the incident as an illustration of his definition of moral injury, but it more accurately captures the concerns of more recent iterations of the concept. As one VA clinician told me, it's important to understand that Shay's definition of moral injury was informed by his work with veterans of the American war in Vietnam—a war characterized by poor training and poor leadership. Today's US military is a very different kettle of fish, the clinician insisted. This is "not Vietnam"; today's military is "well resourced, well trained, and well led." Among psychiatrists and psychologists working with military or ex-military personnel in the post-9/11 era, there is a strikingly different understanding of and attitude towards the military as an institution.

In its more recent iteration, moral injury is attributed to a variety of experiences, the most "toxic" of which is often framed as a betrayal of the self.[28] As articulated by Brett Litz, Shira Maguen, and other clinical researchers, moral injury is not primarily a consequence of feeling betrayed by one's commanders, following illegal orders, or by serving in a military possessed of such warped priorities as using enemy body counts as the measure of success in the war. Instead, in more recent definitions, a soldier can be doing precisely what he is trained for and expected to do, he can be following military codes of conduct and abiding by the laws of war, he can be engaged in *prescribed* killing, and still be traumatized by his actions. Recall Shay's account of the Fallujah incident. The sniper was not following an illegal order. He did not perpetrate an "atrocity" or commit an "unlawful" killing. He acted in accord with how he "understood the Law of Land Warfare and Rules of Engagement." The sniper interpreted the baby as a "human shield," and according to military codes of conduct an enemy using a human shield bears the culpability for the innocent death. He understood his "duty and his loyalty to his fellow marines." He took the shot. And now he has to live with what he did.[29]

The consequences of lawful killings are at the center of explorations of moral injury in the era of the anti-terror state, and those effects of killing are framed by radically different assumptions about the US military and its conduct of war than the ones that motivated Vietnam-era psychiatrists such as Lifton and Shatan, and even Shay.[30] The all-volunteer force is described by many not only as a thoroughly professional military, but also as a moral institution. US military personnel—unlike those they are fighting against—by and large abide by military codes of conduct and act in accord with international humanitarian law, mental health practitioners assume. Soldiers operate according to an "intensely moral and ethical code of conduct," Litz and his collaborators write. "It is important to appreciate that the military culture fosters an intensely moral and ethical code of conduct and, in times of war, being violent and killing is normal, and bearing witness to violence and killing is, to a degree, prepared for and expected."[31]

The psychiatric risks soldiers face in this view are born of *contradictions* that emerge between this intensely moral and ethical code of conduct that has been drilled into soldiers by the military and the very different realities they encounter on the actual battlefields—that is, when confronting enemies not bound by any moral or legal codes at all. And the dissonance can have a "lasting psychosocial-spiritual impact."[32] When the "liberal way of war," in Michael Dillon and Julian Reid's terminology—or, more specifically, when the liberal subject-qua-soldier—comes into collision with realities on the ground, traumatic injuries result.[33] Some clinicians go one step further: The requirement that American troops abide by rules of engagement and the risk of punishment if they do not is potentially damaging. Consider the following exchange among clinicians during a conference session on combat PTSD:[34] One member of the audience, a therapist who works with Vietnam veterans, noted the particular psychological risks of counterinsurgency warfare. During the two world wars, he said, the enemy was clear: soldiers were fighting soldiers.[35] But, as many a veteran has told him, in Vietnam it was impossible to tell the difference between enemy soldiers and ordinary Vietnamese. "And the guys in sandbox one, sandbox two," he continued, they have "the same problem. Who's the enemy?" American troops today face a rather dire problem, he cautioned, because the rules of engagement are too constraining. "Even if you are being fired at, you can't fire back until you are given the order to do so." He asked the panelists, "do the increased restrictions and complicated rules of engagement complicate PTSD?" One panelist agreed; since the two world wars involved "militaries fighting militaries," matters were much clearer—"that uniform ... tells someone else, you are okay to try to kill me, because I represent that nation's military." As to the effects of the rules of engagement, he imagined that more complex rules could exacerbate the risk of PTSD. He then noted, in "Afghanistan the rules of engagement have gotten very, very tricky and very dicey, and service members are certainly feeling the effects." A second audience member stepped in: "It's not just war, it's [the] ambiguity. It's not war itself ... It's not the rules of engagement, it's [from] a change in rules of engagement that I've heard there was the most damage. That when they changed it, that didn't make any sense."

Jonathan Shay may have coined the term "moral injury," but clinicians insist their more recent efforts are novel insofar as they aim to give the concept a grounding in empirical data.[36] In today's radically different disciplinary and political context—in the face of wars that have elicited no sustained public opposition, a military that understands PTSD as but one more cost of making war, and a psychiatric profession that is decidedly clinical and guided by an evidence-based approach to mental health—the political and moral passion that saturates Shay's writing is nowhere to be found. Clinicians are expected to "offer specific treatment recommendations" based not on a "conceptual model" of the problem but on pilot studies that empirically demonstrate the promise of success.[37] They conduct surveys to classify potentially injurious war-zone experiences, develop measurement tools to identify moral injury in patients, and test clinical protocols designed to treat different kinds of PTSD. Whatever might be clinicians' own myriad personal political commitments, politics as such makes no appearance in the design of clinical studies, in clinical treatment protocols, or in their published work. In this clinical version of "support the troops," there is no space for considering whether healing from combat trauma might require either political engagement and critique or the collectivization of the trauma upon which Shay insisted.

A different sense of urgency drives contemporary clinical research. A growing number of clinicians believe that un- or misdiagnosed moral injury could be the cause of the high rates of military suicide.[38] Also widespread is the expectation that the psychological toll of US warfare will continue to rise, in particular since inherent in the concept of moral injury is the assumption that killing is not something that men or women do with ease. The problem appears in redoubled form in light of the US commitment to fighting the kinds of wars that are particularly morally fraught for their combatants. In other words, in focusing on the act of killing, clinicians are suggesting that many combatants pay an acute psychological price for "*carrying out their duties* in a war zone."[39] That weighs heavily on the urgency of figuring out how to respond clinically. And alongside these mental health concerns comes the worry about force protection: Active-duty soldiers' psychological challenges must be treated effectively and efficiently so that they can be rotated back to combat zones.

Recent discussion of how hard it is for soldiers to kill is not the first time American military–affiliated researchers have explored the issue. In 1947, Samuel Lyman Atwood Marshall, a US Army combat historian, published a study of the combat effectiveness among American infantrymen during World War II. Based on "post-combat mass interviews," purportedly with an estimated four hundred infantry companies in the European and the Central Pacific theaters, Marshall estimated that only 20 to 25 percent of riflemen on combat duty ever fired at the enemy.[40] Seventy-five percent of men, he wrote, "will face the danger but they will not fight."[41] Who is the "average, normal man who is fitted into the uniform of an American ground soldier," Marshall asks, and what inhibits him from shooting on the battlefield?[42]

> He is what his home, his religion, his schooling and the moral code and ideals of his society have made him. The Army cannot unmake him. It must reckon with the fact that he comes from a civilization in which aggression, connected with the taking of life, is prohibited and unacceptable ... This is his great handicap when he enters battle.[43]

The dutiful soldier, Marshall writes, discovers in himself a "conscientious objector" when face to face with an enemy combatant, which, he adds, "is something to the American credit."[44] Entirely new methods of training would be needed if American soldiers were to overcome their unwillingness to kill—to increase the firing rate among American troops.

Marshall's interest lay in the psychological-qua-civilizational inhibitions that purportedly had kept American infantrymen from firing their weapons during World War II. He was not interested in the potential psychological or moral harm among those who did. In the mid-1990s, David Grossman, a retired Army ranger, former West Point psychology professor, and the architect of a field he named "killology," returned to Marshall's work. In *On Killing*, he cautions that the "ability to increase this firing rate ... comes with a hidden cost." There is "a powerful, innate human resistance toward killing one's own species." Relying on unelaborated evolutionary evidence, he declares, "We are not naturally killers." *On Killing* explores what Marshall overlooks, "the psychological and sociological processes and prices exacted when men kill each other in combat."[45]

According to Grossman, the result of "sustained combat" for most soldiers is that they "slip into insanity.[46] *On Killing* sets out to explain the "emotional reactions and underlying processes" that lead to that outcome. Reviewing the history of psychiatric understandings of "trauma in war," Grossman takes issue with the emphasis on "the fear of death and injury," calling it "overly simplistic." Fear can indeed be debilitating for military personnel, but fear of what? Often enough, he claims, it is "fear of not being able to meet the terrible obligations of combat," that is, failing to come through for one's comrades-in-arms. Fear of death and injury is "*not* the only or even the major cause of psychiatric casualties in combat." It is, instead, fear "combined with exhaustion, hate, horror, and the irreconcilable task of balancing these with the need to kill" that takes the toll. Echoing Marshall, Grossman writes, "the average soldier's psyche resists killing and the obligation to kill," and within this emotional and physical morass, the soldier finds himself immersed "so deeply in … a mire of guilt and horror that he tips over the brink into that reign that we call insanity." The guilt and horror are only accentuated in the post 9/11 wars, Grossman argues. "Gray-area killings" are common in "an age of guerillas and terrorists," and they pose the greatest psychiatric risks.[47] To be clear, nothing in Grossman's account suggests a critique of American war and militarism, in contrast to anti-war psychiatrists and activists during the 1970s who made similar arguments about the distinct psychological risks of guerilla warfare. That is made eminently clear not just by the absence of such critique in *On Killing,* but by his own apparently lucrative training module ("Bullet Proof") and business venture that draws on his military training to teach police "to kill with less hesitation" and, presumably, with less guilt.[48]

Several years into the US wars in Iraq and Afghanistan, clinicians treating combat trauma at the VA had begun to confront the act of killing head on. "A comprehensive evaluation of veterans returning from combat," insisted Shira Maguen and colleagues in an influential article in 2010, "should include an assessment of direct and indirect killing and reactions to killing."[49] Citing scant clinical research on the mental health consequences of killing in combat, Maguen, among others, maintained that "arguably, the moral conflict, shame, and guilt produced by taking a life in combat can be uniquely scarring across the lifespan."[50] Yet very little statistical data exists on the rates or fact of killing in and of itself, let alone on killing's potential psychological consequences, and this in a military that routinely collects an enormous amount of medical data, including psychological data, from soldiers returning home.[51] Standard surveys and debriefings of returning US soldiers and Marines do not ask explicitly about whether or not they killed in combat, she explained, although over the past decade or so, some at the VA have begun to do just that.

This was not the first time VA clinicians had sought to measure the psychological effects of having killed in a war zone. Writing in 1999, Alan Fontana and Robert Rosenheck published a post-Vietnam–era study still widely referenced today.[52] Accounting for why the military psychiatric community knew so little about killing in the war theater, they argued that research on PTSD was focused on specifying the "reactions" to war-zone stressors rather than on parsing the stressors themselves. As a consequence, it assessed "the *dose* of traumatic exposure" rather than paying attention to "the *types* of traumatic exposure."[53] Dose was calculated according to "combat scales that compressed different kinds of events into a single "index of war-zone stress." Fontana and Rosenheck, however, insisted on developing an "anatomy of traumatic stress in the war zone," differentiating among "fighting, threat of death or injury to oneself, death or injury to others, killing others, and committing atrocities," for example.[54] Referencing Jonathan Shay's concept of the "berserk state," Fontana and Rosenheck hypothesized that "perceived threat ... contribute[s] to killing others, and killing others [contributes] ... to committing atrocities." Killing others, they explained, "violates one of the strongest prohibitions of a civilized society, and so we posit that killing others breaches one of the strongest constraints against committing atrocities." Killing ("killing/injuring others" and "committing atrocities"), the authors conclude, is the *key* mediating factor precipitating PTSD.[55] Moreover, making a point I will return to later, they argued that the central importance of killing to therapeutic work among veterans made it imperative that treatment incorporate a "spiritual component" as an "added axis to the psychological-social-biological" one.

Since the early aughts, clinical researchers at the VA and the DoD have been generating data on killing in a war zone and its traumatic afterlives. This time around, however, there is little emphasis on (or even mention of) soldiers having committed atrocities. One questionnaire designed for soldiers returning from Iraq, for example, poses the following questions: "During combat operations did you personally witness anyone being killed? During combat operations did you kill others in combat (or have reason to believe that others were killed as a result of your actions)?"[56] With 56 percent of respondents answering yes to the first question and 40 percent to the second, Maguen and her colleagues correlated the answers with scores on standard psychological measures for PTSD and other psychiatric diagnoses. They concluded that killing is a "significant predictor" of nearly all mental health and social readjustment problems reported by soldiers, including PTSD.

While most conclusions regarding the psychological effects of killing are based on surveys, one study reported the results of a focus group with twenty-six veterans who had killed, most of whom were veterans of the wars in Vietnam and Iraq. Natalie Purcell and her colleagues report that it was difficult for participants to speak about their "killing experiences, even within the group." When they did, they often spoke in a way that gave them some distance from what they had done—that is, "*it* happened "or "I had a killing experience." And even as many different feelings were expressed, patterns emerged.[57] "The majority cited feelings of satisfaction in the immediate aftermath of killing: 'I liked it. I thought I was Daniel Boone.'"[58] Focus group members described killing as "intoxicating" and "euphoric"; "a power trip"; "almost an erotic feeling"; "When I was there, I was packing —I'm *God*."[59] Others, especially veterans speaking of their "first kill," reported reactions ranging from "nausea and revulsion" to a matter-of-factness that for one veteran was the most disturbing response of all: By the third kill it was just "my job." For most focus-group participants, "conflicted or ambivalent feelings" surfaced later; "they thought about the gravity and significance of killing only after they left the military."[60] Not all participants expressed remorse for having killed.[61] But among those who reported feeling guilt and shame, these were in response "not only to the actions that veterans took in combat but also to the pleasure and power that accompanied those actions."[62]

As detailed in Purcell's study, the psychological aftereffects of killing take many forms. Some veterans spoke of the loss of religious faith, of a sense that they were no longer the same person anymore. Many described the pain of having to confront a "dark side" of themselves, the savage or the monster within. Veterans spoke about experiencing a profound sense of isolation; "they distanced themselves from loved ones because of their experiences with killing, due to fear of what others might think if they knew the truth about their actions." Overall, Purcell and coauthors conclude, "Killing can be a defining experience: It can separate warriors from those who have not killed, *and* it can separate them from their own prewar selves. It brings a potentially troubling knowledge of self and of the human capacity for violence that, for many, is frightening, disruptive, and alienating."[63]

Killing is often described as the most morally toxic compared to other wartime experiences, but it does not stand alone. A diverse field of war-zone moral compromises and crises can trigger non–fear-based traumas, according to clinical research. Witnessing horrifying events, including bearing witness to harms they had a hand in creating—for example, entering a village that has just been leveled by artillery fire, seeing up close the "mass destruction" they caused, as one psychologist told me, can be morally injurious. Soldiers also suffer the aftereffects of having failed to prevent an act that violated their sense of what is right, to return to a point of emphasis for Jonathan Shay. And soldiers discover "things about others" that they may not have known or wanted to know, including feeling betrayed by those in command.

Studies designed to parse this diverse and psychologically treacherous field burgeoned toward the end of the first decade of the new millennium. Clinicians began to articulate a different, perhaps more wholistic view of the psychiatric subject, and they called into question, even if only implicitly, one of the central pillars of PTSD ever since the DSM-III: that the nature of the stressor, aside from being "outside the range of normal human experience" (or, later on, being perceived as a life-threatening event) made no difference regarding PTSD's manifestation or treatment. Clinical researchers started developing "schemes" for "categorizing traumatic military events," attempting to figure out what categories of events are the most damaging and correlating specific classes with specific traumatic afterlives. In one study, for example, 143 active-duty soldiers at Fort Hood undergoing treatment for PTSD were asked a series of questions about a list of "index" events.[64] Stein et al. sorted the index events into six different kinds of stressors: life-threat to self; life-threat to others; aftermath of violence: traumatic loss; moral injury by self; moral injury by others. Are some kinds of stressors more associated with peri-trauma or post-trauma reactions? Which kinds of stressors prove "most distressing and haunting" for active-duty military personnel? Are different stressors associated with "unique patterns of peritraumatic and posttraumatic sequelae"?[65]

I want to pause a moment on the distinctions *in kind* among the heterogeneous stressors identified in such studies. The shift here is not confined to the assumption that not all traumatic "events" involve life-threat to self and others. It raises the question of whether or not all potential stressors compose *an event* at all. For example, the Deployment Risk and Resilience Inventory (DRRI) Combat Experiences Scale was developed "to assess key psychosocial risks and resilience factors for deployed military personnel and veterans deployed to war zones and other hazardous environments." The study pushes back against a particular clinical common sense based on recent attention to "the impact of deployment and especially, war-zone experiences on the well-being of military personnel and vets." Within those deployment-based studies, "exposure to combat, including being fired on and witnessing the death of fellow unit members, is the stressor that has dominated military veteran research." There is an "overemphasis on combat per se," the authors argue, "to the exclusion of other potentially important dimensions."[66] The paper lists pre- and post-deployment environments as "risk" and "resilience" factors: childhood abuse or post-deployment support networks, for example. It then emphasizes "other dimensions" ubiquitous in a war zone, noting there are "more subjective reports of fear and lower magnitude everyday discomforts," the effects of which need to be studied. Consider the following categories of "deployment/war-zone factors" listed in the DRRI: preparedness; difficult living and working environment; concerns about life and family disruptions; deployment social support; general harassment; sexual harassment; perceived threat; combat experiences; aftermath of battle; and NBC (nuclear, biological, and chemical) agent exposures.[67]

Since its first iteration in the DSM-III, a PTSD diagnosis, formally at least, has required an "external event" that is identifiable, discrete, and dramatic, one that overwhelms and shatters the individual exposed to it, if only as a delayed effect.[68] As Bessel van der Kolk describes the experience of one veteran of the war in Vietnam who survived an ambush during which everyone else in his platoon was either injured or killed: "In one terrifying moment, trauma has transformed everything." Many of the experiences listed in above as "deployment/war-zone factors," however, cannot be characterized as a traumatic event, in the sense that "however horrendous," it "had a beginning, a middle, and an end."[69] "Preparedness," for example, refers to the "extent to which an individual perceives that he or she was prepared for deployment"; "difficult living and working environment" includes "personal discomforts or deprivations" that "may include the lack of desirable food, uncomfortable climate, cultural difficulties, inadequate equipment and long workdays." And yet, in exploring the effects of these other dimensions of war-zone stressors, King et al. report "noteworthy" results, including "several associations between lower magnitude deployment stressors and mental health," including diagnoses of PTSD.[70]

In this recent iteration, the etiology of PTSD is no longer required to center on an event—which is "catastrophic, crisis-laden," or an "assault from without" that rips the subject's life—and the subject herself—into a before and after. The DRRI study's "noteworthy" findings torque the concept of PTSD in momentous ways. Many war-zone stressors might be better described as what Elizabeth Povinelli names "quasi-events," which "never quite achieve the status of having occurred or taken place."[71] A growing body of recent clinical research is an effort to aggregate, apprehend, and evaluate such "quasi-events" to better understand the etiology of post-combat mental health disorders and, most centrally, to understand PTSD among American (ex-)military personnel. Such studies not only provide a very different phenomenology of military life in the war zone; they also pose a fundamental challenge to the original defining criterion of PTSD in the DSM-III and since—to the kinds of experiences that can be cited as having generated traumatic afterlives.

## Clinical Protocols and Inconvenient Truths

In *Adaptive Disclosure*, Litz and his colleagues argue that if trauma treatment is to become more effective for military personnel, there needs to be a shift in the "the *zeitgeist* for understanding" PTSD. They call for a reexamination of the "fear conditioning model" that has "guided thinking about war-related PTSD" ever since World War II, offering the following "thought experiment" to explain what they are proposing:

What might promote a service member's healing and recovery from a single life-threatening incident, such as a sniper attack, when no one was hurt? Contrast this with a service member who is plagued by witnessing the aftermath of an improvised explosive device (IED) that killed his best friend (traumatic loss). Contrast that with a service member who is haunted by an incident where he fatally acted out his rage due to a mortar attack that killed his friend the day before (moral injury related to perpetration). Compare that with the experience of a service member who is angry and demoralized over betrayal by a trusted leader whose ruthless and capricious decision led to the unnecessary death of civilians. Does the fear conditioning model fit any case but the first? Is conventional imaginal exposure [PE], or Socratic questioning designed to challenge the accuracy of the service member's beliefs [CPT] necessary and sufficient in promoting recovery and postcombat adjustment?[72]

Unlike the therapies designed for a fear-based model, adaptive disclosure therapy distinguishes among multiple forms of combat trauma and proposes a distinct treatment protocol for each.

Before launching into the specifics of the treatment protocol, however, the authors highlight something else they think essential to effective treatment, namely, the distinctiveness of the *military* as an institution. The chapter "Military Culture and Warrior Ethos" opens with a quote from Admiral Mike Mullen, former chair of the Joint Chiefs of Staff, who had said of the US citizenry,

> I fear they do not know us. I fear they do not comprehend the full weight of the burden we carry or the price we pay when we return from battle. This is important, because a people uninformed about what they are asking the military to endure is a people inevitably unable to fully grasp the scope of the responsibilities our Constitution levies upon them ... We must help them understand, our fellow citizens who so desperately want to help us.[73]

Litz and colleagues invoke Mullen's words, spoken before a graduating class at West Point in 2011, as the opening salvo in a lesson designed for "civilian" clinicians who work with military and ex-military personnel. In a nation in which less than 1 percent of its population serves in the military, there is a cultural abyss isolating military personnel and their families from the rest of the citizenry and that has consequences for clinical care. One reason cognitive processing (CPT) and prolonged exposure (PE) therapies have been "*substantially* less efficacious" in treating "complex military trauma" in comparison to "civilian" PTSD is that "many care providers in the military and the US Department of Veterans Affairs (VA) have not adequately considered the unique cultural and contextual elements of military trauma." Adaptive disclosure (AD) therapy is designed as a counterpoint and it begins with training "care providers to understand, honor, and accommodate the military ethos, and the unique phenomenology of war trauma among service members who may be struggling, yet preparing for their next deployment or their military role."[74]Clinicians who have never served in the military, in other words, are being told that their ability to provide successful treatment depends on their grasp of military culture. "Members of the warrior profession," write the authors, "subscribe, more or less, to shared values and guiding ideals that are uniquely theirs and indispensable to their way of life." Adaptive disclosure "respects the primacy, for warfighters, and their kin, of warrior values and guiding ideals, and it holds the process of reconciling with … [those ideals] to be fundamental to treatments for war-related psychological injuries." Therapists are counseled to approach their patients with "empathic neutrality" and told to refrain from focusing on "the many faults and sometimes glaring hypocrisies of military culture." "Listening without judgment" is what they must learn to do, which "is as vital for successful therapy of a service member or veteran who has suffered a war zone psychological injury as it is for a couple or family system."[75]

As the discourse of a civil-military divide seeps into theories of clinical care, Litz and his colleagues call on clinicians working with soldiers and veterans, as a medical matter, to achieve "cultural competence." They must be proficient in two distinct aspects of military life: first, institutional knowledge (ranks and titles, or "roles, identities and languages") and, second, the more "intangible" elements of what they term a "warrior culture and ethos."[76] "Warriors" are dedicated to defending the social order;

they practice selflessness and are willing to embrace hardship; they have a desire to experience death up close and find "joy in fighting"; and they are bound by an *esprit de corps*. Those are the intangible elements of the military ethos and life,[77] and they shape the moral character of the individual soldier. Military culture, Litz and colleagues insist, is deeply guided by moral principles, and as a consequence, "Unless damaged by moral injury, warriors tend to have highly developed moral identities and to seek every opportunity, on duty or off, to champion their moral values." Out of that complex of values and commitments, both psychological safeguards and risks emerge: "warriors may be particularly resilient in the face of fear-based trauma and at the same time be more vulnerable to the deleterious effects of violations of moral codes or the loss of cherished attachments than others who are less devoted to moral values and guiding ideals."[78]

Without explicitly referencing the literature, in making this argument, Brett Litz and his co-authors draw on assumptions that ground a disciplinary subfield in psychology known as cultural psychiatry. As characterized by Laurence Kirmayer, one of the field's early architects, "to respond to the mental health needs of culturally diverse populations," cultural psychiatry recognized "the impact of social and cultural difference on mental illness and its treatment." Advocates of cultural psychiatry criticize a normative stance that approaches the culture of an individual patient—typically a (post)colonial subject, indigenous person, immigrant, or refugee—as "a sort of baggage or impediment to shared understanding and cooperation."[79] Applied to the treatment of combat traumas, the soldier takes the place of the (post)colonial or indigenous subject. Drawing on the grammar of identity politics, "warriors" are depicted as living within a specific culture and having a distinct identity rooted in the individual's formation by and within military culture. And that sets them apart from American society as a whole, including, apparently, insofar as they abide by a heightened moral sensibility.

In elaborating new treatment protocols designed for adaptive disclosure therapy, Litz and his colleagues specify three types of war-zone traumas: life-threat, traumatic loss, and morally injurious events. They also distinguish among peri-event reactions, affects, and what they term "unfolding needs and corrective elements" for each category of trauma. For example, life-threat traumas elicit "fear, horror, helplessness, panic, dissociation," whereas moral injury elicits "guilt, shame, rage." Traumatic loss manifests as "sadness (or numbness), rage, shock, anguish." More generally, traumatic afterlives are distinct—for example, anxiety and stress follow a life-threat; withdrawal and guilt follow traumatic loss, and self-handicapping and anomie, moral injury. What, then, is required for patients to recover from these different kinds and manifestations of trauma? Those traumatized by life-threatening events, the theory goes, need to reestablish a sense of safety, mastery, and confidence, while persons suffering moral injury need to learn self-forgiveness and compassion. In adaptive disclosure therapy, the right treatment protocol depends on which of the three types of harm a soldier has suffered.[80] And with this innovation, the presumed unity of PTSD—of the traumatic event, of its affective afterlives, and of treatment protocols—is pried apart.

Adaptive disclosure identifies the specific therapeutic needs elicited by the different kinds of traumatic events, and it responds by supplementing the techniques and protocols of prolonged exposure therapy with additional therapeutic strategies. As is the case in standard PE and CPT protocols, therapy begins with the patient being asked to identify "a military experience that is currently haunting and consuming them." But in adaptive disclosure therapy, the experience is then categorized as involving either life-threat, traumatic loss, or moral injury. Regardless of classification, treatment begins with clinicians providing "a sober but hopeful, evocative, and emotionally focused opportunity for service members and veterans to realize how they have changed as a result of combat and operational experiences, to think about who they want to be, and to get a sense of how to get there experientially."[81] AD then proceeds with specific interventions for distinct kinds of war-zone harms.

With respect to life-threat and other danger-based harms, there is nothing novel here, other than the insistence on cultural competence. The life-threat protocol adheres closely to the well-established principles of prolonged exposure therapy; it works to habituate patients to the somatic memory of their trauma and thereby lessen its effects.[82] The innovations of adaptive disclosure are found in its "augmentation" of standard protocols for patients suffering traumatic loss or moral injury. "We assume that [these] patients need to be exposed to corrective experiences that counter core beliefs about blame, being unforgiven and unforgiveable, and the need to suffer."[83] Advocates of adaptive disclosure therapy maintain that "sadness and guilt from loss, shame and self-loathing from personal transgression, or anger about others' moral transgression, cannot be extinguished by repeated intensive processing. For these principal harms, the goal of the exposure is to help reveal their emerging narrative about the meaning and implication of the events."[84]

To help a patient grapple with the meaning of the events that haunt them, AD therapy adds "breakout sessions" to the standard PTSD treatment protocols. In order to explore the "meaning and implications" of particular events for soldiers and veterans, clinicians need to be clear about the contours of military culture and its often-fraught articulation with actual war-zone experiences. Traumatic loss in the context of military culture is specific in that it leads not only to sadness and withdrawal, Litz et al. suggest, but can also precipitate intense guilt: "In many ways, the relationship that service members and veterans have with one another resembles a parent-child relationship more than it resembles other relationships between adults ... Every service member in combat feels a personal and immutable responsibility for the survival and safety of others in his or her unit." Given the intensity of the connection, service members often "react with intense feelings of personal failure and guilt for betraying a trust when one of them is lost, *no matter how.*" Therapists must recognize the reasons for this crippling guilt. Military culture "inculcates the values of agency, power, self-efficacy, and looking out for unit members"; failure to do so can result in immense unresolved grief coupled with crippling guilt. The breakout session for traumatic loss is designed to address the grief, the guilt, and the various self-harming behaviors that ensue through an imaginal conversation with the dead comrade-in-arms. An approach "analogous to the *empty chair* technique in Gestalt therapy, "it is designed to activate "other aspects of self that may be helpful and less punitive."[85]

In an imagined dialogue between a patient and his dead friend, the patient is asked to share the effects of the loss. "This should have the flavor of an emotional and very real confession," Litz and his co-authors write, "of how the patient feels haunted, ruined, guilty, and incapable of having a good and happy life." The patient is asked to imagine how his lost brother-in-arms would respond: "What would he or she want for the buddy if the situation were reversed?" This question, it is hoped, "activates forgiveness-oriented themes that the therapist can then extend and emphasize," by inserting statements such as, "There's no doubt that he (or she) wants you to live the fullest life possible.'"[86] This emotionally charged "encounter" is intended as a way to enable the soldier to forgive himself.

A similar breakout session was developed to address moral injury, the "discovery" of which motivated the architects of adaptive disclosure to explore alternative clinical protocols in the first place. "Morally injurious experiences are among the most psychologically toxic and avoided topics (for both therapists and patients)." In contrast to conventional PTSD therapies, adaptive disclosure "does not assume that anguish, shame, and distress are necessarily caused by distorted thinking." They may be, but just as likely, they may not. In contrast to cognitive processing therapy, AD "is not designed to supplant 'irrational' thought with 'rational' thought … (although this may occur). Instead, the goal is to encourage the mere consideration of other possible interpretations, some of which may be less 'rational' but are nevertheless more adaptive."[87] This isn't a protocol committed to helping the patient change what they believe to be the truth of the traumatic event. As one of its architects told me, in contrast to an adaptive disclosure protocol, CPT is "palliative" care. It may provide "moral reassurance," but it cannot foster "moral repair."

Designed to work in the context of the military's "moral code," in which agency, responsibility, and culpability play significant roles, AD aims to help patients accept themselves as individuals who committed or stood witness to a bad act and to learn to move forward nevertheless. Rather than contextualize what they had done as a way of displacing responsibility and agency onto someone else or the "fog of war," soldiers need to face up to their deeds. At the same time, they need to recognize their own capacity to do good, including by engaging in acts of moral repair. As a therapeutic protocol, this breakout session does not underplay the problem of moral transgression. The goal is to get soldiers and veterans who have been traumatized in this way to understand that who they are is not determined by one act or by a failure to act. AD therapy is "a secular version of Catholic confession," in the aforementioned psychologist's words. "It doesn't matter what you did. If you are suffering, you are not a sociopath, and if you are suffering, you deserve to get help." The very capacity to suffer trauma—in this instance, as moral injury—emerges as evidence of the perpetrator's humanity, a point that echoes Talal Asad's argument about the *liberal* subject and war, whose very humanity manifests through the very capacity for guilt and suffering in the aftermath of having killed another human being (a capacity the "terrorist" presumably lacks).[88] Adaptive disclosure therapy lays the foundation for a lifelong struggle, according to its architects; there is no prior pristine or innocent self to be recuperated here. The struggle involves accepting "responsibility" for what one has done and to move forward by recognizing that it does not define who one is.[89] In contrast to Vietnam-era anti-war activists, however, such talk of responsibility does not imply political engagement or activism in the world, let alone a critique of the post-9/11 wars.

The process of "taking responsibility," of accepting what one has done and moving forward is facilitated by a "dialogue in imagination." Following the exposure elements of the protocol, the patient is asked "to disclose (confess) the morally injurious experience *to the moral authority*," that is, to someone he looks up to as an important moral figure in his life—a priest, a parent, a friend. The patient is asked to close his eyes and use the present tense. Once again, the transgression is relived, as it was earlier in the exposure elements of the protocol, but now with a "key distinction." The patient relives the transgression, this time in the knowledge that "the moral authority is listening and watching." In the "here and now," the patient shares "what the event means about him or her as a human being, given that he or she did (or did not) do something"; treatment requires the patient "to unearth all the raw thoughts, meanings, and feelings, and implications of the transgression." As Litz et al. explain, "This is very much akin to a frank emotional confession." The intent of confessing to an empty chair, to an imagined *compassionate* moral authority, is "to create an atmosphere in which a forgiving and compassionate moral authority, sometimes through the voice of the patient and other times through the voice of the therapist, asks the service member or veteran to consider his or her condemning conclusions in light of the war experience itself and the stressors leading up to the event."[90]

For cases in which the traumatizing event involves acts of commission, that is, "moral injury by self," the protocol incorporates one additional step. The patient must undertake concrete efforts to "move toward decency and goodness" by helping other people. "While it is impossible to 'fix' events in the past and, indeed, any focus on literal repair will likely ring hollow, there is the notion of making amends." Guilt—while "useful [as an] attention getting feeling," is not "a feeling on which to linger or indulge but is instead a call for change, activating the need for some type of corrective action that must be enacted."[91] If, as Michel Foucault argues in *The History of Sexuality*, it was the practice of confession—which has been central to the West since the Middle Ages and was codified largely around confessing to acts of sex—that gradually detached speaking the truth from the requirement that such speech be followed by an act of penance, with adaptive disclosure, the need for some form of penance returns, at least for specific instances of moral transgression.[92] For patients suffering from "moral injury by self," they need to re-enter their communities and make amends, symbolically, not materially or directly, for the violence they perpetrated on others. Are you reopening the question of responsibility? I asked one VA psychologist. "You hit the nail on the head," he said. "And it's not just important for psychological reasons, but also for the culture at large. We can't shy away from culpability. They feel it. We can't be Pollyannish about it." He notes a significant difference between now and how things were after Vietnam. Then service members were blamed by the public for what they did, he told me. People don't do that today, but that's a "double-edged sword." As this psychologist understands it, "All the hero rhetoric doesn't allow someone to have the truth of his/her own culpability." And yet his understanding of (moral) culpability has no necessary relationship to *politics* per se. One might be, or feel, culpable *for a particular act;* there is no talk here of coming to terms with the larger enterprise—the war—of which it was born. And making amends is purely symbolic; there is no call for making amends in relation to the persons or communities one has actually harmed.

With culpability, the problem of guilt, a key issue in post-Vietnam syndrome comes back into clinical understandings of PTSD. While survivor guilt was central to post–World War II understandings of the trauma of camp survivors, over time the notion that Holocaust survivors were paralyzed by guilt became controversial. It was misunderstood to suggest an element "of collusion," as Ruth Leys has argued. Beginning in the 1960s, feminist psychiatrists and anti-rape activists also became increasingly suspicious of the psychoanalytic concept; they feared the ethical, political, and legal implications of ascribing "guilt" to girls and women who had been victims of incest and rape. Taken together with the declining power of psychoanalysis in American psychiatry, guilt receded into the background. In the DSM-III it was named a critical feature of PTSD, but by the DSM-IIIR in 1987, guilt was referenced as merely an "associated and non-critical feature of the condition," and by the publication of the DSM-IV in 1994, it was gone (see chapters 1 and 2).

In her book *From Guilt to Shame*, Ruth Leys details not just the declining importance of guilt but also how, in post-DSM-III definitions of post-traumatic stress disorder, it has been displaced by the concept of shame. Leys argues that the shift speaks to a cultural transformation much larger than the discipline of psychiatry: It indexes a broader culture and politics of shame. Guilt speaks of "actions, that is, what you do—or what you wish or fantasize you have done," while shame is a matter of "who you are." As Leys presents it, the distinction amounts to "a shift of focus from actions to the self that makes the question of personal identity of paramount importance."[93]

The stark dichotomy between guilt and shame—and the abandonment of the former in favor of the latter—has, however, never been entirely true in clinical practice, even as shame has become more prominent in psychiatric theory and practice alike. Guilt never disappeared from the clinical practices of cognitive behavioral therapies for PTSD. For decades now, clinicians working with veterans of the war in Vietnam have grappled with the problem of guilt. By helping patients develop more "realistic" accounts of their responsibility, they held onto the relationship between trauma and guilt. They recognized guilt as a cardinal element of the suffering of soldiers and veterans, even if not the ontic guilt, that is *real,* realistic guilt that Lifton attributed to soldiers returning from the war in Vietnam, discussed in Chapter 1.[94] Nevertheless, the concept of "moral injury" may signal the beginnings of yet another significant shift: Guilt about what one has done and self-handicapping shame (that what one has done now defines *who one is*) are inseparable here. As a theory of trauma, moral injury holds guilt and shame together in a tight, intimate embrace.

Cognitive processing therapies, as we have seen, are designed to help patients generate more "realistic" accounts of what a soldier did or did not do by contextualizing their transgressions in terms of the choices that were actually available at the time. Adaptive disclosure therapy shifts gears. The fundamental assumption in CPT, according to Litz and colleagues, is that "any currently distressing event that does not involve deliberate perpetration of unnecessary violence is caused by distorted thinking that needs to be reappraised." That assumption belies combat realities, and from the adaptive disclosure point of view, it also neglects to integrate the values of military culture and its "warrior" ethos into therapeutic procedures. "In both PE and CPT, attempts at contextualizing war-zone transgressions might be considered moral reassurance rather than moral repair. Moral reassurance is a ubiquitous coping skill in society; we use it to reassure ourselves or others (e.g., 'I did the best I could,' 'They didn't mean to hurt me,' or 'Look at all the things I do right.')." But in the context of "some war-zone transgressions," moral reassurances do no good. They cannot "negate or invalidate troubling and painful moral truths." In contrast, "moral repair" encourages patients to accept "inconvenient truths ... so that a new context can be created for the traumatic events going forward (e.g., by making amends, asking forgiveness, or repairing moral damage symbolically)." Adaptive disclosure aims to "help the patient integrate the discomfort of the moral injury through experiencing forgiveness, self-compassion, and engaging in reparative behaviors.[95]

The architects of this new treatment protocol propose that laying the foundation for healing from moral injury involves coming to terms with the meanings of and responsibility for "a specific action." Patients must find a way to reconcile themselves with what they did or failed to do. And they must accept that what they did does not define who they are. People who suffer moral injury have to learn to let go of, or at least, to live with their guilt and shame.

## Psychiatry's Subject(s)

Moral injury is not an official diagnostic category and, by and large, its proponents are not proposing that it become one. Nevertheless, the concept's influence on thinking about combat-related psychological harms is increasingly evident. A significant shift in the description of PTSD etiology was described in the 2014 report by Institute of Medicine, as noted previously, in recognizing that PTSD can be caused by taking someone else's life. What's more, the report's authors challenged funding priorities for PTSD, questioning the almost exclusive focus on fear-based traumas. Pointing out that shame and guilt frequently accompany PTSD diagnoses, they argue that these "social emotions" are "not modeled or captured in existing experimental models and paradigms."[96] For its part, while holding tight to a life-threat–based understanding of the etiological event, the DSM-5 made a crucial move in removing the requirement that the traumatized person respond to the event with a sense of horror, helplessness, and fear. As the United States enters its twenty-first year of continuous warfare, "civilian" trauma no longer dominates theorizations of PTSD.

These proliferating understandings of combat trauma have implications reaching beyond the question of what PTSD is or, for that matter, what moral injury is. Different psychiatric paradigms have their own ethical and political consequences, *in potentia* if not necessarily in actual fact. Theorizing traumatic loss and moral injury reintroduces notions of agency, guilt, and responsibility that had been sidelined in clinical definitions and common-sense understandings of PTSD once it was redefined as a condition of victimhood. References do get made to the biological underpinnings of moral injury; as William Nash, for example, put it in a workshop: "If some of our moral expectations are genetically rooted in thousands of years of evolution, then a moral injury is something that separates us from that grounding in a universe." Nevertheless, mental health practitioners responding to the moral injury of soldiers are not focused on identifying and treating its presumed biophysiological underpinnings and manifestations, and they are not trying to de-habituate somatic reactions, as is the case in traditional prolonged exposure therapy for PTSD. At least in part, both moral injury and traumatic loss challenge dominant materialist understandings of trauma as they have developed over the past two decades or more.

The zeitgeist that has long undergirded PTSD is a "fight-flight-freeze" response to danger and harm, and that response is understood to be "hardwired"—that is, "richly encoded in memory and conditioned to a variety of peri- and post-event stimuli," Litz and his coauthors argue.[97] According Bessel van der Kolk, beginning in the early 1990s, imaging technologies documented the kinds of physiological changes in the brains of patients suffering PTSD. As a consequence, clinicians have learned that even if helping patients find "the words to describe what has happened to them" is important, it will never be enough. "The act of telling the story doesn't necessarily alter the automatic physical and hormonal responses of bodies that remain hypervigilant, prepared to be assaulted or violated at any time. For real change to take place, the body needs to learn that the danger has passed and to live in the reality of the present."[98]

The relentless focus on physiology, on somatic responses to stimuli continues today in the search for neurological, hormonal, and genetic underpinnings of PTSD. Finding ways to intervene in the processes by which trauma is imprinted on the brain is a major focus of clinical research, as is a quest to find the genetic and neurological underpinnings of who is most at risk for PTSD, how to diagnose PTSD in materialist terms, and who might best respond to which treatment protocols. For example, according to its director, the Strong Star Consortium is conducting research to identify "physiological markers for the detection of PTSD and identifying which treatment a person would respond to best." One hope is to find a "blood test for PTSD."[99] At the 2018 Strong Star conference in San Antonio, one researcher reported on her work identifying "the molecular mechanisms of PTSD," noting how essential that is for designing pharmacotherapies. A second speaker detailed her search for the "biomarkers of treatment response," focusing on how particular neuro-steroids impact treatment response. More generally, the Institute of Medicine's 2017 report recommended neurobiological research, which "might help translate current knowledge of the neurobiology of PTSD to screening, diagnosis and treatment approaches and might increase understanding of the biological basis of evidence-based therapies," as well as studies on the "genomic basis for PTSD [which] is critically important for determining who might be at risk."[100] Researchers at the Defense Advanced Research Projects Agency (DARPA) and elsewhere are exploring brain implants and deep brain stimulation as treatments for PTSD.[101]

More expansive understandings of combat trauma, moral injury, and traumatic loss challenge the biophysiological and, increasingly, neurological paradigm, which has taken hold of American psychiatry and dominates thinking about PTSD. Adaptive disclosure therapy for moral injury and traumatic loss, while drawing on cognitive behavioral therapeutic models, presupposes a very different kind of "disorder" and a different psychiatric subject. "The conversation we're having here couldn't have happened a few years ago," explained William Nash at one training workshop, "not just because Moral Injury was not a term, but because our understanding of what it means to be a person has shifted." What is more, understandings of combat trauma have moved beyond single-event etiologies to explore quasi-events, which is likewise a move away from the hard-wired fight/flight/freeze model of PTSD. Among the circumstances that are not quite "events" are potentially traumatizing experiences—"forms of suffering and dying, enduring and expiring, that are ordinary, chronic and cruddy," to return to Povinelli's words—that do not square easily with understandings of PTSD as a biophysiological disorder of the brain brought on by an extraordinary, discrete, and life-threatening event that elicits a fight/flight/freeze response.[102]

The questions raised by the concepts of moral injury and traumatic loss speak decidedly of the "mind"—that is, of consciousness, the irreducibility of meaning, the experience of overwhelming grief, guilt, and shame. These questions recall the work of Lifton, Shatan, and Shay, among others, with Vietnam veterans. The therapeutic act involves taking seriously the experiences individual soldiers and veterans had and exploring the meanings they take away from them—that is, not trying to "correct" what can be construed as falsely held interpretations or beliefs or to de-habituate their somatic responses. It involves helping patients confront their feelings of grief, responsibility,

guilt, and shame about loss and about what happened or what
they did. So, too, do the prescribed "action plans" for some
morally injurious experiences require "engaging in meaningful
activities, and/or spiritual practices" to reconnect with family
members, fellow veterans, service members, and their communities at large.[103] In this way, the recognition, in particular, of
moral transgression in the war zone has the potential to return
the clinical conversation to the inseparability of trauma from
a civic self. Nevertheless, this is not the civic self previously
described by Shay. Here we see no call for *political* engagement
as a necessary part of healing from an injury born of a decidedly
political act, that is, of fighting a war. For adaptive disclosure's
purposes, the need is simply to draw a line between past and
present by starting to be a better person, which is accepted as a
satisfactory understanding of making amends.

Even as the concept of moral injury and the clinical protocols
being developed for treating it push beyond strictly a biophysiological paradigm of combat trauma, moral injury researchers
conform to the norms and bureaucratic requirements of contemporary evidence-based psychiatry. Their work likewise takes
place entirely inside contemporary political norms. In contrast
to the psychiatrists who worked with Vietnam veterans against
the war and first formulated post-Vietnam syndrome, clinical
researchers today never explicitly question the military and its
conduct of war; they seem to celebrate it as a hyper-moral institution defined by a culture and set of virtues and codes all its
own, even if many are nevertheless skeptical of the point and/
or conduct of the post 9/11 wars, especially the war in Iraq.
Built into the very concept of moral injury is a commitment
to the stance that the military and its personnel are guided by
an especially robust moral code. Moreover, the proponents of
moral injury as a clinical concern were explicit in charging
Shay's initial theorization with falling short of the standards
of evidence-based clinical medical trials. For their concept
and treatment protocols to be accepted by the Department of
Defense and Veterans Affairs, they need to demonstrate the
robustness of their theories via randomized clinical trials. And

in developing clinical protocols, they explore short-term interventions that enable active-duty troops to be redeployed. Force protection, in other words, is a fundamental mental health goal in regard to military trauma, whether it conceptualized as moral injury or PTSD.

A tension stands at the heart of clinical work on moral injury. On the one hand, there is talk of transgression, of wrongdoing, of wounds to the soul, of guilt and shame, and not as mere misrecognitions in need of correction. On the other hand, the meaning of "the moral," as the concept is deployed, is decidedly slippery. Is what is moral in the war zone distinct from what is moral in "civilian" life? Is moral transgression ever simply a fact, regardless of context? A report on a clinical trial to develop a Moral Injury Events Scale (MIES), for example, summed it up this way: "The MIES indexes only perceived contradictions between remembered behaviors and post hoc moral expectations in the necessarily complex moral context of modern warfare; it does not index wrongdoing in any form."[104] Moral injury advocates are obliged to stress that point as a condition of having it recognized by the Navy (renamed "inner conflict") and for the Department of Defense to fund research on it. And yet, despite public statements affirming the possibility of suffering moral injury without having committed moral wrongdoing, *in actual clinical practice*, the question of good and bad—of right and wrong—occupies center stage.

The concept of moral injury is politically and ethically Janus-faced. Its advocates do not speak the language of political critique that was at the core of the Vietnam-era articulation of the trauma of perpetration—of having committed atrocities, of the kinds of militarism, racism, and imperial power that made such acts possible in the first place, that made the war in Vietnam as a whole both possible and a crime. Quite to the contrary, moral injury is understood to stem from the contradiction between the strength of the military's moral code (and its strict enforcement of the rules of engagement) and the far more ambiguous and brutal realities of counterinsurgency warfare, failing to consider the reality that the laws of war themselves are as important in *enabling* some forms of violence in war as they are in outlawing others.[105] Drawing here on Talal Asad's analysis of the assumptions underlying the distinction between terrorism and just war, the argument could be made that moral injury indexes the US military's liberal-qua-moral foundations. In contrast to the (Muslim) terrorist, Asad writes, the "just modern soldier incurs guilt when he kills innocent people."[106] More accurately, the just modern soldier (a liberal subject) *might* develop feelings of guilt in response to the legitimate and legal, if nevertheless morally ambiguous, acts of violence inherent in fighting a counterinsurgency war. That is, they might develop feelings of guilt even for killing an enemy combatant—perhaps in response to the pleasure they may have experienced at the moment of the kill. But for all this talk of guilt that cannot simply be "corrected," it is not Robert J. Lifton's concept of real guilt, nor is it Martin Buber's "ontic" guilt, as discussed in Chapter 1. In contemporary moral harm theory, cultural relativism replaces political and ethical judgment.

What we see in adaptive disclosure is not a call for political engagement, in the sense of undertaking action in the world that directly addresses the US wars and the harms they have wrought on others. Anti-war veterans in the Vietnam era, in collaboration with psychiatrists who worked with them, insisted that radical political action and psychological healing were cut from the same cloth. They organized and acted to *end the war*. As they understood it, repairing the self and ending imperial harm went hand in hand. Healing was constitutively and unavoidably political. But as represented in the AD protocols, the corresponding concept has become "making amends," defined in terms that are all but entirely personal, in that it "means drawing a line between past and present, and in some way changing one's approach to living, in order to move toward the positive and toward better behavior."[107]

Still, the concept of moral injury troubles the foundations on which a diagnosis of PTSD has relied since the mid-1980s. Its architects recognize that combat trauma—in its heterogenous etiologies and manifestations—will never be contained fully within a biophysiological or even a purely medical paradigm. The person is damaged in far more complex ways, morally and spiritually, and the resulting afterlives of trauma cannot be reabsorbed into a "manifestation of traumatic Pavlovian conditioning and response."[108] This is a suffering neither easily overcome nor easily treated, let alone healed.

Most generally, for all its political and ethical ambivalences and shortcomings, the concept of moral injury does not simply set moral and ethical questions aside. It reminds us instead that what is "normal" in a war zone, what soldiers are trained to do, can be inherently injurious to those who carry out acts of war. Yes, killing is the job. Yes, soldiers experience, witness, and wreak destruction. And yes, many walk away unscathed. Nevertheless, "combat normal," the architects of the concept caution, never really becomes normal for many military personnel. It raises questions about technoscientific fantasies of making soldiers so resilient that they will go to war and incur no psychological harm. Moral injury also reminds us to push back against a view of the military as but another job, as "service," with all the ethically positive connotations the word carries in tow. As one psychologist told me, despite his deep anti-war activism during the era of the war in Vietnam, today he sees that people who "*work* in the military" get "an identity, a sense of purpose," and as such he has more appreciation of the military today (my emphasis). Likewise, asking her readers to accept such a description on its own terms, anthropologist Zoë Wool writes, "At war and at home soldiers talk about what they do as 'a job' or 'work' more often than anything else".[109] By re-centering the moral and ethical questions that trouble many soldiers on returning from war, the concept of moral injury contains the kernels of a very different message. It allows us to remember, *to insist* that making war *is not just another job*. And it is politically and ethically essential to reject such (self-)narrations, at least if one recognizes that we must also consider, that we might need to *prioritize,* the perspectives and experiences of those persons and communities on the receiving end of what American soldiers do.

# PART THREE
## CONSCRIPTING CITIZENS

# 5

# Caring for Militarism

The Department of Defense and Veterans Affairs are not alone in responding to the combat trauma of American soldiers who have returned from the wars. As I elaborate over the next two chapters, the American public is also engaged— or is being called upon to become more engaged—in helping veterans heal from war. When it comes to formal, institutional veteran care, nongovernmental organizations and, in particular, faith-based organizations are key. But nongovernmental institutional involvement is also symptomatic of a broader sense—or, perhaps, a broader *rhetoric*—of civic obligation, often framed as a corrective to how soldiers were treated upon their return from Vietnam. The American public, it is said, needs to respect, listen to, and care for those who went off to war in its name, not just in institutional contexts, but also as individuals (Chapter 6). The space for political critique is dramatically narrowed in this discourse and its attendant practices, as I will show, producing, even if unintentionally, what one might name a militarist sensibility. Within that sensibility, the concept of moral injury figures prominently, and in contrast to most clinicians who work with patients suffering combat trauma, it is framed by many as an injury distinct from PTSD.

Inside the military and the VA, chaplains have long insisted that no treatment for PTSD shorn of "spirituality" is ever going to work, and that call has become louder and perhaps more felicitous over the past decade or more with the influence of moral injury on discussions of combat trauma. For their part, an expanding network of charities, churches, local community groups, and nonprofits holding similar beliefs have taken up that call, working to heal combat trauma framed as a spiritual injury, an injury to the soul. Nongovernmental groups, prominent among them Christian-based charities and churches, play an essential role in veteran support and reintegration, an outcome of the outsourcing of social welfare responsibilities to the private sector, and more specifically to religious organizations that began in the 1980s. But lest this move to the spiritual seem an entirely religious affair, arts-based organizations have also taken up the work of healing and reintegrating veterans back into the national community to which they have returned, and they do so with a secular sensibility not so far removed from the more formally Christian-based approach. As viewed from the arts angle, combat trauma is likewise damage to the self, to the soul, not a medical disorder; moreover, ritual, which is collective and communal by its very nature, is considered essential to the work of healing and coming home.[1]

The work of this complex array of actors and institutions raises, yet again, substantive questions about the character of combat trauma. How might combat trauma be better understood? Where, how, and in what kind of setting might healing occur? In this wider landscape, facilitating psychological and moral repair is approached outside of, or at least adjacent to, a mental-health frame and it incorporates an array of practices: writing workshops, theatrical performances, pastoral care, and rituals of healing, penance, and self-forgiveness. All are driven by a sense of a moral imperative to attend to the pain and suffering of the American soldier and veteran. For those not in the military—that is, for those working specifically with veteran populations—it is also driven by a commitment to reach across and repair the so-called civil-military divide, as detailed in the introduction.

Recognizing the psychological pain and suffering of the victim of violence has been central to the new humanitarianism of the past several decades.[2] In part, this has manifested as the "medicalization of politics," to borrow Miriam Ticktin's words; care and compassion replace earlier critiques of structural inequality. The name of the game is intervening in the moment of "emergency," in responding to what Slavoj Žižek has named "subjective violence"—the spectacular violence, which is to say, the more obvious or apparent violence, like a terrorist attack or the effects of an improvised explosive device.[3] What is overlooked in such endless attention to the emergency, Žižek insists, is the "objective" or "structural" violence that undergirds it, the grinding poverty that capitalism of necessity generates, and, in this instance, the not unrelated imperial power and hubris that enables the United States to conduct its wars so very far from home. Such humanitarian priorities have been accompanied by a focus on the victim, as I elaborated in the introduction. Caring for and giving voice to those who have been harmed stands at the heart of the moral, and presumably post-political imperative that drives such work.

As this new humanitarian sensibility meets the project of caring for American troops and veterans, however, the question of victimhood becomes far more complex. Are soldiers and veterans heroes? Perpetrators? Are they victims? If so, of whom? In what ways is the larger "community"—the American public, most of whom are and have always been "civilians"—responsible for the suffering that veterans now endure? And what about the actual victims of American military forces? What about their needs for care? If the new humanitarians, such as those who founded Médecins Sans Frontières, understand themselves as not bound by the borders and obligations of the nation-state, the "new American humanitarianism" is unequivocally the child of national-imperial politics. And yet, like the humanitarianism we see acting on the international stage, it remains focused on "alleviating pain in the present moment" and it does so, by and large, while insisting on its "political neutrality"—that is, by refusing to take a stand vis-à-vis the post-9/11 wars.[4]

In tracking nonclinical practices of healing and care, this chapter explores a range of engagements with pain, suffering, and repair as they move among both religious and theologically based discourses and practices, as well as secular ones within the military and beyond. In contrast to the Vietnam era, when the psychiatric approach to healing combat trauma developed in the context of a robust political critique, similar conversations today are far more likely to be framed within a moral discourse often explicitly shorn of political judgment. This tends to be a conversation about suffering souls, moral pain, sin, repentance, and moral repair. In what follows, I explore the various kinds of obligations, questions, and practices all this talk of moral and psychological suffering has generated, and I consider a turn to ritual as a collective and spiritual alternative to clinical protocols, a different means of repair. Throughout, I give an account of a project of care that, despite moments of political critique that break through, suborns the work of American militarism and war.

## Souls in Anguish

Theologians and progressive activists Rita Nakashima Brock and Gabriella Lettini recount how, in the context of their experiences working with traumatized soldiers and veterans in the early years of the wars in Afghanistan and Iraq, they "were searching for some approach to moral questions of war that went deeper than the ideologically polarized pro-war versus pacifist positions that characterized many debates about war."[5] They helped organized the Truth Commission on Conscience in War (TCCW), which was imagined as following in the footsteps of the Winter Soldier Investigation organized by the Vietnam Veterans Against the War.[6] Its goal was to put "the moral issues [emerging from the wars] before the public."[7] As Brock recounted to an audience several years later at a workshop on moral injury at the Union Theological Seminary (UTS) in Manhattan, during the planning process for the TCCW, a Catholic priest at the Boston VA shared an unpublished paper on moral injury with the organizers. "Wow," she recalled thinking, "this is what we are talking about." At the close of the TCCW forum, organizers and participants called for public education, especially within religious institutions, about the phenomenon of moral injury. Brock, Lettini, and Herman Keizer, a retired US Army chaplain, committed to the task, and in June 2012 the Soul Repair Center of the Brite Divinity School in Fort Worth, Texas, was born.

The Soul Repair Center and Rita Brock herself quickly became crucial actors in a network of largely Christian-based organizations and individuals devoted to recognizing, studying, and publicizing moral injury as a form of combat trauma and helping soldiers and veterans heal.[8] Clinical researchers had been urging the importance of involving "larger systems that can facilitate recovery from moral injury ... particularly across disciplines that integrate leaders from faith-based and spiritual communities as well as other communities from which individuals seek support."[9] In ventures like the Soul Repair Center, theologically motivated activists and religious service groups have taken up the call. And they have developed a conception of moral injury that moves beyond what we have seen in clinical settings: It constructs spiritual damage as caused explicitly by transgression and sin.

"To violate your conscience is to commit moral suicide." With these words, Brock and Lettini open their 2012 book, *Soul Repair*. Even though clinicians consider forms of moral injury in their treatment protocols, they rarely provide specific definitional criteria for the elements understood to be responsible for it, such as moral transgression or a violation of conscience. When approached theologically, in contrast, the meaning of "the moral" and the character of the "injury" are elaborated more explicitly. "Veterans with moral injury have souls in anguish, not a psychological disorder," write Brock and Lettini. "Feelings of guilt, shame, and contrition were once considered the feelings of a normal ethical person. However, secular approaches tend to view them as psychological neuroses or disorders that inhibit individual self-actualization and interfere with 'authentic' feelings and urges." The problem, from this emerging point of view, is that many veterans do not "believe their moral struggles are psychological illnesses needing treatment"; "they experience their feelings as a profound spiritual crisis that has changed them, perhaps beyond repair."[10]

Military chaplains, nonmilitary clergy, religious institutions, and congregations working with active-duty soldiers and veterans tend to share a view about the proper role of clinical medicine in the aftermath of combat trauma. "The fields of psychiatry and psychology provide invaluable insight into combat operational stress injury and posttraumatic stress disorder," writes Beth Stallinga, a lieutenant commander in the US Navy Chaplain Corps. "At the same time, mental health practitioners are often ill-equipped to address many of the recurring spiritual concerns increasingly identified with trauma." Moral injury, as she puts it, refers to "operational stress injury and trauma that affects the mind and spirit."[11] Or, in the words of Paul D. Fritts, a major and chaplain in the US Army, "moral injury is a psychologically descriptive label for the normative problem of sin," which is "an offense against religious or moral law," whether intentional or accidental.[12] And no injury matching that description is conceptualized under the standard clinical view of PTSD.[13]

Whether experiences of psychologically debilitating guilt, shame, and contrition signal neurosis or signal the suffering of a "normal ethical person" reiterates a now long-standing struggle over the meaning of PTSD. Is it a sign of pathology or a normal human response to an extreme situation? However, figures such as Brock, Lettini, Stallinga, and Fritts reframe and extend that question: Moral injury signals a soul in anguish. If this is so, what do we mean by "the soul?" For those who root their care of soldiers and veterans in a Christian ethic, referencing the soul represents a rejection of—or at least, a supplement to—a secular conception of combat trauma as we have seen it thus far in clinical practice. The soul, according to Stallinga, is "the nexus of our deep connection with all that is good, true, and beautiful: our connection with the rest of creation, and our connection with God." Wounds to the soul "result in a diminishment of everything meaningful to the person."[14] As such, chaplains rather than clinicians are best positioned to care for those suffering spiritual wounds.[15] After all, as one participant put it at a moral injury workshop I attended in Kansas City in 2015, pastors "are very often in the role of accompanying those at a spiritual impasse."

The spiritual, according to scholar of religious studies Winnifred Fallers Sullivan, is a complex concept in American society. It is "deeply entangled in various religious and secular histories, social structures, and cultural practices."[16] She quotes a pair of Christian theologians who explain that the human spirit "is more than a set of fixed traits and characteristics; it is an animating impulse—a vital, motivating force that is directed to realizing higher order goals, dreams, and aspirations that grow out of the essential self. In this sense, the human spirit organizes people's lives and propels people forward."[17] Even as the typical conception of the human spirit in the United States is shaped by a decidedly Christian history and theology, she argues, the "spiritual" signals a religiosity that is taken to be "democratic, innocent of political partisanship, and open to the sacred in its many incarnations," as necessarily befits a military culture and chaplaincy that does not (and cannot constitutionally) officially conceive of itself as Christian.[18]

Within this discourse, "religiosity" is understood to be an essential part of what it is to be human, without regard for any specific ontology.[19] As iterated by the Army's spiritual fitness program, "we define spirit as the existential core of the individual, the deepest part of the self, and one's evolving human essence."[20] As for what spiritual *fitness* refers to for the Army, in the words of Captain Chad E. Cooper, it denotes "the development of the personal qualities needed to sustain a person in times of stress, hardship and tragedy. These qualities can come from religious, philosophical or human values ... [and they form] the basis for character, disposition, decision making and integrity."[21] Or in the words of an Army chaplain interviewed by Sullivan, "Soldiers that had just come back from combat ... viewed Iraq as the Wild West: 'If they don't look like me I can shoot them and there will be no consequences.'" "Spiritual fitness," as Sullivan sums up the remark, is what "separates soldiers from outlaws."[22]

There are structural reasons that explain why active-duty soldiers in distress most often turn to military chaplains as their "first-line responders." Founded on July 29, 1775, following a decision of the Continental Congress, the Army Chaplain Corps has been an integral part of the US military ever since, expanding from its initial appointment of protestant chaplains to including Catholic, Jewish, and, more recently, Muslim and Buddhist "chaplains" into its ranks.[23] Military chaplains are noncombatant commissioned officers, bearing a "rank without command." They deploy to the battlefields so they are on hand when soldiers need them.[24] As one former Navy chaplain explained to Sullivan, the job of a military chaplain required her to "fully enter into the life of the marine—into their muddiness and danger and ennui. She would only be trusted if she was one of them." This is more than the cultural competence with respect to the "warrior ethos" deemed essential to effective clinical care, as discussed in the previous chapter. The chaplain's authority is rooted in her *having been there* with soldiers, having shared—at least to some extent—their experiences at war. This is a "ministry of presence"—a presence as literal as it is figurative: The chaplain "lives the life of the soldier," is "there for all in those moments of need. Listening. Understanding. Supporting"; *ministry* here refers to a "suffering with."[25] Finally, whereas mental health professionals working in the military are obliged under certain circumstances to report up the chain of command, conversations between soldiers and their chaplains are confidential. As such, "the chaplain ... is recognized by active military personnel and returning veterans as a trustworthy source for healing moral injury."[26]

The "trust" established between military chaplains and the troops carries over into post-military life, at least according to RAND's report on the work of faith-based organizations (FBOs). There is no stigma attached to speaking to a chaplain; and, as explained by one person interviewed for the report, "The chaplain is someone you can go to who isn't going to tell your story everywhere." The military chaplain is trusted and, in contrast to mental health practitioners in the military, is institutionally permitted to offer confidentiality. Perhaps trading on that military experience and "familiarity" with chaplains, RAND reports, nongovernmental faith-based organizations have "developed reputations as safe places for veterans, providing supportive, judgment-free environments."[27]

Trustworthy. Confidential. And with respect to military chaplains, Present. But there is far more going on here, or so theological redefinitions of combat trauma as moral injury insist. Military chaplains, students and scholars of theology, and leaders of churches and faith-based nonprofits share the view that religious figures are best positioned to address war-zone trauma because many soldiers experience combat as a theological crisis. Wollom Jensen and James Childs, for example, insist that "soul injuries" are "not medical or psychological in nature and therefore require ... a faith-based modality." Spiritual and theological injuries at their core, they need to be "treated with the tools of religion," and that "puts faith communities, congregations, clergy and faithful laity on the front lines of spiritual triage and treatment."[28] Taking such arguments a step further, Army chaplain Timothy S. Mallard levels a scathing critique at the clinical concept of moral injury. It "borrows a manifestly theological concept such as transgression—which in Christian theology is tied to the antecedent concept of sin and the descendent concept of forgiveness—without any linkage between the three." Deeply skeptical of a secular definition of morality, Mallard proposes thinking instead in terms of a "spiritual injury" as the "intra and interpersonal damage to souls brought on by significant trauma, including the rupture to foundational religious values, beliefs, and attitudes, the inability to healthfully participate in an immanent human faith community, and the temporary or permanent loss of a transcendent relationship to God (manifested particularly in questions about forgiveness, doubt, truth, and hope)."[29]

But advocating for "pastoral care" as essential to healing war trauma does not necessarily mean dismissing the role played by psychiatric medicine. Some advocates attempt to disentangle the "psychological" from the "spiritual" in combat trauma; others, like Army chaplain Paul Fritts, seek to marry "science" and "religion" in treatment protocols. At one moral injury workshop, William Nash, the former Navy psychiatrist we met in Chapter 4 as one of the key architects of clinical treatment protocols for moral injury, represented the latter view. Other speakers addressed the spiritual dimensions of combat trauma and the role of theology in understanding it and religious practitioners in responding to it, but Nash laid out the phenomenon in clinical terms, even as he recognized the need for other kinds of interventions, including religiously based ones, to supplement the clinical approach. Regardless of how the lines are drawn between the psychological and the spiritual, however, all efforts to parse the detailed nature of spiritual wounds produce them as their own kind of thing.

During the aforementioned 2015 conference, I participated in a workshop on moral injury led by a professor of pastoral theology and pastoral care at a divinity school in the south. Drawing on Judith Herman's arguments from her book *Trauma and Recovery* (noted in Chapter 2), the professor insisted on "the importance of ... offering sanctuary ... a 'safe space.'" She framed Herman's approach as one that involves working through "frozen grief" by "providing space for remembrance, so you begin to see if you can let that ice cube melt, that frozen grief melt, or that unspoken story" be told. I intervened with a question. In a book largely about incest and child abuse, Herman was not merely writing about stories that are unspoken. She was writing about memories that are repressed—that is, unknown and inaccessible. Was it possible that soldiers and veterans may not know the stories they are supposed to recount? "Honestly ... I'm not working at that level with the veterans," she responded. "What I do know from working with survivors of sexual abuse [is] that that kind of trauma is *for a skilled therapist* to address."[30] Or, as Rita Brock remarked in explaining the difference between PTSD and moral injury at the 2017 conference in Manhattan, "PTSD is actually the loss of memory," which is "a dissociative experience," while moral injury is not dissociative because "it's a memory you know. You are in time and space but it's something deeply painful." For Stallinga, moral injury comes to the surface—becomes accessible to treatment—only after psychological disorders have been dealt with. "The spiritual distress related to operational stress injury cannot be treated effectively until baseline issues concerning depression, anxiety, and substance abuse are addressed by the appropriate provider." Doctors have a role in treating those psychiatric problems—"the physical and behavioral aspects of the wound"—but "chaplains ... will be called upon to walk with those for whom the 'dark night of the soul' feels endless, and those for whom 'the knowledge of suffering' may seem at times too heavy to bear, certainly too heavy to bear alone."[31]

Advocates of faith-based healing modalities tend to address the wars in which the injuries take place from within the so-called post-political sensibility that scholars of the new humanitarianism have identified as characterizing its forms of reason.[32] From the 1970s through the 1990s, feminists, including Judith Herman, understood themselves to be engaged in an explicitly political project when they fought for the recognition of incest and rape as traumatizing experiences and as crimes in need of legal redress. In contrast, the discourse today among advocates looking to respond to the unrecognized spiritual trauma of the American soldier home from war displaces that language of the political with a narrowly circumscribed moral vocabulary. Similarly, we rarely see war being critiqued the way it was by Robert J. Lifton or Chaim Shatan, in terms of imperial overreach, militarized racism, and colonial (and, sometimes, male/patriarchal) violence.

Within the faith-based discourse of souls in anguish and spiritual pain, war often appears as a confrontation with "evil," the source of which is never specified. To be clear, this is not the evil with a "small e" of which Lifton spoke—evil that is historically specific, a product of politics and power.[33] Instead, it is "radical suffering, radical evil that some of these veterans see way too close for comfort," as the aforementioned workshop leader at the Kansas City conference put it. In Jensen and Childs's words: "In theological terms it seems totally plausible to say that moral injury is an encounter with evil so radical that it evokes the problem of evil as a deeply existential reality rather than simply a theological conundrum."[34] Or, as Timothy Mallard writes, "War is the most anti-human of experiences. It degrades, rends, and tears at us as people both in body and in soul. It degrades, rends, and tears at human societies in our familial and collective relationships and the created order." And yet none of that is to say that war is necessarily bad or wrong. For Mallard, "despite its destructiveness, war remains an enduring and necessary reality because it checks unrestrained evil, corrects injustice, and restores, if only temporarily, a semblance of social cohesion and stability."[35] One treats the wound. One provides a "ministry of presence"—sitting with, listening to, providing a space to heal. And for some, especially among military chaplains, one nevertheless acknowledges that war is a necessary evil, that "violence 'must' be done." For those less willing to concede war's necessity, pastoral care provides "a minimalist, almost ephemeral, form of empathic spiritual care," which enables caregivers to sidestep the political and ethical judgments that psychiatrists like Lifton and Shatan, alongside the veterans with whom they worked, insisted were unavoidable.[36]

Evil, radical evil, unrestrained evil—such talk references the problem of experiencing a world in which meaning and moral expectations have collapsed. In developing an account of how evil is framed in "modern thought," moral philosopher Susan Neiman asks, "What's the difference between calling one action evil, and another, a crime against humanity?" They may seem interchangeable, but "a crime is something for which we have procedures—at least for punishing if not for preventing." It fits "in some manner into the rest of our experience." In contrast, Neiman argues, we name an action evil when it cannot "be ordered or fit into our experience, so that it "threatens the trust in the world that we need to orient ourselves within it." Hannah Arendt challenged precisely such a conception when she sought to give *an account of evil,* to make it intelligible from a philosopher's point of view. As Nieman notes, she pointed to its "banal" character, to make it clear that its "sources ... are not mysterious or profound but fully within our grasp."[37]

In the conversations I have encountered about war as (radical) evil while doing fieldwork among members of both faith-based and secular organizations and practitioners, references to evil heed far more closely to Nieman's description of evil in modern thought than to Arendt's historical-philosophical account. When evil's source(s) or intelligibility is referenced, it tends to be with reference to the "barbarity" of the opposing forces—abominable cultural mores, a refusal to respect the laws of war. More commonly, since the idea that "war is evil" is just presumed to be common sense, it seems to require no further engagement or elaboration. There is little if any interest in producing an account of what the Israeli philosopher Adi Ophir understands as evil's modes of production.[38] He asks, for example: What are the "structures" of evil "that need to be fought"? How is evil produced?[39] Instead, in the discourse I encountered about evil, war, moral pain, and injury to the soul, to come face to face with (radical) evil is just what war is, especially today when the wars the United States fights are counterinsurgency ones. In contrast to Ophir's insistence that we approach the problem of evil not metaphysically but as a thing in and of this world, these conversations are focused on the consequences for American troops of having confronted evil on the killing fields of the post-9/11 wars.

Those who point out that American soldiers encounter evil in the theater of war are not claiming that American soldiers go into war unconstrained by moral rules and expectations. As Jensen and Childs insist, echoing many others, including the clinicians I discussed in the previous chapter, the military is guided by and grounded in a strong moral code that emphasizes loyalty, duty, respect, selfless service, honor, integrity, and personal courage, all of which are understood to be trademark Army values. And, they write, "Integrity or honor as a core value for the military is indeed a beginning point for the type of moral and ethical reflection that is essential to the spiritual well-being of a warrior."[40] If during the Vietnam war era the military was widely regarded as a place of moral degradation, as we saw in Chapter 1, it is celebrated by many today on both sides of the civil-military divide as a superior moral setting, as "a place of better values than the world from which recruits come."[41]

The strict limitations on legitimate violence contained in the rules of engagement are significant, in this view, for reasons that reach beyond matters of mere legality: "The Rules of Engagement adopted by the military of the United States and other countries are a modern attempt at limiting the dimensions of chaos in war and thereby mitigating the damage *to the humanity of warriors* caused by armed conflict." And, as Jensen and Childs argue, "While it would be an absurd presumption to view the military of the United States as a Christian organization, it is nevertheless the case that much of the moral and ethical thinking with regard to the waging of war by the United States has been and continues to be deeply influenced by the just war tradition." *Jus ad bellum* requires that war "must be declared by a legitimate authority," that it "must be fought with the right intention," and that it "must be a last resort." *Jus in bello* requires that "war must be waged in respect for the lives of noncombatants" and that "the means used must be proportionate to the ends." These criteria, together with the "benevolent treatment of prisoners" and the principle of "no means mala in se" (that soldiers cannot use "weapons or methods that are inherently evil") make up the essential content of the *Department of Defense Law of War Manual*.[42]

A fundamental tension characterizes this discourse about the military, war, and damage to the soul. On the one hand, soldiers are not to kill indiscriminately; they are bound by a moral code and laws of war that delimit the contexts in which and the means by which killing is permissible. On the other, at least for many soldiers, the military code cannot wholly supplant the values with which they were raised. For those raised to believe the Judeo-Christian commandment "thou shalt not kill," the argument goes, the act of killing remains forever morally questionable. At the 2017 UTS workshop mentioned previously, for example, Brock expanded on those moral tensions: "What I call spirituality [involves the fact that] you are not alone in the universe, and this vast universe is part of what makes you who you are. [It is a] larger world of meaning to which [one] has a responsibility." That world is "your moral house," and over time the house changes. It changes as you integrate disruptive experiences; "that's a normal process." The military, however, disrupts one's moral house in a very specific way, because "virtually every society in the world has a serious moral prohibition against killing," even while the job of the military is "to teach you how to desire killing." Basic training is "a lot like monastic training," she said. The military takes away everything new recruits already know and value, and it tells them what to do and what to desire. It undertakes "a complete remodeling" of their moral house. Brock was careful here to qualify her words: she was not saying that the military was in the business of producing bad moral houses; serving in the military, after all, involves serving "a higher purpose." It requires "caring deeply about people in your unit. How many of us have a friend who would die for us? ... That's part of military experience." Learning to kill, indeed, desiring to kill, Brock explained, "comes in a context with a lot of meaning attached to it."

On the one hand, in Brock's account, the "moral" is equivalent to "obedience to any law that is given from the outside," what Immanuel Kant placed strictly outside the realm of morality.[43] On the other hand, the laws of war, even if and when they are enforced, may not seamlessly override a deeper moral code—for example, a blanket religious prohibition against killing—and thus is moral injury born. Army chaplain Paul Fritts puts the contradiction starkly: "the US Army wants Soldiers who are moral and at the same time able to kill enemy combatants."[44]

Setting aside the fact that the commandment "thou shalt not kill" is not the only properly Christian relationship to killing, as evidenced in the long history of "holy wars" and "just wars" waged in the name of Christianity, this tension between conflicting moral codes is argued to run deep.[45] Soldiers must be taught to kill; indeed, they must be taught to desire to kill, or so many of these same thinkers and practitioners argue. As explained by an ex-Marine to an audience during a civilian and veteran dialogue event held in New York City in 2019, "In boot camp, every time we do something you have to say kill, so that gets embedded in your brain ... Make your bed. And I would say, Kill ... Either yes, sir; or kill; or martial arts training—every time you kick, hit, you yell kill."

Some argue that the *purpose* of training is not actually to teach soldiers to kill but to meld them together into an effective military unit, even though it is impossible not to recognize that the soldier's job, at least in part, is to kill, and the distress it causes can be very real. At one workshop I attended, for example, a participant noted that being in the military causes "a shift in your moral compass. To kill is good ... you want to destroy the enemy." A veteran of the war in Vietnam objected: "Killing is ancillary in the military. You don't train to kill, you train to work as a unit, and while you're doing it, you may kill. And that skews things. You are brought up, 'thou shalt not kill.' That's the moral injury."[46] Or take Wollom Jensen's account of his training for the American war in Vietnam:

> Hours are spent on the rifle range, in hand-to-hand combat training, and at the bayonet course. This training not only teaches the applicable techniques and skills of using weapons but also helps to set the mind-set necessary for war.
>
> "What's the Spirit of the Bayonet, Company?" the drill sergeants would shout. "To KILL, Drill Sergeant!" the company would respond.
>
> "What are the two types of bayonet fighters, Company?" the drill sergeants would respond. "The quick and the dead, drill sergeant!" we would shout back in reply.
>
> Then we would be off to impale with our bayonet and butt stroke with our weapon the dummies that lined the bayonet course.[47]

According to Fritts, "The Army's dilemma is that the institution demands moral excellence of Soldiers in order to maintain discipline but at the same time requires that combatants be prepared to perform the morally injurious act of killing human beings." And to overcome the predicament, "Army culture encourages quick trigger fingers, for example, by dehumanizing enemy combatants with insulting terms such as "Raghead,' 'Gook,' and 'Kraut' in the belief that killing Ragheads, Gooks, and Krauts is easier than killing spouses, siblings, and parents."[48]

An audience member at the UTS workshop grew more than a little agitated as he listened to Brock's account of the military and its moral codes. He objected to the whole tenor of the conversation about morality and the military. "If training is to no longer see these people as human, then how is the training moral?" How can a "moral standard" be maintained in the context of "training people to see other people as inhuman"? It's "a very complicated, twisted thing," Rita Brock responded. The soul is "one's moral conscience" and moral conscience is born of the human capacity to "feel what happens to other people"—of empathy. Indeed, she continued, being connected to other human beings "is our conscience." If the military involves shutting off empathy for one group of people, it fosters an "intensified empathic relationship to those in your unit." In combat, it is "not just you dehumanizing them" but them dehumanizing and putting at risk people you love. Soldiers still have that empathy in them and when that empathy is restored vis-à-vis those they previously dehumanized, moral injuries can emerge. To summarize Brock's point in Susan Nieman's words, "Indifferent souls are rarely troubled by the thought" of the moral transgressions they may have committed.[49]

Moral injury—understood as spiritual pain, as a wound to the soul—is caused by many different kinds of events, as typically discussed within and among the faith-based practitioners. Regardless of their cause, however, the idea is that moral injuries are experienced as a fundamental rift within the self. It is a "moral distress" that "occurs when one knows the ethically or professionally prescribed action to take but doing so violates" one's moral code, according to a guidebook for clergy and lay ministers produced by Military Outreach USA. As an example, the guidebook cites a "study of soldiers during the early period of the Iraq war" showing "that they soon began to question the process of 'kicking in a door' to a home and only finding a family. These 'minor moral wounds or distresses' soon got to a point where some could no longer justify the policy of their commanders."[50] Or take the following story recounted by a veteran of the war in Iraq at a conference I attended:

Around April 2004, I was in Baghdad. I stood anxious and waiting by a truck as my team leader went downrange to look at some ordinance ... As so often happens, some kids approached me as I stood there ... and they asked me for candy, as they often did. I didn't have any candy, but we had some bottles of water in the truck, and they were actually still pretty cold from the freezer that morning. I thought to myself, I'll do a good thing and I'll give these impoverished kids some water. So I got it out of the truck and I went to hand a couple of bottles to the lead kid. The boy, probably about 8 years old ... refused the water. He had, after all, asked for candy. But his turning down the water made me angry ... Here I am risking life and limb, my team leader risking life and limb ... and this kid won't take the water I'm offering out of the goodness of my heart. So I ripped the cap off the ... bottle and I dumped some at the ground, cursed at him, and I threw it at him. A man who was most likely his grandfather came up and grabbed him and he pulled him away, and I remember looking at him ... His eyes were full of fear. He was afraid of me. And I didn't recognize that look because I didn't recognize myself. My mind bucked, I was one of the good guys up. [Up] against that image of fear in the man's eyes, [I] rejected it.

Moral injury, as described here, is a pervasive grief resulting from an irreparable schism between the soldier's previously perceived moral self and his actions on the streets of Baghdad. People are morally injured in moments of profound recognition, having witnessed themselves failing to live by their own moral convictions in circumstances that subject their convictions to the most profound demands. They experience a schism in the self. "War teaches the veteran something about herself that she did not know before and that she cannot unlearn ... The main take away is that I am not who I thought I was. I am something different. Something I never planned on being."[51] For this particular veteran, the awakening—the pain—led to a radical politics: He became a vocal critic of the war.

As such examples illustrate, killing is not the only cause of moral distress. Tyler Boudreau, the Iraq war veteran introduced in Chapter 3 as the author of the article "The Morally Injured," has pointed out that the violence of a military occupation consists not only of actual bloodshed, but also of many "smaller" and persistent kinds demeaning interactions.[52] Nevertheless, among faith-based practitioners, as we have seen to be true of clinicians as well (Chapter 4), the archetypal event precipitating moral injury is understood to be the act of killing. "A basic moral obligation, perhaps THE basic moral obligation with respect to moral injuries of combat veterans is: you shall not kill (Exodus 20:13) ... Even in a best-case scenario in which the Soldier, on a rational level, understands that she killed in order to prevent being killed, on an emotional level she feels as though she broke God's commandment," Fritts declares.[53] And as Brock told her UTS audience, many a veteran has asked him- or herself whether there is only one way to kill. "What does it take to kill someone? Do you have to be the shooter?"

In broad strokes, then, the faith-based discourse on moral pain and spiritual crisis replicates the logic of the clinical literature: moral injury is born of a contradiction between a person's personal "conscience," on the one hand, and military orders, codes of conduct, and the everyday realities of war, on the other— given, as always, the proviso that the particular wars we are talking about are ones in which avoiding moral transgression is effectively impossible. To borrow Hannah Arendt's critical reading of moral philosophy, moral conduct and moral conflict "seem ... to depend primarily upon the intercourse of man with himself." Arendt writes that the problem with "doing wrong," going back to Socrates, is that "I am [then] condemned to live with the wrongdoer in an unbearable intimacy."[54] As framed here, the spiritual rift caused by having killed—or demeaned or injured—others in war is precisely the inability to live with the self, with the person that one has become. Through the operation of conscience—the seat of self-knowledge and of knowing right from wrong—an unbearable intimacy comes to the fore.

This (Christian) spiritual discourse speaks of moral suffering while effectively sidestepping the question of moral evaluation and judgment. Or at the very least, it frequently exhibits a deep discomfort at the prospect of going over that precipice. Judgment—in the sense of any substantive invocation of religious metaphysics, as would be expected among theologians and faith-based practitioners—is set aside in a variety of ways. One possibility is to shift the burden of responsibility onto "the enemy." Terrorism, guerilla warfare, "collateral damage," wars without borders or defined battle lines all challenge the moral code set forth in the Just War Doctrine. It has become more and more difficult to abide by the code of the warrior.

A second possibility is to become a cultural relativist. The military is its own "culture" with its own moral values and codes, which we have seen not just in Brock's earlier words but also in the framework used by architects of adaptive disclosure therapy discussed in Chapter 4. A participant at the UTS moral injury workshop challenged Brock's argument that the US military has its own "moral house": "Maybe because I am a first-generation immigrant from a colonized country, I see the American military as always doing harm to another country. So is morality always culturally [constituted]?" Brock replied: "Moral content is civilizationally determined. The capacity is universal." The military is "an alternate cultural universe ... in which forms of sanctioned killing are moral, because if the purpose is to protect the constitution, then some kinds of force are required." There is little space here for political critique, and certainly not the political perspective of the self-described immigrant from a colonized country.[55]

Contradictions that arise among competing moral codes, between the laws of war and realities on the ground, between a military culture steeped in the "warrior code" and the realities of counterinsurgency warfare, dominate conversations about

moral injury among the largely Christian faith-based organizations and other religious leaders, thinkers, practitioners, and
activists working with soldiers and veterans. So, too, does talk
of the soul and of sin. And yet, this is "sin" with a twist. As
Palmer puts it, soldiers "may perceive they have committed a
sin. It is that perception of sin that can cause a *moral injury* to
that person."[56] Left unstated, perhaps because it is assumed to
be obvious, is that the soldiers' perceptions might be wrong. Sin
appears here as a subjective judgment, as appearing in the eye
of the beholder. This is a concept of sin appropriate to the spiritual work carried out by "a ministry of presence," as discussed
previously in reference to Sullivan. It is "minimalist, almost
ephemeral"; this is sin without "code, cult, or community," with
no "metaphysics."[57] It is a concept of sin—and of spirituality
writ large—fit not just for a post-political world, but perhaps
for a post-ethical one as well.

## Reclaiming Ethics

Not everyone engaged in this conversation is willing to refrain
from judgment. Not everyone is willing, as Arendt states it, to
reduce the moral to "a set of mores, customs and manners, which
could be exchanged for another" or to define sin subjectively as
a matter of individual perception.[58] Brian S. Powers, a veteran
of the wars in Iraq and Afghanistan, reframes the conversation
in his 2017 essay "Moral Injury and Original Sin." In its current
framing, he writes, moral injury gives no account of the ways in
which moral values are "twisted and distorted in the axiological
universe of [a] military endeavor," for example, "the creation of
a moral world in which all that mattered was the pursuit of the
enemy." As it now stands, the concept also provides no account
of how it might be that the very "roots" of moral injury may
reside "in the exhibition of military power itself." Powers draws
on Augustine's understanding of original sin and human willing
to propose an alternative frame: moral injury is not "merely the
violation of an interior value, but rather ... a more profound dis-
tortion of our deepest internal understanding of what is 'good'
and 'right.'" Once we understand moral injury "as the pursuit

of distorted and poisoned moral goods" we can recognize it for what it is: "the realization that one's moral orientation, to which one commits his or her willing, is aligned toward a 'good' that is ultimately false." And the pursuit of that false good is the source of sin.[59]

Powers notes the crucial question that arises from his fundamentally Christian perspective on moral injury, which is how individuals come to have committed their willing to a false good in the first place. He echoes Adi Ophir's perspective in *The Order of Evils* in insisting we examine the structures through which superfluous suffering, which for Ophir is evil, is produced. In search of an answer, Powers turns to the experiments conducted by Stanley Milgram in the 1960s at Yale, widely understood as demonstrating people's shocking degree of moral malleability when acting under the influence of authority. Powers credits Milgram with having "found that a distinct majority of his test subjects obeyed a white coat-clad experimenter's commands to shock another individual, often over the agonized screams or disquieting silence of the 'victim.'"[60]

The question, of course, is why they became willing parties to cruelty, and Powers accepts Milgram's explanation citing "antecedent conditions." The test subjects had already accepted the legitimacy of the authority figure giving the orders—in this instance, the person in the white laboratory coat. "It is not difficult to envision how military members are conditioned through antecedent factors to accept the 'good' of the military enterprise," Powers writes. The "US military has long held a sacred place within American society and this sacredness permeates our cultural ethos." In the successions of wars being fought, each one is portrayed as an absolute good: The "survival of Christian civilization" was at stake, as Churchill assessed the situation in World War II. Or in George W. Bush's justification of the post-9/11 wars, the United States was in an existential struggle against the "axis of evil," invoking, of course, the "axis powers" of World War II. Moreover, Powers insists, what conditions the soldier's will goes far beyond a general "cultural ethos" surrounding the military. Invoking David Grossman on how the US military trains soldiers to kill, he concludes that "what is being carefully yet subtly altered in these techniques is the presentation of killing—it is no longer a necessary moral ill, but an exemplary and perhaps even obligatory moral good"; "if the willing of military members is conditioned in this way, then moral injury can be understood as the commitment of one's active willing in a powerful and compelling moral orientation that is understood at some point to be false."[61]

Powers is not alone in his attempt to rescue the concepts of moral injury and sin from relativist or minimalist framing. So, too, does Warren Kinghorn, a professor of psychiatry and pastoral and moral theology at Duke University.

> The concept of moral injury, designed especially by [Brett] Litz and colleagues as a psychological concept, cannot ultimately remain there; it beckons beyond itself to a thicker contextual account of proper human ends than modern scientific psychology, bound to liberal presuppositions, can or will provide. The reality is that "moral injury" names a call for something that the modern clinical disciplines structurally cannot provide, something like a moral theology, embodied in specific communities with specific contextually formed practices. And, because this is the case, Christian moral theology can offer depth of context to moral injury that clinical psychology cannot.[62]

In contrast to Powers, who makes no mention of it, Kinghorn recognizes the pragmatic value of a "medical model." It is useful "in the design of treatments, and ... reduce[s] stigma that permeates killing." Nevertheless, the existing medical model falls woefully short: "Moral injury provides an important reminder that attention to the traumatic effects of war on soldiers and civilians cannot be separated from the more theoretical considerations of war's moral justifiability, and vice versa." (Note here, Kinghorn mentions civilians, that is, *civilians in war zones,* a referent strikingly absent in almost everyone else's speech.) Such a conception of trauma is not new, he notes. "Robert J. Lifton and Sarah Haley both recognized that in their work."[63] If moral injury pulls psychiatry toward theoretical questions about the war's moral justifiability, Kinghorn continues, it challenges Christian ethics to move from "abstract arguments about just war and pacifism toward closer consideration of the concrete psychological and individual costs of war." And in an attempt to bring discussions of just war down from its theoretical heights and into the muck of war's very real human and material consequences, Kinghorn insists, "*Jus in bello* is important not only within abstract considerations of just war but also because civilians and noncombatants die, and veterans suffer permanently and irreparably, even when such constraints are observed and particularly when they are not."[64]

It is thus beyond the capabilities of clinical medicine, in Kinghorn's view, to confront foundational moral questions that are causally related to war-zone traumatic injuries. The disciplines of psychiatry and psychology limit their frames of reference to "psychological and cognitive terms: unlike moral theologians, they cannot engage in thick description about the appropriate ends of human life ... They cannot pass judgment on the validity of the moral rules and assumptions that individual soldiers carry, since to do so would be to venture into the ethics of war." And quite crucially for Kinghorn, in the medical model, the object of therapy is "the reduction of *all* moral suffering," which means that psychologists are "unable to distinguish between meaningful and nonmeaningful moral suffering." But from a Christian perspective, moral suffering can be meaningful and productive, and as such, the aim cannot be to eliminate it by any "technology" available, be it psychotherapeutic or pharmaceutical. The "proper Christian response is not to deny [the suffering] ... or to hurry past it but, rather, to lament and, as John's Jesus adjures, to remain," by which he means dwell in the awareness of it in order to learn and grow, morally and spiritually.[65]

The exceptional place occupied by the military in American society—made manifest in a widespread if not wholly undisputed refusal to exercise judgment—was striking at nearly all the conferences, workshops, and panel discussions on combat trauma and moral injury in which I took part. Quite remarkably even among participants who considered themselves on the progressive end of the political spectrum and who often personally opposed the wars, most commonly the war in Iraq. At one workshop focused on veterans and the incarcerated, two overlapping populations understood by its organizers to suffer moral injury, one of the first speakers started off by posing a series of questions:

> What is owed in moral terms to our vets? What is owed in ethical terms to our citizens returning from incarceration? What is owed to those serving on our behalf, those serving in the most racially stratified incarceration system? How can communities respond to the invisible and very real wounds of moral injury?

The *political* critique implicit in the second question about prisoners ("those serving in the most racially stratified incarceration system") was a recurring theme throughout the three-day training workshop. How is it that primarily black men end up in jail? In what ways is the US legal system systemically racist? A priest who has worked for over a decade with violent offenders at a high-security federal prison began his session by offering the following writing prompt: "Those who are incarcerated are smart and very aware of the forces that have led to their reality and often their own culpability. Their voices are erased. How to address that erasure? The question of the humanity of those not understood as human beings by the public?" (We also had the option of writing about "the last time I was in jail.") In his work with prisoners (all of them "violent offenders") this priest took due note of what they had suffered, but he also asked them to come to terms with they had done and take moral responsibility for their actions. In the priest's view, these men needed to face their victims, to apologize, and to encounter the pain of the victims of their crimes, often relatives of those they had killed.

No equivalent conversation about either veterans or the wars they fought took place. The tone, more than merely respectful, seemed reverential. Barely a mention was made of the global structure of power, which is itself also deeply racialized and enables the United States to conduct wars with little consideration of the Others whose lives and homes they destroy. One speaker did mention responsibility for the wars at some point, by addressing some collective "we" and referring to "our" responsibility toward the soldiers sent into the fight: "We are now in two very long wars—it's hard to imagine what winning is and yet *we are still sending people to die*. And we have to face it, because a democracy cannot go to war without the public supporting it ... Iraq, Afghanistan, it all began with support."[66] At a different moment during the workshop, the aforementioned priest made a comment that stood out for its political edge: "Instead of psychologizing those who are deployed for questionable reasons," he said, "there is a need to speak truth to power. Where are those weapons of mass destruction in Iraq, for example?" These were two of very few notable exceptions, while otherwise any hint of the harm caused by American militarism remained tightly sealed within the national "we."

One of the workshop's three days happened to fall on September 11, and we were given another writing prompt to begin the day: "Where were you when the Towers fell? How did it impact you? What meaning can you make of it?" The workshop organizers spoke of our duty to remember those who were killed on that day, the soldiers who were sent off to war in response, and, among the latter, the ones who are "still there." A prayer was said and a ritual of remembrance held that evening for the Americans who died and for those Americans who are still at war. Of Iraqis and Afghans there was no mention at all, nor of the Pakistanis and others that the US military has harmed and killed in response. These others, quoting Margaret Urban Walker, did not appear to the speakers as "worthy of consideration"—and this in a room filled with a racially diverse collection of individuals, many of whom consider themselves social justice advocates. The deafening silence on this point was broken finally by a young African American woman. She had deployed to Iraq as a prison guard. "Saddam's prisoners," she told us, helped her; they befriended her and protected her. "We both felt imprisoned, but I volunteered and got paid ... They didn't have a choice. I came home and felt bad. I didn't want to be a part of that."

## Humanitarianism at Home

For American veterans of the post-9/11 wars, faith-based organizations do a lot of the work of care, a fact symptomatic of a broad shift in the provision of social services in American society over the past several decades. Legislation passed in the late 1990s and then again in 2001 increased federal funding for faith-based organizations in providing social services, and not only to (ex-) military populations.[67] As argued by Melinda Cooper, President Clinton's welfare reforms were part of a larger shift toward a greater role of religious nonprofits in the delivery of social services. The welfare reform act of 1996 not only permitted the outsourcing of all aspects of Temporary Assistance to Needy Families (TANF) to third parties, it also included a "Charitable Choice" provision that allowed "federal and state governments to contract with religious nonprofits without infringing on their rights to religious expression." Religious nonprofits began to play a prominent role in delivering "soft skills," such as job training and substance abuse programs, alongside "a whole host of new programs in moral instruction."[68]

"Faith-based welfare" came into its own under the presidency of George W. Bush, who invoked executive powers to establish a White House Office of Faith-Based and Community Initiatives and set up satellite offices in various federal agencies that were explicitly instructed "to facilitate collaborations between faith-based organizations and the federal government." Driven by a combination of fiscal conservatism and a desire "inject moral purpose into social policy" as a way of appealing to conservative Christian donors, the Bush administration engaged in a "massive political effort to reconstruct the social safety net around religious providers and their methods." With these measures, social welfare was remade, not only in the way it was provided but also in its purpose. In Cooper's description, "the ambitious [federal] antipoverty programs envisaged by the Great Society" had been replaced "by a system of domestic humanitarian relief designed to manage rather than eradicate the problems of homelessness and hunger."[69]

Neither the military nor Veterans Affairs were spared these shifts in structure and value. As documented by historian Jennifer Mittelstadt, the 1980s saw the "rise of the military welfare state." With the express aim of reconstructing the US military in the aftermath of the American defeat in Vietnam and key to his conservative revolution, Reagan had his administration invest large sums of money in building support for military personnel and their families. The military expanded entitlement benefits for its personnel at the same time fiscal and ideological support for welfare programs for the poor continued to decline precipitously. The argument was made that the very survival of the volunteer Army depended on improving the provision of social welfare services to soldiers and their families. Or, in Army lingo, the "Army Family" would "Take Care of its Own."[70]

These commitments began to shift with the end of the Cold War in 1989 and the fall of the Soviet Union, which "ushered in an unprecedented era of austerity for the military." Outsourcing military contracts for services falling under the category of "soldier care" was one way to cut costs. President Clinton's welfare reform project authorized private contractors to provide a variety of services previously handled in-house by the military. While in the 1980s, 30 percent of military support services was outsourced to private contractors, by 1999 that number had risen to 45, and as Mittelstadt documents, the biggest contracts for service provision were awarded in "military welfare," including healthcare, social work, and counseling. Echoing the ideology behind the neoliberal "welfare to work" programs, now came the worry that soldiers and their families had grown overly dependent on the military. In the aftermath of the Gulf War of 1991, the military commitment shifted more and more to fostering "self-reliance" instead of "dependence."[71]

Faith-based organizations have also become critical resources for soldiers who have left the military. Referring to the Charitable

Choice provision of 1986 and President Bush's faith-based and community initiatives, Laura Werber and her colleagues report "religious congregations and other FBOs [faith-based organizations] are increasingly recognized as important partners for delivery of health and social services, especially in light of current funding constraints." Faith-based nonprofits play "important roles ... not only in providing social support and addressing members' spiritual needs but also in providing social services to members and local communities." They are "especially well situated to assist veterans," because of the "ubiquity of these organizations in local communities."[72]

On February 27, 2012, the Subcommittee on Health of the Committee on Veterans Affairs held a congressional hearing devoted to building bridges between VA and community organizations to support veterans and families. Given the "impending influx of returning veterans," even the "historic increase in VA spending" will not be enough, avowed Michael H. Michaud, the ranking Democratic member of the committee. If veterans are to be adequately cared for, the federal government will need to "collaborate" with the private and nonprofit sectors. And even though the hearing was framed to address the need for cooperation between the VA and the nonprofit sector in general, three of the four speakers were clergy.[73] There was a discernible focus on the role and value of religious institutions, including mention of the fact that one key element of the partnership between the VA and faith-based organizations is offering training for clergy, so they are can provide appropriate care for veterans.[74]

Faith-based organizations provide specific kinds of help to veterans who come through their doors. Not surprisingly, they focus on spiritual healing, which they assume to be the proper response to moral injury. Spiritual healing, for its part, takes various forms: "pastoral care, spiritual guidance, healing retreats."[75] Whether the idea is to propose an alternative to clinical care or to provide ways to supplement it, this conversation about how to improve the ways in which spiritual wounds are treated often references the values and limitations of adaptive disclosure therapy, with the therapists' use of the empty chair as the object of sustained and nearly unanimous critique. Can confessing to and asking forgiveness from a merely imaginary moral authority be meaningful or effective? Faith-based practitioners tend to reply with an unequivocal no. As Joseph M. Palmer, author of the *Outreach USA Manual*, puts it: Why *imagine* a moral authority figure when there is an obvious one to whom one can appeal? "Only one institution" is equipped to provide both forgiveness and support, as well as the service opportunities crucial to adaptive disclosure therapy, Palmer insists, and that is "a house of worship." If moral injury is a sin, "a transgression against the word of God," as Palmer believes it is, there is a well-established practice for healing, in the form of forgiveness, in the presence and word of God. For his part, interested in integrating clergy into the therapeutic process, Paul Fritts argues, AD therapy *is* pastoral care. "All of the basic ritual elements in the Sacrament of Reconciliation are also present in the AD therapeutic frame," and insofar as they are, the presence of a chaplain at the moment of confession should be an obvious choice.[76]

Regardless of divergences, including those between avowedly Christian or "spiritual" based organizations and practices already discussed, and a decidedly secular one that I turn to shortly, there is a shared conviction that soldiers and veterans will not heal from moral injury in the absence of community, and here the presumed healing powers of ritual, broadly construed, come to the fore. At the heart of the theological reinterpretation and appropriation of the moral injury concept stands the community's obligation to respond to suffering.[77] No style or amount of clinical care can alleviate moral suffering. The only way it can be addressed is through the reintegration of the sufferer into the community of believers and/or, as we shall see, the nation.

## Rituals of Care

Pastoral care, spiritual guidance and retreats, purification rituals—these are among the myriad nonclinical interventions for the care of veterans' spiritual wounds that faith-based organizations and other community groups are developing. By the late aughts, rituals, retreats, and other kinds of nonclinical practices were being suggested and offered with increasing frequency as an alternative to the more individualized therapeutic relationship typical of clinical care.

One workshop leader at a conference on moral injury brought up the importance of ritual and its healing powers by referencing Christian history: "In the first millennium of Christianity … anybody returning from war was expected to enter into a year of penance, a year of being at the edge of the community and engaging in ongoing conversation with a priest … Ritually, this was expected," she said. While more cautious in his historical reading—we don't really know to what extent such rituals took place, he notes—Kinghorn likewise points to the importance of this tradition, seeing the rituals as providing a "formal, liturgical space and time for veterans to reflect upon, lament, and possibly even to mourn their war-making practices without repudiating their necessity or the necessity of the campaigns of which they were a part."[78] One can imagine that such practices were to some extent communal, he writes.

Christian penance, Native American rituals, variations on rituals during the annual Christian and American national calendars (Lent, New Year's Day, Veterans Day, Christmas) or rituals designed for the specific purpose of letting military personnel or veterans "let go"—these are among the practices being promoted by faith-based organizations and thinkers to either replace or supplement a clinical-therapeutic approach.[79] Several participants at a training session on moral injury shared rituals in which they had participated personally, in each case with the goal, as originally described by Judith Herman, of letting go of "frozen grief":

> We take a big pile of rocks and they pick up a rock that is a metaphor for the burdens that they bring and they carry it and leave it, but then we treat the rocks as sacred, and they're washed and cared for and left, and we hold each of those burdens as something that has been carried and let go of. Some of them pick up a couple

little rocks, but some of them pick up big boulders, and some of them can't put them down. They come back out with them.

A second participant shared a ritual hosted by his veterans' service organization:

> We started a monthly ritual with a labyrinth ... Veterans enter the labyrinth and they take ... an honor walk ... They write the name of a battle buddy on a card and they walk it into the center and if they can let go as they're walking, let go of grief and let it go, and honor the veteran that died or someone by placing it, there's like holy water in the center and all that ... What I've been told is that veterans ... as they go into the center ... they experience out of their unconscious life, memories of the veteran or the relationship, good, bad, and ugly, and it comes out and there's a lot of tears and weeping.

Such rituals of grief and healing are not confined to American soil. In *What Have We Done*, journalist David Wood recounts a cleansing ritual staged for members of an Army unit as their tour of duty in Iraq was coming to an end. The chaplain "was afraid that he and his soldiers were contaminated by war trauma; that, unless they began cleansing now, once they got home their moral wounds would suppurate, perhaps for decades, until the pain would finally erupt." He asked participants to jot down a few words about their twelve months in combat: "write down what you want to leave behind." According to Wood, "They wrote fast, words of sorrow and anger, regret, shame, guilt, grief." The chaplain then instructed them to bring the cards forward and place them in a baptismal font—"a dry stone bowl recovered from the weeds where it had been tossed years ago when Iraqis had converted this former British army chapel into a mosque ... The bowl rested on a plywood stand, and one by one the soldiers approached, dropping in one, two, even three cards."[80]

Why *ritual*? What is ritual understood to be or do? For Fritts, "rituals demarcate safe, albeit temporary, space to experiment with new possibilities for living."[81] Take Rita Brock's description of a healing ritual designed for veterans that she recounted during the 2017 moral injury conference at UTS in Manhattan. The ceremony was held in a church, with three to four hundred people in attendance, including veterans and active-duty military personnel. There was a table representing the fallen and the missing. The ritual began with a Muslim call to prayer, followed by a service of lamentation and hope conducted by rabbis and members of the Christian clergy. "This is one thing religions know how to do," Brock explained, which is "process grief. Lamentations are crucial for processing grief. You can't process grief alone." A ritual "is outside of ordinary space and time ... within it there is a narrative arc ... and it gets you back out of grief, doesn't leave you in grief."

At the heart of such (proposed) practices of ritual healing are not only specific Christian theological concepts of sin, transgression, and forgiveness, there is also a commitment to the healing properties of community. And in this sense, the turn to ritual marks a profound querying, if not outright rejection, of a clinical model, which, in Kinghorn's words, treats moral injury as something that occurs "within an individual."[82] Moving from a general reference to "community" to write about an explicitly sacred one, Jensen and Childs quote Mircea Eliade's definition of the sacred, insisting that the "'experience of sacred space makes possible the founding of the world.'"[83] It allows for the construction of a "cosmos" in the face of "chaos." For "wounded warriors," in this estimation,

> sacred space is not a place of our own creation but exists wherever God reveals God's self in the gathering of two or more. American Legion and Veterans of Foreign Wars (VFW) posts, churches and pubs, coffee shops and athletic fields, workplaces and foxholes, high places and low, in the presence of angels or demons, in places sacred and places profane, God finds us where we are as our ally.[84]

Descriptions of the healing power of such rituals are not uncontested, however. A member of the audience at the UTS workshop intervened following Brock's description of the church ceremony recounted above. "I'm very angry right now," he said, straining to calm his voice. "In that ritual, loss of the fallen—on that table—was there recognition of those who were murdered ... so we don't keep helping ourselves feel better but keep doing things to the other side." In other words, he asked, what about the grief for those US soldiers have killed? Not in that ritual, Brock said. "The military doesn't often go that far." And yet, as Fritts himself remarks, "the prerequisite of mutual forgiveness between transgressor and transgressed" is only *in relation*—that is, in relation to the person or community one has harmed.[85] If that is the case, healing from moral injury faces what might be an unresolvable impasse.

Some Vietnam veterans have met with the relatives of victims they wrongly killed to seek forgiveness, Fritts writes, albeit he is not entirely sanguine about the results. And yet, the practice of American veterans of the war in returning to Vietnam to connect with and sometimes engage in service projects with Vietnamese finds few parallels these days.[86] Even if such encounters were to occur, the matter of seeking forgiveness and making amends for a war—more specifically, for an imperial war—is not so simple, nor has it ever been. Elaborating on the problem of absolution, Fritts quotes from the final chapter of Brock and Lettini's *Soul Repair*: "In drawing its emotional power from nostalgia, absolution denies economic, racial, linguistic, and national power differences and the devastations of war that continue in the present—in effect, using greater power to demand that those who have been harmed assuage the guilt of their conquerors."[87] Rather than going down that rabbit hole of differential power relations between the conquerors and those whose land and homes they invade, however, Fritts turns inwards. He proposes that insofar as the church is a "'community whose raison d'être as a community is the mediation and attestation of the universal face,'" it serves as "the best venue for exploiting the healing power of community"; "as mediators of the universal face, the church meets the transgressor in relation thus offering the hope of forgiveness in the reconnection occurring with the mutual recognition of the face."[88]

Failing to imagine what it might mean to seek forgiveness in the absence of any *relation with* those one has harmed, the Self-Other distinction—and the emphasis on community and obligation—is displaced onto a very different field, namely, a binary between Americans who have and who have not "served."[89] We return here to the civil-military divide. "Previously we have emphasized that the concern of the Christian ethic in relation to military life include the moral responsibility the citizenry in general and faith communities in particular have for the support of those who we send to war." A particular and politically crucial slippage occurs here: Moving from the role of military chaplains, nonmilitary clergy and religious service organizations devoted specifically to working with veterans, a theologically inflected therapeutic—a pastoral—relationship emerges as the model for "the citizenry" writ large. There are various ways "such ownership can find expression," Jensen and Childs continue. In discussing Just War Doctrine, they include *jus post bellum*, shifting its general purview in order to focus on an obligation to care for one's own soldiers and veterans.[90] Alongside chaplains and the church, "we need to recognize that our faith communities, which are part of our civilian society, share in the reality of a divide that exists between the military and civilian life. This divide hampers a better level of civilian understanding, concern, and involvement in the needs of those in military service." Chaplains, clergy, and the faith-based organizations that veterans "encounter as they return to society," Jensen and Childs conclude, are "key to bridging the gap between the two worlds."[91]

## War Stories

"I've heard for quite a long time that there is something healing about storytelling. I'm in the mood for a little healing, so I'm going to tell you a story." This was Tyler Boudreau, whom we have encountered before, opening his remarks at the 2015 moral injury conference in Kansas City. He is not alone in framing storytelling as a therapeutic practice; the idea can be found everywhere from community-based groups like the Warrior Writers to the VA's Healing Arts Network and Operation Homecoming, a project sponsored by the National Endowment of the Arts, which has held writing workshops at Walter Reed as "part of a formal medical protocol to help soldiers heal."[92] Projects encouraging soldiers to share their stories reflect a widespread commitment to narrative as its own form of healing trauma. As Judith Herman proposed decades ago, telling the story is a lifeline for the traumatized.[93]

The particular iteration of storytelling to heal trauma that I want to focus on here, however, is a different one. Founded in 2009, Theater of War came out of Brian Doerries's belief that ancient Greek tragedies have something to teach us about suffering and pain today. Noting the importance in Greek tragedy of "suffering," he argues that by "portraying physical pain and emotional anguish, tragedies were designed to elicit powerful emotions." The goal was catharsis—the "purification of dangerous emotions ... of their toxicity."[94] The Greeks performed tragedy as "a means of establishing *sophrosyne* [a healthy, balanced mind] in the Athenian populace, which for whatever reasons—repeated exposure to war, pestilence, or death—had careened off balance." The public performance of Greek tragedies, he ventures, was nothing other than "mass therapy" in public, ritual form.[95]

Although Doerries was born and raised in Newport News, VA, a city "surrounded by bases," he didn't have much contact with or concern for the military growing up. Replicating the grammar of the civil-military divide, Doerries notes that this detachment and indifference continued into adult life: "In an effort to ethically distance myself from the [post-9/11] wars," he writes, he "had largely ignored stories about returning service members and veterans." But that was to change. Upon reading a *Washington Post* story on the dysfunction at the Walter Reed National Military Medical Center, Doerries's "willful ignorance" was finally pierced.[96]

Doerries had already experimented with the healing power of tragedy. Following a staged reading of *Philoctetes* "in the basement of the Culture Project, an Off-Broadway theater in the East Village," a physician expressed interest in using the play "to frame conversations about doctor-patient relations at a teaching hospital at a medical school." The doctor organized a reading for medical students and faculty at the Weill Cornell hospital in New York, and the *New York Times* covered the event, describing *Philoctetes* as "a case right out of a chronic-care ward in a Veterans Administration hospital." A light went off for Doerries: Could he work with military and ex-military personnel? "Philoctetes, after all, wasn't just a chronically ill patient. He was a veteran who had been abandoned by the nation that sent him to war."[97] Thus was born the Theater of War project, which proposes that ancient Greek drama

> was a form of storytelling, communal therapy, and ritual rein-tegration for combat veterans by combat veterans. Sophocles himself was a general ... The audiences for whom these plays were performed were undoubtedly composed of citizen-soldiers. Also, the performers themselves were most likely veterans or cadets. Seen through this lens, ancient Greek drama appears to have been an elaborate ritual aimed at helping combat veterans return to civilian life after deployments during a century that saw 80 years of war.[98]

It took time for Doerries to break into the halls of military power. William Nash finally opened the door, inviting him to present the project at the US Marine Corps Combat Stress Conference in 2008. Following extensive negotiations, Doerries then signed a contract with the Department of Defense to stage one hundred performances over a twelve-month period on military bases in the United States and abroad, representing "an unprecedented partnership with the US military to resurrect an ancient general and bring his healing message to thousands who needed to hear it."[99]

Theater of War launched its first official tour on US military bases on October 16, 2009, and over time its engagement with the post-9/11 wars has expanded to include performances for "mixed military-civilian audiences." Doerries hoped to answer a call issued by Jonathan Shay, "to communalize the experience of war." He set out to create "a vehicle that would help Americans come together to share the burden of the pollution of war."[100] By 2015, Doerries reports, Theater of War had performed before 300,000 people.

Theater of War stages scenes from two of Sophocles' less canonical plays, *Ajax* and *Philoctetes*, chosen by Doerries because he believes they speak most specifically to post-combat experiences in the new millennium—for example, the unprece-dented survival rates for wounded soldiers, who then are faced with years of suffering and pain, and the high rates of soldier suicide.[101] In staging dramatic readings of scenes from these two plays, the project draws on the talents of a long list of established, often famous, actors, who volunteer their time.[102] Each reading is followed by a panel assigned to respond to the play—a com-bination of veterans, spouses of veterans, and mental health care practitioners, who "serve the role of the ancient Greek chorus, intermediaries between the play and the audience."[103] Following the panel's intervention, Doerries poses questions to the audi-ence, engaging in an extended give and take. The performances, according to Doerries, are but "catalysts for the discussions" that follow.[104]

## The Scene of Suffering and Healing

Doerries recalls addressing

> a crowd of war-weary infantry soldiers after a reading of Sophocles's *Ajax* at a US Army installation in southwestern Germany, [where] I posed the following question, one that I have asked tens of thousands of service members and veterans on mili-tary bases all over the world: "Why do you think Sophocles wrote this play?"

After some time, a "junior enlisted soldier" raised his hand: "He wrote it to boost morale?" Doerries asks, "What is morale-boosting about watching a decorated warrior descend into madness and take his own life?" The soldier replied, "it's the truth … and we're all here watching it together."[105]

The Theater of War project is framed by a particular reading of ancient Greek tragedy, which harkens back to Jonathan Shay's reading of the *Iliad*. The "core of the story is betrayal," Doerries explained at a master class on the project held in New York City in 2019. It "radiates out and ultimately Ajax betrays himself because of it." Following the first reading before a military audience in San Diego in 2008, there was a long silence before anyone in the audience stepped up, he recounts in his book. A woman—a nun, as it happened, who worked with the Canadian military—walked up to the microphone and said, "I would like to repeat a line from the play *Ajax* that I have heard countless young men say to me over the decades of serving alongside them in multiple wars: 'Witness how the generals have destroyed me!'" The room exploded. The wife of an assistant commander objected: "How dare you say that! Our husbands made this conference possible. This is about healing, not assigning blame!"[106]

Perhaps surprisingly, the woman's intervention did not put an end to the discussion. One panelist, the wife of a Navy seal, jumped in. "I can definitely relate to that line, too. Over the years, my husband has said things like that to me. He's felt that way on many occasions."[107] More and more Marines approached the microphone, speaking about leadership failures and recounting other ways in which Sophocles' words reflected their own experiences back to them.[108] According to Laurie Sutton, a psychiatrist and former brigadier general in the US Army and currently New York City commissioner for the Department of Veterans' Services, Doerries came along at a moment when the military needed "out-of-the-box solutions to problems of stigma and shame." And out of the box this certainly is. "I'm a psychiatrist," she told the audience at the aforementioned master class, "I've seen a lot of approaches over the years. I've never seen an approach that can take total strangers … and then the magic happens … [the] candor of sharing and vulnerability that happens under those circumstances."

The performances are powerful. Waiting for the reading to

begin, it is hard to imagine the intensity that is about to unfold. The stage is bare but for a table and chairs set up for the actors. The actors sit with scripts in their hands and microphones in front of them, and then they begin. They deliver animated readings: loud and emotional; they weep, they scream. The performance of Tecmessa is often the most difficult to watch. Her pain is almost unbearable. And that is the point. As Sutton sees it, "Sophocles wrote these plays to comfort the afflicted and affect the comfortable."[109]

At one performance I attended at Columbia University, the actors presented two scenes from *Ajax*, the first following upon Ajax's slaughter of the animals and the second was the suicide scene.[110] The audience was transfixed. Doerries had introduced the scenes before the actors began, and when they finished he summarized the rest of the play: the brother who arrives too late to save Ajax asks himself why he failed to be there when Ajax needed him. "To a lot of our veterans, that sounds like survivor's guilt, but I don't think survivor's guilt quite captures what is at stake," said Doerries, without explaining any further. He then recounted the burial scene, raising a question he had found still resonates today: "How do we honor and show respect for people like Ajax who sacrifice everything, including sometimes their mental health, without honoring the violence that sometimes takes over their lives?" Following the panel discussion, Doerries posed a question to the audience: "Given everything you know about the play, written 2,500 years ago by a general, performed for 17,000 soldiers ... what do you think Sophocles was up to when he staged this play? What was he trying to say?" A few students raised their hands: "Sophocles is seeing the experiences of soldiers. He thought they needed to be seen on a larger stage, and to get it out there and put it down for generations." A second student focused on minor characters: "I think it was representing all of the other people affected by war—the little boy who is put up in his father's face, which is covered with blood, and doesn't have a word to say. I wonder what was he thinking." Doerries notes that the little boy grows up to become the king of Ajax's land.

Many of those who intervened—young and old, students and community members—identified themselves as veterans before they spoke. "The thing that hit me most, something that I see in society today, where the general is the one in the back that no one ever sees. The soldier—the grunt—the one that's out there doing it gets nothing. That's something we as vets have been going through forever." Doerries posed a second question: "If Ajax were someone you knew, loved, cared about, swore you would never leave behind ... and you knew that person was on a sand dune with thoughts and demons struggling in the way Ajax was at end of play, and you had a chance to be with that person, what might you say or what would you do?" A veteran's hand shot up: "I would listen. In the play everyone was trying to be direct, and give advice ... sometimes what a person needs is somebody just to listen." Someone else jumped in, "I think we don't give enough recognition to our veterans. There are some veterans out there who don't get as much love as they deserve." Yes, Doerries responded, the "problem Sophocles was dealing with is compounded today since only about one percent serve in military. That creates an opportunity for people to feel not respected or cared for." Another self-identified veteran-student intervened: "We call on soldiers to engage in violence, but then belittle the violence." Visibly struggling to contain his anger, he continued: "Maybe we are all anti-war here; and then [Ajax] goes and kills these animals; [that's] exactly what you expect someone who is put in this situation would do ... You have PTSD, you have a disorder." Rather than pathologizing the soldier, "we should be saying, you are reacting to this situation in a way that ... [anyone might while being put] in these extreme, impossible circumstances."

In an audience that included scholars of the classics, not everyone was so ready to get on board with Doerries's decidedly therapeutic reading of Sophocles' plays. One professor intervened: At the time Sophocles was writing, he was living in "a society and culture defined by nationalism ... I register this play as a critique [of that] and of the fame and glory [attached to war], while neglecting those who suffer." Yes, Doerries answered, one way of reading these plays is a "as a way to treat trauma"; another is as an "articulation of their nationalism." Tecmessa, Ajax's supposed wife, Doerries then noted as almost an aside, was not actually his wife. She was a slave, a foreigner captured in war. Another member of the audience, someone old enough to remember the American war in Vietnam, became agitated and stepped in:

> "A lot of what we've heard is heartfelt but ... I found myself looking for clarity and what came back to me was a memorandum by a Colonel Robert Heimer, in 1971, at the height of Vietnam conflict, where he said, the US Army was no longer able to fight, because it was either in rebellion, on drugs, or other elements that kept it from being a fighting force. Therefore, the US had to withdraw from Vietnam. *They withdrew because the army rebelled*. This is what I call clarity ... To organize in the military against these things is what I call clarity."[111]

Doerries replied: "It's not the job of the veterans to stop the war; they are not in charge of the policy. But there is nothing more powerful for talking about war and condemning war than hearing veterans talk about war and share their story." A self-identified student and Marine veteran quickly contradicted Doerries's point about listening to veterans talk about war as the way to arrive at its most powerful condemnation. There is this stigmatization around the war in Vietnam, he said. But "what we are saying today is [this is] not Vietnam. [These are] totally different circumstances ... What we are fighting for. People forget [those differences]. Pro-war or anti-war, I don't think that is the right way to think about it."

Let me return now to Tyler Boudreau's story that he told because he was "in the mood for a little healing." It "takes place in Iraq in a little place we called Camp Suicide. We called it Camp Suicide because it was a dangerous place to be. Every day we would get these rockets and mortars flying in ... It was just a matter of luck whether you got hit or not." Skimping neither on humor nor dramatic flair, Boudreau related the tale of the mortar attack and the Pop-Tart. While living on forward bases, the meals were all MREs (ready-to-eat), which, "contrary to political propaganda ... do not really taste that good. One out of the 24 meal selections ... has a Pop-Tart ... a highly coveted item." One day, he opens his MRE and much to his delight finds one, a surprise not to be taken lightly. Rather than scarfing it down, he devises a plan to maximize his enjoyment. He finds an isolated place, sits down on a chair, holds up the Pop-Tart, looks at it, is about to open it—when in come the mortars. He shoves the Pop-Tart under his chair, runs off to get his gear (flak jacket, Kevlar helmet), and with five or ten others, lines up "in one direction behind the beam, you know, just in case it happens to land right over there." And then they wait. Finally, the all clear. Boudreau thinks the danger is over, "and I tear off my flak jacket and throw it down and go right back to my chair." The Pop-Tart is gone! The rest of the story is about his fury about the missing Pop-Tart, his search for the guilty party, and finding out, while venting his rage at his commanding officer that he was face-to-face with the perp.

Boudreau paused upon completing the tale. "So now what I want to know is, what about that story is healing? Hm ... I keep hearing people talking about stories and they're saying something like, what makes a story healing is that it allows you to build some meaning around an experience that maybe was feeling meaningless ... And I've also heard that there's something cathartic about the story, get it out, purge it." But something about this "formula" was not adding up: "What we know about stories is that they're all about choices. You choose where to begin the story, where to end the story. You choose which characters to bring forth and which to leave in the background. You choose what actions you're going to show, you choose all of the descriptions, and the decisions, and the ideas, and the conversations."

Revisiting the story of the Pop-Tart, Boudreau asked, "What didn't I include in my little story?" Then he gave an answer: "A 122-millimeter mortar flew over the wall and hit a friend of mine right in the chest and he was engulfed in a white ball of flame. The only thing left of him was this coating of charred [flesh] ... *Do you feel that, do you feel that weight?"* There was something else he did not include in the original narrative, we then learned. "Sitting right there in the middle of the line of us —remember we were all lined up—two of the guys in that line were that very day being investigated for war crimes, two of them ... We've had a short-term detention facility, like a tent, with cages in it. And these guys were guards. And they decided to cut the extension cord, and strip the wires, and start zapping the detainees. They weren't asking them questions, they weren't interrogating them, they weren't trying to find out some valuable thing to save American lives, they were bored. And they get caught."

> So, here I am, the moment, right now, with the rockets and the mortars falling: What is my commitment to those two individuals? In the moment, not now, then? ... They do something that I think is morally despicable, they are war criminals ... what is my commitment to them...? Maybe that's a question I don't really want to deal with. Maybe that's a question I'm not ready to deal with. Maybe I'll just tell you about the Pop-Tart. We'll all laugh.

In that Theater of War narrows the reading of *Ajax* and *Philoctetes* to matters of veterans' suffering, pain, and healing, explaining soldier suffering and suicide with exclusive reference to the "core" theme of "betrayal" (by those higher up the chain of command), the same questions can be asked of it. Who and what is being left out of the narrative? What are the stories, questions, truths, and perspectives that Doerries and so many in his audiences are not ready to face? Who and what is extruded from this theatrical-therapeutic encounter?

After the fall of France to Hitler's Germany in 1940, Simone Weil wrote an essay on the *Iliad*. A decidedly ethical engagement with the ancient play, her work, *The Iliad, or the Poem of Force*, has been read in terms of the way it brings into focus the "sinister psychological changes" that come of the experience of war. But that is not at all Weil's reading. "The true hero, the true subject, the center of the *Iliad* is force ... that turns anybody who is subjected to it into a thing," and for Weil the transformation is as true for the ones possessing and wielding force as it is for its victims.[112] Force rather than betrayal stands at the center of the *Iliad,* for Weill. And in understanding force as its own subject, her reading engages as much with the victims of force (the conquered) as with its (always temporary) possessors (the conquerors, the executioners). Force "crushes" its victims and "intoxicates" its possessors, at least for a time. "These men, wielding power, have no suspicion of the fact that the consequences of their deeds will at length come home to them—they too will bow the neck in their turn." Retribution, Weil insists, is "the soul of the epic." Destiny "by its very blindness ... establishes a kind of justice."[113]

Doerries's Theater of War project builds on Jonathan Shay's reading of the *Iliad*, as mentioned previously, and already in that earlier reading the question of justice and the innocent victims of war have been sidelined. The "conquered," the "vanquished"—more specifically, victims of all sorts of American military violence—seem not to matter. The order of the day is to heal the pain and suffering of the perpetrators of violence and to make the nation whole. There is no opening here for a discussion of the ways in which force, the violence enacted by American troops, turns not just themselves but their victims into objects, as Weil makes clear. During the Theater of War master class, a veteran of the war in Afghanistan shared a story that has become an all-too-common trope about the insensitivity, ignorance, prurience even of "civilians." With more than a little bit of edge in his voice, he recounted a time when a fellow student at college had asked him if he had killed anyone while at war. The sense of outrage was palpable in the room, with most everyone aghast that someone had asked him such an insensitive question.

For my part, I found myself wondering about the student. Who was she? Was she an Iraqi or Afghan? Was she someone who had experienced war as a civilian, perhaps even in one of the many countries that have been targeted by American drone strikes? Is it really so outrageous to ask of military personnel who have returned from war in which so many have died whether he killed any of them? Might that depend on the context? On who is asking and why? Such questions, however, are not easily posed. If, in Weil's reading, an "extraordinary sense of equity breaths through the *Iliad* ... [such that] one is barely aware that the poet is a Greek and not a Trojan," there is absolutely no such equity here.[114] For Theater of War, as in the many other contexts of caring for militarism previously discussed, the tragedy is a categorically American one.

# 6

# The (American) Civilian

Standing in the White House briefing room in October 2017, John Kelly, the White House chief of staff, delivered a defense of his commander-in-chief. Responding to criticism of then-president Donald Trump for his allegedly insensitive comments during a phone call with the wife of a soldier killed in Niger, Kelly's remarks were steeped in references to the so-called civil-military divide, even if he did not name it as such. And his was no simple empirical description:

> Who are these young men and women? They are the best one percent this country produces. Most of you, as Americans, don't know them. Many of you don't know anyone who knows any one of them. But they … volunteer to protect our country when there's nothing in our country anymore that seems to suggest that selfless service to the nation is not only appropriate but required.

At the end of his prepared statement, Kelly announced he would take questions only from "someone who knows," a Gold Star parent or sibling or someone who knew one.[1] He closed the briefing with the following words: "We don't look down upon those of you who haven't served. In fact, in a way we're a little bit sorry because you'll never have experienced the wonderful joy you get in your heart when you do the kinds of things our service men and women do—not for any other reason than they love this country. So just think of that."²

In the shadow of the ongoing wars on terror, public discourse in the US is saturated with references to a civil-military divide. And in engaging the apparent abyss between those citizens who have served in the military and those who have not, a lot of effort— among scholars and journalists, politicians and pundits, and sometimes among military personnel and veterans themselves —is spent explaining who these soldiers are, what they have experienced, and how they are different from the rest of the American population, even if not in ways that stereotypes might suggest. But what about the "civilian"? Who are these Americans who "don't know them"? And what is their obligation toward those who have served?

In *The Image Before the Weapon*, Helen Kinsella develops a genealogical account of "the civilian" in common usage and in the laws of war. While the meaning of "combatant" has been quite stable since the twelfth century, she argues, not so for the civilian. Only in the nineteenth century did the term come to refer to someone "who is not a member of the armed forces." But as Kinsella rightly insists, focusing on *who* a civilian is belies a more fundamental question as to *what* a civilian is and that question cannot be answered by any simple reference to an individual's status as a noncombatant. Kinsella traces how the figure of the civilian emerges—in different times, in different contexts of warfare—out of "threads" that weave together specific discourses about gender, innocence, and civilization.³ As my argument unfolds, I focus on a discourse of innocence.

If at the most basic level, a civilian is she who is not a combatant, that means something quite specific in the context of a state that for well over a century now has waged its wars on foreign soil.⁴ In the American vernacular, and quite specifically, in conversations about the post 9/11 wars and the civil-military divide, the term "civilian" is widely used not with reference to a noncombatant in a war zone, but rather, to describe an American who has never experienced war.[5] What's more, this "civilian" is someone *who can never truly know war.* The advocates of adaptive disclosure therapy, discussed in Chapter 4, called on civilian clinicians to become competent in "military culture" to be able to treat soldiers and veterans suffering the traumas of war. But here, in talk about the civilian, the purported ignorance seems far more absolute. Among US citizens are those—soldiers and veterans (and in a different way, their families)—who know war and those who do not. The divide is stark. An epistemological and moral abyss separates these two kinds of citizens, and all sorts of work about national obligation, responsibility, and civic value and virtue gets done in the space in between. American civilians are innocent. But theirs is an innocence with a twist. Their innocence is suspect, pernicious even. It is a guilty innocence. The innocence of American civilians operates as an accusation: In addition to being ignorant about what war is really like, civilians are naive about the evils that exist in the world. Civilian innocence signals a privilege that those sent off to wars on their behalf do not have.

As this chapter unfolds, I explore this figure of the (American) civilian in the time of the War on Terror—who she is, what roles she is supposed to perform—through a reading of three intersecting phenomena that were most prominent in the early to mid-2010s: a public discourse about soldier trauma, the gesture of thanking soldiers for their service, and a repeatedly iterated call to the American public to care for soldiers and help them heal. I illustrate an economy of suspicion that haunts the civilian-citizen, she who is tarnished by a moral and epistemological lack, she who is obliged to support those other citizens who have gone off to war and sacrificed in her name. This civilian-as-suspect-citizen is a constitutive element of what Andrew Bacevich has called "the new American militarism," as I argue by tracing the discursive practices and demands through which the suffering soldier appears as the sole *acknowledged* subject of concern and action in the public domain.[6] Drawing on Hannah Arendt's writings on representative thinking, judgment, politics, and collective responsibility, I explicate and question an American political common sense in which "we" *must* "support the troops." And I do so by exploring the forms of attention and care that support is supposed to take, as well as the grounds—epistemological, moral, and political—on which the demand is made.

As elaborated in the previous chapter, caring for soldiers is a constitutive labor of American militarism in the post-9/11 era. While the people involved in faith-based organizations and other nonprofits work directly with soldiers and veterans, here I examine a call to the public at large. About a decade into the wars, a public discourse about soldiers and veterans began asserting an obligation on the part of civilians to acknowledge soldiers' suffering while refraining from judgment in regard to the American wars that are responsible for it. While presented as a politically neutral act and an unequivocal ethical good, caring for traumatized (and injured) soldiers—in this instance, more an ideological stance and rhetorical gesture than a practical matter—captures the American civilian, liberal and conservative, pro- and (presumably) anti-war in its distinctly imperial gaze. From this angle, the post-9/11 wars appear only in and through the costs accrued to American troops. The American soldier, although always the hero of war, appears also as its victim. No one else rises to the level of significant ethical or political concern.

## War Trauma

"Five months after carrying Sergeant Emory down the stairs in Kamaliyah," he could no longer shake off all the hurt and harm of war. On his third deployment in Iraq, Adam Schumann was done.

> His war had become unbearable. He was seeing over and over again his first kill disappearing into a mud puddle, looking at him as he sank. He was seeing a house that had just been obliterated

by gunfire, a gate slowly opening, and a wide-eyed little girl about the age of his daughter peering out. He was seeing another gate, another child, and this time a dead-aim soldier firing. He was seeing another soldier, also firing, who afterward vomited as he described watching head spray after head spray through his magnifying scope. He was seeing himself watching the vomiting soldier while casually eating a chicken-and-salsa MRE.

He was still tasting the MRE.

He was still tasting Sergeant Emory's blood.[7]

Schumann, diagnosed with depression and PTSD, and thinking about suicide, was sent home.

David Finkel, an American journalist who embedded with the 2-16 Infantry Battalion of the US Army during the "surge" in Iraq, beginning in the spring of 2007, tells Schumann's story in *The Good Soldiers*. This Pulitzer Prize-winning account of war reads like a diary of specific days and moments—the excitement and patriotism, the gore (of IEDS, of dead bodies, of killing), the anger and the hatred, counterinsurgency tasks like handing out soccer balls, and the psychological pain of the (mostly) very young soldiers who carry it out. In Finkel's telling, Schumann is not exceptional, in that the military's own studies "suggested that 20 percent of soldiers deployed to Iraq experienced symptoms of PTSD." He also reports that "in the culture of the army, where mental illness has long been equated with weakness," such diagnoses were not easily recognized or accepted. There remained "a lingering suspicion of any diagnosis for which there wasn't visible evidence."[8] And yet injuries for which there is no visible evidence are ubiquitous among troops and veterans of these wars—as recounted by journalists and scholars, as represented on TV shows and in movies, as described in novels and poetry written by veterans who have returned from war. And in a discourse that passes over the military's primary concern with force protection in favor of talk of a national moral obligation, those so-called invisible injuries are examined and explained to the public at large—so they can be understood and healed, so that proper attention to "the war" is paid on the home front.

David Wood, another American journalist (and author of the book *What Have We Done*, discussed in Chapter 5), embedded with a Marine unit in Afghanistan and some years later, in March 2014, published a lengthy essay on moral injury in the *Huffington Post*.[9] He opens with the following questions: "How do we begin to accept that Nick Rudolph, a thoughtful, sandy-haired Californian, was sent to war as a 22-year-old Marine and in a desperate gun battle outside Marjah, Afghanistan, found himself killing an Afghan boy? That when Nick came home, strangers thanked him for his service and politicians lauded him as a hero?"[10] Wood continues,

> Can we imagine ourselves back on that awful day in the summer of 2010, in the hot firefight that went on for nine hours? Men frenzied with exhaustion and reckless exuberance, eyes and throats burning from dust and smoke, in a battle that erupted after Taliban insurgents castrated a young boy in the village, knowing his family would summon nearby Marines for help and the Marines would come, walking right into a deadly ambush.

In case we cannot imagine it, Wood does so for us: "Nick ... spots somebody darting around the corner of an adobe wall, firing assault rifles at him and his Marines. Nick raises his M-4 carbine. He sees the shooter is a child, maybe 13. With only a split second to decide, he squeezes the trigger and ends the boy's life." As for Nick, he struggles with the dilemma: "He was just a kid. But ... I'm trying not to get shot and I don't want any of my brothers getting hurt ... You know it's wrong. But ... you don't have a choice." This, as Wood informs his readers, is the essence of war trauma as it frequently appears among soldiers who have fought these latest American wars.

In choosing this particular event to open a series of essays on moral injury, Wood ascribes a young American Marine's trauma to a decision made during a battle reportedly instigated by a barbaric act. Stories of barbaric acts, culturally incommensurable values, and an enemy who does not respect the laws of war characterize many accounts of the wars on terror and the kinds of war trauma, including moral injury, that come in tow.[11] The way Wood understood the situation in Afghanistan, "some ugly aspects of the local culture and the brutality of the Taliban rubbed American sensibilities raw, setting the stage for deeper moral injury."[12] He quotes Rudolph as an example:

> You see the Afghan tradition of basically boys dance for grown men and they give them money and the guy who gives the most money gets to take the boy home. We are partnering with guys who are basically screwing the neighbors' kids, 6- and 7-year-olds, and we are supposed to grin and bear it because our cultures don't mesh? ... When I really want to fuckin' strangle those dudes?"[13]

Other kinds of stories about moral injury are also told, some more critical politically, such as the one recounted by an Army veteran at a conference on moral injury discussed in the previous chapter. He recalled being shaken to the core by his own cruelty toward an Iraqi child. An adult came over to protect the child, and the speaker did not recognize himself in the man's terrified eyes.[14] Moral injuries can result as well from seemingly banal acts of carrying out an occupation—kicking in doors, scaring the family, and frequently enough finding no insurgents at home.[15] Soldiers tell of mistaking noncombatants for insurgents in the heat of battle or having no opportunity to discriminate, at a checkpoint, for example, with a car speeding at them that fails to stop.[16] For the most part, these narratives are framed by a set of shared assumptions about the inevitable moral ambiguities of counterinsurgency wars. Occasionally they are offered—almost exclusively by veterans—as a political critique of America's wars, which they now oppose.

War stories told about combat trauma by journalists and scholars who were "embedded" with American soldiers in the war zone or spent time with veterans back home[17] are generally narrated from the soldiers' point of view.[18] Readers are typically admonished to recognize their obligation to face the *realities* of war, to confront rather than evade the question of what "we" have sent "them" to do, while, at the same time typically sanitizing the extent and brutality of American military aggression. Wood describes the "scowling young killers of Uganda and Congo" he encountered previously as a war correspondent; a few pages later, he writes of American troops carrying "immense responsibility"; handling it "well and with passion." "At war, I have seen Americans at their best. In a very personal way, I admire and honor their service."[19] One has to wonder what he has seen and heard in the midst of battle and in its aftermath that he leaves out of his story. A parallel question might be asked of recent anthropological accounts of the war, narrated from the soldiers' points of view, in which case ethnography as method operates to some extent as the functional equivalent of embedded journalism. What might the soldiers with whom various anthropologists have "embedded" stateside chosen not to share?

In "The Life and Lonely Death of Noah Pierce," Ashley Gilbertson takes a different tack in her account of the kinds of actions, sensibilities, and affects that drive combat, as well as its horrors and traumatic afterlives. Noah Pierce was an Army veteran who committed suicide in 2007 and whose war experience Gilbertson reconstructs based on his diary and letters home he wrote from Iraq. She wants to know what pushed Pierce to suicide. "It could have been the memory of the Iraqi child he crushed under his Bradley. 'It must have been a dog,' he told his commanders. It could have been the unarmed man he shot point-blank in the forehead during a house-to-house raid, or the friend he tried madly to gather into a plastic bag after he had been blown to bits by a roadside bomb, or … it could have been the doctor he killed at a checkpoint." The "moral ambiguity of house-to-house raids" haunted Pierce.[20] He wrote about how he and others in his platoon would "blow off steam" by "abusing prisoners." "I'm so pissed off right now," he wrote to his parents, relating how "beatin' a sandnigger unconscious would help but we will get in serious trouble if it happens again." He stole money from Iraqi civilians and sent it back to his parents. "Well staying here as part of the postwar occupation has had one good impact on me," he wrote in another letter.

I no longer regret what I did during the war. I have so much hatred in me I could go murder more sandniggers and I would just smile. That goes for almost everyone here. We had sympathy for them after the war but now we have absolutely nothing but hatred for them. We should have killed more during the war. I let all kinds of "'innocent" people go when I should have just mowed them down.[21]

Or as he recounted in his diary,

So far, this has been the worst month of my life. With all this work I have been ready to snap. I don't know how much I can take. A car pissed me off last night. The fucker kept flashing me and when he pulled off the road I almost ran him over. I changed my mind though, I could have gotten away with killing that mother-fucker though. My transmission was going out and I could have blamed it on that. I am just waiting for a good opportunity though. I am just waiting for the chance where I know people will die. I am not going to swerve at them, but I am not going to avoid it like I have been. The only reason I have avoided it so far is there have been women and children in the cars coming at me.

"I am a bad person," he bemoans.[22]

## The Obligation to Listen

In the preface to a well-reviewed book on moral injury, a retired general asks, "What does the nation owe its citizens-who-become-soldiers?"[23] That question organizes the discourse about soldier trauma as it appears in the combat-trauma imaginary I have been tracing, often tethered to the alleged fact of a growing civil-military divide. Less than 1 percent of the total US population serves in the US military, as discussed in detail in the introduction, and that number captures but one element of the isolation of military personnel from the country at large. Almost 50 percent of those serving in the military live in only five states, and an increasing number are coming from families with deep, often multigenerational ties to the military.

Talk of the civil-military divide indexes more than straightforward statistical facts, as Kelly's performance at the White House press conference makes clear. It iterates a political judgment, in which a virtue attaches to military personnel and a critique to citizens who have not served. As Phil Klay, a novelist and veteran of the war in Iraq, recounted in the *New Yorker* after the fall of Afghanistan to the Taliban in August 2021,

> a buddy of mine ... recently admitted to having an instinctive recoil against men our age who didn't serve in the military. "It's unfair, but I feel that," he said. "Who excused you, you know? ... Why did you think you had a choice? I know it's a volunteer army but, the volunteer army is a trick question, you know? You're supposed to say yes if you have any honor."

Klay continues, "More of us veterans feel that than we publicly admit."[24] Moreover, talk of the civil-military divide stages a call to citizens who have not gone to war to step up to the plate and support those who have. As philosophy professor Nancy Sherman put it at a multidisciplinary conference on trauma, "Even in a city like ours, those who wear uniforms are exotic, on campuses like mine, exotic. So, my work is in a sense helping us to come out of the bunker on both sides. I don't think you can only talk to your fellow buddies over a beer if you're coming home from war."[25]

What is involved in coming out of these respective bunkers? More specifically, in such rhetoric about war, troops, civilians, and combat trauma, what kinds of practices, obligations, and responsibilities are being called for? Let me return to David Wood's *Huffington Post* essays. In defining moral injury as "the signature wound" of the post-9/11 wars, he does more than simply elaborate its contours as the form of combat trauma typical of counterinsurgency wars. A second theme structuring his narrative is the existence of an epistemological and moral chasm separating civilians from soldiers. And, indeed, his account of moral injury is presented as an attempt to help bridge that divide. Echoing some of the distinctive features of military culture described by advocates of adaptive disclosure therapy (see Chapter 4), Wood notes a special kind of closeness and love that exists among members of a combat unit. Given such intimacy, he insists, the "traumatic loss of someone you love [a fellow soldier] is not fully understandable by a civilian." Wood quotes Amy Amidon, a psychologist who works with active-duty Marines, saying that "civilians are lucky that they still have a sense of naïveté about what the world is like … The average American means well, but what they need to know is that these [military] men and women are seeing incredible evil, and coming home with that weighing on them and not knowing how to fit back into society." He tells of one veteran's experience of civilians: "People say, 'Thanks for your service.' Do you know what I did over there? It just seems like you're being patronized. Don't do that to me."[26] Or, as Timothy Kudo recounts in his essay "On War and Redemption": "When I returned from Afghanistan this past spring, a civilian friend asked, "Is it good to be back?" It was the first time someone had asked, and I answered honestly. But I won't do that again. We weren't ready for that conversation."[27]

"Thank you for your service." Critiques of this prevalent gesture occupy a lot of space in the literature on war, soldiers, civilians, and homecoming. While no doubt received and interpreted in various ways by (ex-)military personnel, *as a trope* the act stands for the fraught relationship between soldiers and civilians in the same way that the image of civilians spitting on Vietnam veterans or calling them "baby killers" does for that earlier war, a parallel that makes quite clear that the notion of a civilian public detached from "its" military is not as new as this post-9/11 discourse suggests. Thanking soldiers and veterans for their war service is treated as a sign of support, a signal that the American public has learned the lessons of Vietnam. As argued by Elizabeth Samet, a professor of English at the US Military Academy:

Whether anyone ever spat on an American soldier returning from Vietnam remains a matter of debate ... Apocryphal or not, this image has become emblematic of an era's shame and of the nation's failure to respond appropriately to the people it had sent to fight a bankrupt war. The specter of this guilt—this perdurable archetype of the hostile homecoming—animates today's encounters ... "Thank you for your Service" has become a mantra of atonement.[28]

Nevertheless, according to many commentators on the practice, this supposed gesture of public gratitude tends not to be all that well received by (ex-)military personnel. It has become a "mechanical ritual," Samet writes. "After the engagement, both parties retreat to separate camps, without a significant exchange of ideas or perspectives having passed between them."[29] Or, as *New York Times* reporter Matt Richtel puts it, the "thank you for your service phenomenon," more often than not "comes across as shallow, disconnected, a reflexive offering from people who, while meaning well, have no clue what soldiers did over there or what motivated them to go, and who would never have gone themselves nor sent their own sons and daughters."[30] Being thanked "can feel self-serving for the thankers, suggesting that he did it for them, and that they somehow understand the sacrifice, night terrors, feelings of loss and bewilderment. Or don't think about it at all."[31] David Finkel's book, *Thank You for Your Service,* now a major motion picture, is an intimate account of the lives of veterans who have returned from fighting in Iraq, and it is largely a portrait of broken lives, and psychological and physical pain that stands in glaring contrast to the book's title. Finkel's fundamental question appears concisely on the back of the book: "When we ask young men and women to go to war, what are we asking of them? And when they return, what are we thanking them for?"

In *Afterwar*, Nancy Sherman proposes an alternative frame for thinking about the gesture—the "ritual," as she calls it—of thanking soldiers for their service. "[One] element in the moral background that is never far from us is the legacy of Vietnam.

'Thank you for your service' is a national reaction to a past negative reaction." But, Sherman asks, "How can gratitude be substantive when its expression is so trivialized in a pat, easy-to-say 'Thank you'?"[32] In contrast to many other commentators, she nevertheless refuses to dismiss the gesture out of hand and instead considers what a civilian is doing when she thanks someone for their service. The ritual is "a public enactment and recommendation of a norm," Sherman insists. "Our gratitude shows others how to respond" and "in showing gratitude, we ourselves come to feel gratitude." Thanking soldiers for their service is a practice of ethical self-fashioning—in other words, the cultivation of a morally appropriate disposition on the part of the public in the face of those who "have served." In this spirit, Sherman describes her book as a call to (civilian) readers to engage with those who went off to war. It is "a manifesto for how to engage in moral repair, one on one, with individual service members and veterans so that we can begin to build a new kind of integrated community."[33] Sherman elaborates:

> This book is about homecoming from the wars in Iraq and Afghanistan and the struggle to find inner peace afterward. It is an intimate look at a handful of the 2.6 million women and men who have served in these longest wars in American history, and what it feels like to return to a country that hasn't really felt war. There has been no war tax and little economic pain.[34]

"We've been at war while the country has been at the mall," Sherman reports having been told by soldiers. That is a well-rehearsed trope—and accusation;[35] in Sherman's reading, the civil-military divide has consequences, "for all of us, on a personal level. For many of us don't know how to begin a conversation with a veteran, how to ask where she's been and what she's been through, and how things are for her now. Each side feels the distance." Sherman is not yet ready to argue for "national service," but she is prepared to insist on "the moral necessity for each of us to be personally engaged in the largest reintegration of American service members into civilian society since Vietnam. The mil/civ walls have to come down. It is critical for the moral healing of soldiers."[36]

Sherman develops her argument by asking her readers to understand widespread "resentment" among (ex-)military personnel, a call to step up to their civic responsibilities. Rather than recoil from encounters with soldier and veteran resentment, the American public should understand it and fashion a productive response. Sherman insists that she is not talking about *ressentiment* in the sense of the Nietzschean critique. Instead, she understands resentment as "holding another to account, of demanding respect, of calling out another for due attention and recognition as part of a shared moral community. It is a way of saying another is responsible *to you*." Implicit is the "complaint that civilian fellow citizens ... fail to assume an adequate degree of moral responsibility for the wars that they (indirectly or directly) help wage, and for the afterwar—the arduous veteran recovery that follows in the wake of going to war."[37]

I want to unpack Sherman's account of resentment, civilians, responsibility, and moral healing, which is but one iteration of a much broader discourse. She demands that the American public recognize a national collective responsibility for (some of) the afterlives of the ongoing American wars. But what does a "one-on-one" obligation to help soldiers heal not only entail but also preclude?

## Civilian Responsibility and Therapeutic Citizenship

In *What Have We Done: The Moral Injury of Our Longest Wars*, David Wood tells a cautionary tale about clinical treatments for moral injury. He quotes one of the most prominent clinical researchers on moral injury as having told him, "You have these treatments that are really not hugely better than nothing at all." For Wood that "confirmed a conviction that had been growing since I began studying moral injury," that "true healing of veterans with war-related moral injuries will only come from community … peers, neighborhoods, faith congregations, service organizations, individuals. That means it's up to us."[38]

Whether moral injury is best treated by clinicians, or even framed in medical-psychiatric terms, is far from a settled question, as I illustrated in the previous chapter. As the concept circulates beyond clinical practice, some see possibilities for rebuilding community or repairing a divided nation by getting the public to engage with and take responsibility for American soldiers returning from war. For others—for example, Tyler Boudreau, the ex-Marine quoted previously, who returned from Iraq and became a critic of US global military power—the concept opens a space for political engagement:

> PTSD as a diagnosis has a tendency to depoliticize a veteran's disquietude and turn it into a medical issue. What's most useful about the term "Moral Injury" is that it takes the problem out of the hands of the mental health profession and the military and attempts to place it where it belongs—in society, in the community, and in the family—precisely where moral questions should be posed and wrangled with. It transforms "patients" back into citizens, and "diagnoses" into dialogue.[39]

There is nothing inherent in the concept of either PTSD or moral injury that precludes *a priori* the possibility of radical political critique. Nevertheless, Boudreau's is a rare voice in this public conversation.

Wood's account of war trauma among veterans of the post-9/11 wars is far more typical. After arguing that healing takes place in the context of community, Wood instructs his readers on how to get involved. "*Let's set aside the question of war itself,*" he begins. "Like many others, I have considered the idea that killing and destruction are something we should never under any circumstances impose on others. Nor should we send our youngest generations into wars in which we ourselves are too squeamish, or too wise, to engage." He sketches his long and fraught relationship with war, an initial condemnation rooted in his "life as a Quaker," and then years as a war correspondent during which he "found war captivating ... in war I have seen individual acts of breathtaking generosity and quiet nobility. But from a larger perspective, it's clear that good rarely comes from war. The human misery and the wreckage are hard to over-state." Amid war's "criminal waste," however, he has "found harmony with those who have fought in combat, for they have the keenest appreciation of the ugly depravity of mass state-justified bloodletting."[40]

Criminal waste, depravity, misery, wreckage: in whatever terms the "horrors" of these wars are described, there seems to be (near) unanimity on the particular "lesson" of the American war in Vietnam. "We have learned that we are supposed to sep-arate the war from the warrior," writes Sherman, "we have a sacred obligation to those who serve, whether or not we agree with the cause of those wars and whether or not those who serve agree with them."[41] And that sacred obligation is to be enacted through people's willingness to listen. Bill Edmonds, an American advisor and trainer at an interrogation center in Iraq where prisoners were tortured, concurs. He asks, can "warfight-ers who are unable to reconcile what they've seen or done with the person they once were, ever fully come home? That is, can wounds to moral identity ever truly heal?" They can, although "the obstacles are daunting":

> It's possible to change course, and the most important first step is for warfighters to accept their hidden injuries and to take charge of their own healing. This is where communities can help, and their role is so very simple and requires such minimal effort: listen. Attend to the stories of those whose injuries are less *visibly* apparent, in whatever forms those experiences are communicated. Provide for them, in any way you can, a safe, nonjudgmental, and compassionate space in which to share their experiences, and an environment where they can, possibly, [engage in] self-forgiveness.[42]

For his part, Wood recommends a program developed by a clinical psychologist at Harvard: "her idea was to match veterans with volunteer civilian listeners for a long session of uninterrupted, intentional listening." Intentional listening is "listening with validation." It is "listening without judgment; saying,'*Yeah, that was fucked up*. But also ... *I honor your service.*'"[43]

Listening without judgment. What are the political effects of enacting a one-on-one obligation to listen to soldiers and veterans not only regardless of one's own position on the wars but also, as Sherman requires, *regardless of theirs*? And what can it possibly mean to take collective responsibility for (a) war and yet simultaneously "set aside the question of war itself"? In a therapeutic context, listening without judgment is regarded as fundamental, and it assumes a particular form in clinical protocols designed to treat moral injury.[44] Listening without judgment is also the foundation of pastoral care.[45] But what does the demand to listen without judgment—in contrast, say, to Tyler Boudreau's call for "dialogue"—entail, signal, and do when extended to the demands of (nonmilitary) citizenship? I want to begin by considering the problem of epistemology it signals, one that returns us to the question of civilian innocence.

A tension is to be found at the heart of this call on the American public to *just listen*. At the same time that "civilian"-citizens—generally interpellated in this discourse as a "we"—are being called upon to listen, the prevailing conviction among psychiatrists and psychologists, among journalists and philosophers, and among many a soldier and veteran is that civilians will never *really be able to hear* what someone who has been in combat has to say, at least not if hearing implies the possibility of coming to know, let alone understand. "The difference between what the ... soldiers know about the world and what most American civilians know about the world is often at the center of their encounters with each other," notes anthropologist Zoë Wool. She is "reminded of many soldiers' insistence that there was no point in talking to psychiatrists who hadn't been in combat."[46] Or, to return to Amy Amidon's formulation, civilians have the privilege of not knowing and not having to confront the evil that exists in the world.

Such sentiments echo through the writings of Wood and Sherman, through accounts by veterans and the psychiatrists who work with them, as well as a growing canon of war literature emerging out of these still ongoing wars. Only the soldier knows war, and that truth—his truth—as Roy Scranton would have it, makes him a "trauma hero."[47] To be clear, however, not just any soldier stands in as the figure of the trauma hero. While most military personnel never see combat, in this entire discourse of virtue and suffering that detail is overlooked. The soldier-as-subject is imagined as the infantry "grunt," someone who has experienced ground-level combat, and that (frequent) misrecognition facilitates the stark epistemological and moral divide between the soldier and the civilian—he who has sacrificed, suffered, and *knows*; she who does not. An entire epistemological politics about war, knowing, and truth lives in and through that distinction.

### You Who Was Not There

As recounted by historian Yuval Noah Harari, "The quintessential late-modern western war story ... describes the experience of war as an experience of learning the truth about oneself and about the world." War was not always represented as a revelatory experience. Rather, a "master narrative" of war as experiential revelation emerges during what Harari views as the "long" Romantic period, 1740 to 1865. In contrast to the "tame experiences of peace" and to life as a civilian, "war experiences reveal the truth precisely by blowing apart all prior cultural constructions."[48]

The epistemological authority of war rests, according to Hariri, on a particular kind of witnessing. "Eye-witnessing ... is factual and can be ... easily conveyed to other people," he argues. But being at war involves "flesh-witnessing," and that emerges as a "potent new source of authority."[49] A flesh-witness can never really transmit her knowledge to other people. And if war is impossible to understand for those who were never there, so, too, is it impossible for them to judge: only she who has "flesh-witnessed" war's extremities and horrors can "speak about *and judge* what she witnessed."[50]

During one workshop on PTSD and moral injury led by a VA psychologist in 2015, one participant told the rest of us, "if a combat veteran is gracious enough to share his or her story with you, be very careful to respond in a nonjudgmental way. You weren't there." At nineteen years old, he told us, his son deployed to Afghanistan, at a time when "it was the Wild West." They lost thirty of the one hundred members of their platoon. One day, the son recounted to his father, his unit was taking mortar fire; they were ordered to "put steel into that village until they quit shooting at us." They flattened the village and then went in. "There's not a living thing in it, there's not Taliban, there's not man, woman, child, goat, nothing." What should he say to his son, this father wondered? "You're a terrible human being! You killed a bunch of civilians! How could you do that?" The workshop leader responded to this father's obvious and profound pain: "Yeah, that's a good question." Judgment is "absolutely not the way to go, because if people grace you with telling you bad things that happened to them, it's very easy to think, oh I would've behaved differently, or how could you have done that, and that is incredibly disrespectful and absolutely not therapeutic for the person." At the same time, the psychologist cautioned, "easy answers"—you were just following orders, you did what you had to do—are "not a very good response either." Another participant spoke up: "Can I say something? ... I haven't been in that situation, but I think that the only thing that I would want to hear is, I cannot *imagine* what that would be like. Because it's the fucking truth."[51]

Joan Scott has written critically about historiography that attempts to "enlarge" the picture by "rest[ing] its claim to legitimacy on the authority of experience, the direct experience of others." She argues that given orthodox history's commitment to a referential understanding of evidence, "when the evidence offered is the evidence of 'experience,' the claim for referentiality is further buttressed—what could be truer ... than a subject's own account of what he or she has lived through." But, Scott cautions,

> When experience is taken as the origin of knowledge, the vision of the individual subject (the person who had the experience or the historian who recounts it) becomes the bedrock of evidence on which explanation is built. Questions about the constructed nature of experience, about how subjects are constituted as different in the first place—about language (and discourse) and history—are left aside.

As a consequence, "the evidence of experience ... reproduces rather than contests a given ideological system."[52]

A parallel invocation of the truth of experience characterizes calls upon the American public to just listen to those "who have served." But in contrast to historians who believed in their capacity to understand and re-present experience as history, the evidence of experience operates here to reinforce the dividing line. "You who never was there," to borrow Walter Benn Michaels's turn of phrase, can never know.[53] The belief that only the soldier knows war is not new, as mentioned above,[54] but, I suspect it carries far more moral and political weight in a society with no draft, one that is so often argued to be cleaved in two by a civil-military divide. Moreover, in a moment of trauma's empire,[55] this epistemology is harnessed to a form of citizenship modeled on the therapist's couch. Civilian-citizens are called upon to attend to the "individual suffering" of returning troops, to listen to their moral and psychological pain, all the while refraining from judgment (Was he involved in war crimes? Was the war just?) because they cannot know.

Listening, attending to the needs of the suffering soldier, appears here not merely as a way to recuperate and recognize his humanity, as it might in the work of humanitarian psychiatry.[56] The suffering soldier is no simple *victim*, an object of care in whose name humanitarian workers and advocates act and speak.[57] The soldier, the only one who knows, is also the only one *entitled to speak*. He is the virtuous *subject*, the "super-citizen, the true patriot" to whom a national debt is owed.[58] Humanitarian reason not only reproduces the virtue and value of the soldier-as-ideal citizen; it is harnessed to the work of restoring a coherent national body politic.

## On Politics as Judgment

What kinds of stories must the American public be willing to listen to? More precisely, what are so-called civilians being encouraged not to judge? And what kinds of words or speech acts might be taken as signaling judgment? David Wood quotes a veteran reporting the following encounter: "Even though you're home you don't feel at home. When you try to talk to someone, they don't understand, they start making their own assumptions about, like, 'Well, I don't think we should have been fighting that war in the first place.' Really?"[59] The veteran's incredulity, as re-presented by Wood, marks the statement that the US should never have gone into Iraq in the first place as an inappropriate speech act, a failure to credit and defer to the soldier's first-person report of his experience. But there is another possible reading here: What if the individual was expressing sympathy for a former Marine's suffering by recognizing that it was caused by a war that should never have been started in the first place?

The American public is to support the troops regardless of its— or *their*—political position on the wars. Is it also enjoined from expressing any political judgment on the wars themselves—that the wars were sustained more by a politics of militarism and its attendant profitability than by security needs, even if the attacks on 9/11 were the grounds on which they were launched,[60] that the Iraq war was started on an outright lie—even if that judgment is not directed at the soldier per se? And what, precisely, in the things that soldiers and veterans have done, or have desired to do, or enjoyed doing should their fellow citizens not judge? Killing a thirteen-year-old child holding a gun, which Nick Rudolph had "no choice" but to do? Kicking in doors and raiding homes as part of the everyday work of carrying out an occupation? The torture at Abu Ghraib? Does it also include not judging the pleasure some soldiers take in the work of war and the act of killing? "War is a gift from God," one of Wood's interviewees, Jim Gant, declared. "The opportunity to prove yourself on the battlefield. In Iraq we were killing people every day. There's a lot of satisfaction in the hunt, getting a target, going after a specific person, which I did many, many times, and like I said, I enjoyed it a lot." Some people, this former officer in the Army's special forces explained, will not fire their weapons, although most people in combat will fire when they feel threatened. "It takes a completely different person to hunt another human being down and shoot him in the face," says Gant. "For me, it was a lot of enjoyment and satisfaction."[61] And now, he tells Wood, he suffers moral injury.[62]

Many decades ago, Hannah Arendt faced an onslaught of criticism for her coverage of Adolf Eichmann's trial in Jerusalem. One criticism spoke to Arendt's willingness to hold Eichmann to account: "There was a whole chorus of voices that assured me that 'there sits an Eichmann in every one of us' ... The only true culprits, it frequently was felt and even said, were people like ... myself who dared to sit in judgement; for no one can judge who had not been in the same circumstances under which, presumably, one would have behaved like all others."[63] Under the repressive and terrifying conditions produced by the Nazi regime, can anyone be sure that they would have acted differently? Are any of us sure that we, in contrast to Eichmann, would not have "followed orders?" That same logic structures the demand for the American public to refrain from judging US soldiers and veterans and it divides citizens into two national kinds: those who "serve," and those who do not; those who may speak and those who must listen (at least, when face to face with a soldier or veteran); those who really know, and those who cannot know and therefore must not judge. If politics presupposes an obligation to think from someone else's point of view, as Hannah Arendt has insisted, to have the "willingness to imagine how the world looks to people whose standpoints one does not necessarily share," in the injunction to listen to soldiers, that obligation is borne by "civilians" alone.[64] *Pace* Boudreau's call for *dialogue,* this civil-military encounter is not imagined as an actual conversation. Soldiers/veterans have the right to talk; everyone else has the obligation to listen.

"Civilians" must not judge. The demand is rooted in an epistemological politics that insists that only soldiers know war—only soldiers have been in situations in which they have had to make choices unfathomable to those who have never been there. It is, however, also grounded in a particular rendering of the American civilian and of her responsibility for the wars. Rita Brock reminded her audience at the workshop on moral injury at the Union Theological Seminary discussed in the previous chapter of just that responsibility: This is a "civilian-controlled military, after all." But just as the military cannot be lumped into one generic category regardless of rank and leadership, something that Brock reminded her audience in reference to the torture of prisoners at Abu Ghraib,[65] neither are "civilians" a homogenous category. *Which* civilians—what kinds of civilians—control the military? How is civilian responsibility differentially distributed across the population at large? At one point in his book, Wood breaks down the generic category of "the civilian" and asks, "What is the accountability for those who engineered the wars? Of the politicians who pushed for and funded the fighting year after year? Of those of us who silently accepted the rationales for those in power, and paid our taxes?" He continues: "Instead of just war, these conflicts became war justified by war. And we let it happen. Not only was there no serious antiwar movement, there was precious little questioning of the moral justifications of the wars at all." Even though by 2006, the Iraq War was regarded as "a mistake" by a majority of the American public, "voters kept returning to office politicians who were determined to press ahead with the wars."[66]

Wood is correct. In the era of nationalist hype that followed the attacks on September 11, 2001, there was no significant antiwar movement. Those who raised questions about the US foreign policy that preceded and informed the attacks, or who criticized the drumbeat of war coming out of Washington, were subjected to immense public criticism and scorn. In 2008, Barack Obama ran on a pledge to withdraw from Iraq, if not from Afghanistan, and ultimately succeeded at neither. Nevertheless, to echo a question Roy Scranton asks of Sherman's book *Afterwar*: Who is this "we" on which this narrative relies? The easy correlation between the desires or "will" of the American public and the decisions made by the United States government, Scranton argues, is specious, especially when it comes to military action. "It is disingenuous to presume that soldiers are acting on behalf of 'the American people.'"[67]

Nevertheless, the American public—"civilians," in this discourse—does bear responsibility for these wars, even if not equally so and even assuming a far less Pollyannish view regarding whose "will" the US government represents or enacts today. But what about "those who served?" Cannot many of the same questions be asked about (ex-)military personnel? If there was no substantial civilian anti-war movement to speak of, for which the American public should be called to account, what about soldiers and veterans? Despite the stereotype of the Vietnam veteran being subjected to the scorn of anti-war activists, veterans also participated in—they were powerful actors in—that fight.[68] That cannot be said about the post-9/11 wars. No significant or widespread organized dissent or anti-war politics has appeared among soldiers and veterans.[69] And did not military personnel also vote for those very same politicians, the ones who sent them to and kept them at war?[70] Did not (many) military personnel *also believe in the wars,* even if a large number left disillusioned, wondering what the fight was for, and angry at "civilians" for sending them into the fray?[71] From within the logic of the discourse that speaks of the civil-military divide, combat trauma, and the obligation to care, such questions are placed out of bounds. More precisely, in being tethered to the "problem" of the civil-military divide, the discourse dismisses from consideration alternative, anti-nationalist and anti-imperial forms of accountability.

While calling for one form of accountability, the discourse of combat trauma renders a different one ever more difficult to mount and sustain. If there is to be any exit from the national-imperial frame, we need to insist on one basic distinction, at the very least. Returning to Wood's anecdote, in our encounters with soldiers and veterans, we must separate out "yeah, that was fucked up" from "I honor your service." Certainly, it is plausible to express compassion for someone's suffering—even if that suffering is born of *what he has done*—without simultaneously honoring his service. Also plausible, appropriate even, is being openly unable or unwilling to feel compassion for anyone who speaks of the pleasure he took in killing or, for that matter, believes that the wars are politically or morally right.

The call to "support the troops" and to honor their service—regardless not only of one's own position on the wars but also regardless of theirs—is not the correct "lesson" learned from the American war in Vietnam, contrary to what Sherman and so many others insist. That mantra is a consequence of the conservative reconstruction of the US military defeat that accompanied Ronald Reagan's rise to power in 1980, as I discussed in Chapter 2.[72] It is a consequence of the reconstruction of the armed forces as a "professional" military, with the purported discipline, virtue, respect, and abilities needed for winning wars. This valuation of the soldier as ideal citizen has become a political common sense, continuously interpellating the American public—right and left, liberal and conservative—into the new American militarism.[73] As Robert J. Lifton told me, it is "as if serving in a war is the highest and bravest activity a young person can engage in, even if often the kids who serve have nowhere else to go," and this regardless of what one "thinks of the wars themselves." The attitude Lifton describes echoes through articles and books written about combat trauma. And it echoes through the ritual of thanking someone for their service, in which, as Sherman understands it, "we are recognizing character—*courage tied to public service.*"[74]

In a review of *Afterwar*, Iraq War veteran Roy Scranton asks of Nancy Sherman: "What kind of community expresses gratitude for such behavior? Who is the 'we' that ought to 'integrate' such vile acts?" Scranton invites his readers to think about Sherman's discourse of gratitude, so replete with references to psychological and moral pain, in comparison with that on the Black Lives Matter movement:

> Imagine that instead of having a conversation—insufficient as it has been—about systematic racism, we were having a conversation about the moral and psychological stress American police suffer in the course of patrolling their communities. Imagine instead of talking about how Black Lives Matter, we were talking about police health care, police pensions, and police suicide rates ... Imagine that instead of trying, however inadequately, to address America's long history of racial violence, we were spending our time trying to educate civilians in their obligation to "bridge the police-civilian divide." You don't have to imagine: that's the very conversation we've been having these last fourteen years about war.[75]

Scranton may have spoken prematurely about a conversation that was scarcely to be imagined at the time vis-à-vis the Black Lives Matter movement. Nevertheless, his analogy captures the grammar undergirding this soldier/civilian discourse of character, gratitude, obligation, and (non)judgment.

The discourse relies not only on a militarist ideology in requiring the American public to respect and be grateful for the troops' service.[76] It also relies on a fundamental slippage and misrecognition. Despite what are sometimes explicit claims to the contrary, nonmilitary citizens are being asked to respond to soldiers and veterans as if they occupy the subject position of the victim. In fact, the claim to victimhood echoes rather loudly through Sherman's explication of the role and value of resentment. Resentment, pain, healing, recognition—Sherman's account of moral injury and public obligation invokes the contours of what Wendy Brown termed "politicized identity." As compared to Sherman's discourse about soldiers, Brown's analysis focuses on a very different configuration of identity politics. She elaborates

the historical conditions of possibility within which marginalized subjects struggled to "secure a place for [themselves] ... in a
humanist discourse of universal personhood," and she identifies
the political failure she understood to be installed at the very
heart of this explicitly emancipatory project.[77]

All the talk of soldiers suffering, of the untranslatability of
a soldier's experiences and pain, of the importance of recognition is not an emancipatory project, not even in its conceit.
Nevertheless, it mimics the grammar of identity politics that
found form in the 1980s and 1990s in the United States, and
it remains in accord with Brown's understanding of how
Nietzschean *ressentiment* operates (if not necessarily with its
generative conditions). Suffering emerges "as the measure of
social virtue," and "good fortune ('privilege,' as we say today)
as self-recriminating, as its own indictment in a culture of suffering." In the terms of this contemporary grammar of the soldier
as injured subject—a politicized identity shorn of any emancipatory political desires—it is almost impossible to abet against
what Brown cautioned could become, and we have certainly
seen in the post-9/11 combat-trauma imaginary, "the steady
slide of political into therapeutic discourse."[78]

Sherman draws on an essay by Jean Améry to develop her
analysis of soldier resentment. A Holocaust survivor famous
for his refusal to relinquish his resentment, Améry argued that
only a victim of the Nazi regime could apprehend "the moral
truth of the blows." Sherman does not seamlessly assimilate
what she names Améry's "moral injury" with the suffering of
American soldiers and veterans, who themselves do not tend
to appropriate the victim identity in any explicit or coherent
sense. Nevertheless, given her analytic frame, she cannot avoid
ascribing traumatized combat veterans the subject position of
victimhood. "Resentment, at its most basic," Sherman writes,
"is a bid for respect, *a demand of the person who caused the
injury*, or who contributed significantly, to acknowledge one's
standing."[79]

In his essay, Améry includes in his call to moral account for
Nazi atrocities victims who have chosen to forgive, a German

public that wants to bury the past and begin anew, and himself. He explores resentment as something other than pathology; it is not a psychic *inability* to move on. Améry insists on the value of his resentment: It is a way to hold both himself and the body politic to account, to argue that Germany should not be allowed to simply move forward, to be assimilated into the new order of nations, *to construe themselves as victims*,[80] to see Nazism as just one more iteration of the state violence endemic to European states and empires. He writes:

> I hope that my resentment, which is my personal protest against the antimoral natural process of healing that time brings about, and by which I make the genuinely humane and absurd demand that time be turned back—will also perform a historical function. Were it to fulfill the task that I set it, it could historically represent, as a stage of the world's moral progress, the German revolution that did not take place.[81]

The philosopher J.M. Bernstein also turns to Jean Améry to elaborate a concept of moral injury, although his differs markedly from Sherman's. For Bernstein, Améry's "confession and description of the essential elements of his existence as a victim are what make his account invaluable." In his explication of the moral truths born of his torture, Bernstein locates the value of Améry's position in the fact that it "rewrite[s] morality *from the perspective of the victim, from the perspective of moral injury.*"[82] In contrast to Sherman, Bernstein begins from the ethical ground on which Améry builds his argument—*the victim's* right to resentment, to her moral truth. In contrast, Sherman's appropriation of Améry's argument requires that she muddle the cardinal question of victimhood. What Sherman fails to recognize, to quote Roy Scranton, is that "Simply put, the victims tortured by the wars in Iraq and Afghanistan weren't American soldiers, but Iraqis and Afghans."[83]

For all the talk of killing and moral transgression we have seen in the prevailing combat-trauma imaginary, the question of US military aggression is still overlooked—which is to say, the acts through which "one person"—the American soldier —"violates another" remain unacknowledged.[84] Iraq War veteran Tyler Boudreau is an exception. He writes, "without the Iraqi people, the troops can have no moral injuries to speak of. And the only way Americans can fathom the meaning of this term, 'moral injury,' is to acknowledge the humanity of the Iraqis."[85] Far more commonly, when the discussion of combat trauma—and of moral injury—references the Iraqi, the Afghan or, for that matter, the Pakistani, the Yemeni, the Syrian, and the ever-proliferating list of Others on whose territory the "War on Terror" is being waged, the drama continues to revolve entirely around the American self. The Iraqis and Afghans that American soldiers have wounded or killed, whose cities and villages Americans have destroyed, and whose families they have decimated emerge as but object lessons in a moral understanding of combat trauma in which American troops occupy the role of the suffering and injured subject. We are told stories of Iraqi doctors shot at checkpoints, children killed, people humiliated, heads that "spray," and we hear of Afghan villages that were flattened, but we are admonished to listen for the purpose of comprehending the moral pain US soldiers and veterans bear for having carried out or witnessed such brutality. These war stories call on the public to identify with—to listen to, to help—those whom Allan Young termed "self-traumatized perpetrators." And while Young was wrong in arguing that focusing on perpetration as traumatic was a way to unite a divided nation and normalize what had been done in Vietnam, as I argued in Chapter 1, in the context of the post-9/11 wars, his argument is spot on: The figure of the self-traumatized perpetrator allows American citizens—soldiers and "civilians" alike—to set aside pressing political and ethical questions about the reasons for the post-9/11 wars and, even, about their conduct.[86]

I want to be clear. It is not that the "facts" of the suffering Other are not *known*. The US press has covered civilian casualties on the battlefields of Iraq and Afghanistan, at least to some extent, and on the killing fields in other countries subjected to US drone and special ops warfare. In fact, as Afghanistan fell to the Taliban in August 2021, and as thousands of Afghans tried desperately to flee the country from the one remaining egress, the international airport in Kabul, there was suddenly sustained, if ultimately fleeting attention to the dangers and risks to Afghan allies left behind. One prominent thread of that short-lived public attention, however, was not about Afghans at all. It spoke of the mental health consequences for American veterans of the chaotic exit from Afghanistan, that is, of the trauma and moral injury that "abandoning" their allies would inflict.[87]

More specific to the contemporary combat-trauma imaginary, the traumas that soldiers suffer presuppose and often require mention of the people and communities who have been injured, killed, and had their lives and worlds destroyed by US military personnel. Moral injury in particular, after all, appears most clearly in the context of soldiers *confessing to* acts of (perceived) moral transgression. The facts are known, but they do not rise to the level of public concern. They do not seem to merit consideration and judgment. To use a distinction invoked by Stanley Cavell, the facts about how many Iraqis and Afghans—as well as people in other countries on the receiving end of American military violence—have been killed and what they have suffered are (well enough) *known*.[88] What they are not is *acknowledged*. They are but "meaningless particulars"[89] in (most) public discussions of American military violence unleashed on foreign soil. The public knows *more than enough* to render judgment on the wars, if only it decided it mattered.

Stories of "evil shit" recounted by some soldiers and veterans appear in the discourse as narratives that must be heard, even revered.[90] For example, in his introduction to a panel of veterans, a military chaplain at a conference I attended instructed the audience to "put down your pens and listen with your hearts ... This is not an interrogation." The veterans are "making a gift to us." In bestowing their "gifts," I must emphasize, two veterans expressed profound remorse for what they had done in Iraq and they spoke critically of American imperial violence. But throughout this three-day conference, these two veterans were the only ones I heard bring up "the Other" with any sense of awareness of what had been done *to them*. The few references to injured Iraqis or Afghans made by the other speakers occurred as part of a call for the rest of "us" to empathize with and listen to the American veteran now suffering moral damage, sometimes stemming from his own transgressions. The role of "civilians," we learned from one workshop leader, was "to bear witness and to validate their loss and pain." And to be clear, the organizers and most participants at this conference were positioned on the liberal-left of American society. It was not a particular *political* position on the wars that produced the deafening silence about the damage caused abroad by US militarism. It was a focus on our shared "respect" for those who had served and the unquestioned assumption that citizens who have not gone to war have neither the authority nor the right to judge, or perhaps really even to speak meaningfully about war, especially not when face to face with a soldier.

## Caring for the World

In her essay "Collective Responsibility," Arendt sketches the philosophical and theological genealogies of the distinctions to be drawn between the political, the legal, and the moral. My interest here is in the distinction she draws between the moral and the political. Over centuries, Arendt argues, the moral has been understood as concerned with the self, while the political indexes a care for the world. Arendt's exploration of political and moral standards was driven, of course, by a particular history. Writing in the aftermath of Nazi Germany, she grappled with the "collective and vicarious responsibility in which the member of a community is held responsible for things he did not participate in but which were done in his name."[91] All the talk of combat trauma speaks similarly to the question of collective and vicarious responsibility. But in this case, aside from the exceptional speech acts coming almost exclusively from a relatively small number of anti-war veterans, the call is for the American public to live up to their collective and vicarious responsibilities *toward those Americans who fought the war.* Heeding closely Arendt's description of the difference between the moral and the political, what we see being staged in today's combat-trauma imaginary, in other words, is a morality play that is all about the US national self.

It is not a single self that I reference here, of course. There is the self of the soldier who must learn to live with himself. Whether articulated in secular or theological terms, combat trauma is understood to cause a painful split within the self, echoing Arendt's description of moral conduct since the rise of Christianity as "concerning the individual in his singularity" and depending "primarily upon the intercourse of man with himself ... [that is,] not a matter of concern with the other."[92] There is also the self of the nation, where the split appears in the form of a divided house to which unity must be restored. In neither variation do we find talk of reparations. There is no talk of responsibility toward the millions of people American soldiers have harmed, directly or indirectly.[93] The Iraqi or Afghan is mentioned, if at all, as an afterthought, someone to be gestured toward and then set aside, and, of course, only the Other *civilians* (the apparent moral equivalent of the US soldier), not the Other warriors, have any visibility at all. As Wood puts it in an author's note in the early pages of *What Have We Done*:

> This book is about the Americans we sent to war in Iraq and Afghanistan and the moral injuries they sustained there. In those conflicts, civilians were also caught up in the fighting, as willing or unwilling participants or as bystanders ... The moral injuries of the Afghan and Iraqi people are beyond the scope of this book but not, I trust, out of our thoughts.[94]

In *The Order of Evils*, Adi Ophir rightly argues that any given moral discourse frames "only some of the existing evils and let[s] only some of its victims come into presence and assume their own voice."[95] In today's discourse of soldier trauma, existing evils appear through the figure and voice of the suffering American soldier, and the responsibility for disrupting that order of evil is displaced onto an American public that is duty-bound to care for those "we" sent off to war. There is no call for a *jus post bellum*, no sense of obligation toward those whom "our" troops have harmed and whose lands "our" military has destroyed. To recognize any such obligation, after all, would require judgment. In approaching the soldier and in imagining and responding to combat trauma, the question of the war itself could no longer be set aside.

The problem of responsibility, both individual and collective, dominated much of Hannah Arendt's thinking, especially in the aftermath of the Eichmann trial and the criticism she received for how she covered it.[96] Arendt did not address collective responsibility from within a moral framework, however, but through the language of the political. Responsibility is "always political," she writes, "whether it appears in the older form, when a whole community takes it upon itself to be responsible for whatever one of its members has done, or whether a community is being held responsible for what has been done in its name."[97] There is no escaping political responsibility:

> No moral, individual and personal, standards of conduct will ever be able to excuse us from collective responsibility. This vicarious responsibility for things we have not done, this taking upon ourselves the consequences for things we are entirely innocent of, is the price we pay for the fact that we live our lives not by ourselves but among our fellow men, and that the faculty of action, which, after all, is the political faculty par excellence, can be actualized only in one of the many and manifold forms of human community.[98]

From an Arendtian perspective, taking collective responsibility requires an act that Wood and Sherman preclude *a priori*. Along with the many others calling on "civilians" to *just listen* to suffering soldiers, they evade what Arendt finds unavoidable, namely, the human responsibility to judge. We must try to think from others' points of view—which is an *imaginative* rather than an impossible act; then we need to deliberate and evaluate together, and in public, with (imagined) others. The risks of not doing so, for Arendt, were monstrous: "Out of the unwillingness or inability to choose one's examples and one's company, and out of the unwillingness or inability to relate to others through judgment, arise the real stumbling blocks ... Therein lies the horror, and at the same time the banality of evil."[99]

Emerging in and through all this talk of war, combat trauma, and civilian obligation is what Miriam Ticktin has named a "moralist anti-politics."[100] "Civilians" are called upon in their capacity as citizens to attend to the "individual suffering" of returning troops. They are told they cannot possibly know or ever understand the experience of war—that is, war from the soldier-qua-grunt's point of view. "We" are asked to receive their words as "gifts," to set politics aside, to set aside the question of war itself. In effect, citizens, who are now "civilians," are called upon to disregard what Arendt names the "*care* of the world," a decidedly political, rather than an anti- or post-political obligation for her. Indeed, care or concern for the world is the political act *par excellence,* for Arendt; it is how we, as humans, as specific communities of humans, collectively engage one another and build the common—the political—world in which we live.[101] In contrast, the civilian's (re-)engaged citizenship imagined here takes the form of the therapist's couch.

It is certainly possible to support the need for institutional care for (ex-)military personnel and yet reject the therapeutic model and the moralist anti-politics that undergirds the call on the American public to just listen, to help heal those who fought, perhaps did horrible things, and who may well still think what they did was right or even enjoyable. Stacey Pearsall, a combat photographer in Iraq, reports being unable to get herself to say "that Iraq was not worth it, because then I would be diminishing the sacrifices my friends made on the battlefield."[102] But I have no problem saying it. It was not worth it. And it was not worth it not simply, or even primarily, because of the American troops who suffer(ed) and died. It was not worth it because of the hundreds of thousands that American troops killed and wounded (directly or indirectly), and because of the everyday worlds they shattered, and which remain in violent disarray today, two decades hence. There is no statistical equivalence by any measure between the harms suffered by the Iraqi and Afghan populations and those suffered by American troops. Perhaps there is no moral equivalence, either.

This moralist anti-politics is not without exception what is being asked of the American public by (ex-)military personnel, nor is everyone insisting that the American public cannot possibly comprehend. I do not want to imply that there is no space at all in public discourse today for political critique or judgment. A National Public Radio story (aired June 23, 2021) opened with the following question: "Can a civilian understand what it means to be in combat?" Elliot Ackerman, a veteran and novelist, gave a detailed account of being pinned down in a candy store with his platoon during the second battle of Fallujah in 2004, after which the reporter wondered whether Ackerman "rejects the idea that civilians can't possibly relate." Ackerman says, "You know, you ever been involved in something tragic? Ever been in a car accident, crisis? It's the same thing, totally the same thing."[103] Or, as a former Green Beret told Matt Richtel, it is not only that civilians have no skin in the game, but that they seem not to have any "real opinions either." "At least with Vietnam," as Richtel quotes the soldier, "people spit on you and you knew they had an opinion."[104] For that matter, some of the same writers—journalists, scholars, veterans—who call upon "civilians" to step up to their responsibilities and listen also ask "us" to step up and take a position on the wars—we are a democracy, after all!—just not, so it seems, when actually face to face with someone "who has served."

Nevertheless, there remains a profound, perhaps irresolvable tension in mainstream discourse, in that it is impossible to elevate the figure of the American soldier while at the same time decrying the war. And, crucially, if the goal is to articulate a robust political critique of the war, the truth of the soldiers' experience must not be taken to be the truth of war. In its epistemological conceit, the American soldier's perspective is inherently not only nationalist but also imperial. As a frame of war,[105] it is only possible for a state that has the privilege of fighting its wars on someone else's soil. The experience of war on the part of enemy combatants never appears from within its gaze. Neither do the lives and experiences of the civilians who get caught in the vortex of US military violence—and who certainly and constitutively "know" what war is like. To quote Viet Thanh Nguyen, "There is neither power nor glory in the stories of civilians killed or maimed or forced to flee or orphaned by war. [And yet it] … is in civilian experiences, similar to what many Afghans are now going through, that we truly find war stories."[106]

Tim O'Brien, a novelist and war critic who fought in Vietnam, views the ritual of thanking troops for their service as mere "patriotic gloss"; "we're thanking without having the courage to ask whether the mission is even right."[107] But, while courage may well be lacking, I want to insist that there is a far deeper problem: the lack of epistemic and moral authority on the part of anyone in the contemporary American public sphere who has not enlisted in the military and fought in the wars, which often seems to be taken to be the same thing. Combatants, as the privileged witnesses to war, are the nation's super-citizens, while the rest of the public is duty-bound to honor and care for them. The overriding moral commitment to care for the troops that is assumed in the prevailing discourse (rather than, say, do no harm to Iraqis) values national unity at the expense of all else, with the responsibility for restoring that unity residing with so-called civilian-citizens obliged to act in particular ways to re-suture the nation across the abyss that is the civil-military divide. The citizen responsible for this re-suturing is an always already suspect subject (she who did not serve; she who cannot know), who must listen and never judge, who must care for and console. The new American militarism has found—indeed, it has forged—the civilian-citizen that it needs.

# Epilogue

On Sunday, August 15, 2021, on the heels of rapid military victories throughout Afghanistan, the Taliban walked into Kabul. Afghan soldiers put down their arms. The president, Ashraf Ghani, fled. Helicopters lifted American diplomats off the rooftop of the US embassy in the Green Zone, invoking an iconic image of the final chaotic and desperate evacuation of Saigon as it fell to the Viet Cong nearly five decades earlier. US soldiers retreated to the airport where, over the next two weeks, they would oversee the largest evacuation in US history.

The US defeat in its longest war was dramatic and undeniable, a defeat that should have come as no surprise. In February 2020, the Trump administration signed a peace deal with the Taliban, effectively conceding that America had lost the war. After Joe Biden's election to the presidency, he agreed to abide by that treaty, even as he delayed the draw-down of US troops by four months, moving it from May 1, 2021, to September in order, according to the administration, to facilitate a more orderly withdrawal. As the summer of 2021 progressed, however, the Taliban took city after city at a speed that few in the US intelligence community had predicted. In the end, the American retreat was anything but orderly.

For the next two weeks, the American press paid rapt attention to Afghanistan, at long last. The war itself, that is—what was unfolding *on the ground*—was in the headlines. Many Americans, if newspaper and social media coverage and comments were any indication, seemed to take notice that Afghan lives, and not just those of American troops, were at stake in this long and brutal war, perhaps even that the US might owe something to those who had worked for its military and other American government or affiliated institutions over the past two decades. The pandemonium that unfolded as thousands of civilians fled to the Kabul International airport seemed to hold much of the public transfixed. Images of desperation were broadcast around the clock on US television and shared on Twitter and other social media: Crowds pushing frantically to enter the airport; Marines standing on a wall over a gutter, reaching down to snatch babies and young children out of parents' arms and lift them to safety.

Images of desperate Afghans and valiant American soldiers at the airport were supplemented by other stories of heroism and other figures of suffering, many of which are far more typical of how the war has appeared over the past two decades on the home-front. There was account after account of American veterans working selflessly around the clock, using every contact they had, to get their former colleagues into the airport and onto planes. There were stories upon stories about how, as they watched city after city fall to the Taliban, many veterans were re-experiencing the trauma of war, mourning sacrifices that now seemed in vain. What's more, watching their Afghan brothers-in-arms abandoned to their own fates, many a veteran suffered moral injury anew.[1]

Over the next few weeks, the American public was exposed to an excruciating display of American failure and the myriad costs of war. As recounted in one NBC news report on that first fateful day, "within hours of the Taliban takeover, chaos erupted at Kabul's international airport as desperate Afghans raced to flee their country. A harrowing video ... showed Afghans storming the military side of the airport and clinging to a US Air Force plane as it attempted to move down the tarmac." The reporter lamented, "some people appear to fall to their death as the aircraft takes off." It was hard not to be reminded of "Falling Man," the Associated Press photograph of a man falling to his death from the burning Twin Towers on September 11, 2001, as the American war in Afghanistan, launched as a response to that horrifying day nearly two decades ago, came to an official end.

On August 16, President Biden took to the White House podium to address the American retreat from Kabul and to reframe American defeat. The military had invaded Afghanistan twenty years ago with a very clear goal, he said: to "get those who attacked us on Sept. 11, 2001, and make sure Al Qaeda could not use Afghanistan as a base from which to attack us again." *That war* was not lost; it was accomplished a decade ago, and yet, administration after administration failed to withdraw American troops. "Our mission in Afghanistan was never supposed to have been nation-building. It was never supposed to be creating a unified, centralized democracy."[2]

Embracing the formal end to American military presence in Afghanistan, Biden then shifted responsibility onto Afghans: its political leaders "gave up;" its military folded without a fight.[3] The story of sacrifices made by Afghan military personnel —not to mention those made by Afghans who joined the war effort by working for the American military, the US government, or NGOs—is far more complex than Biden's dismissal suggests. Approximately 66,000 Afghan military and police died in the war (compared to 2,448 American military personnel and 3,486 American contractors),[4] to say nothing of the approximately 46,319 civilians who died, a number that is a likely a serious underestimate given the difficulty of counting the dead.[5] Nevertheless, Biden's message was clear: This is not an American failure. At worst, it was American folly to believe one could build a modern, democratic nation-state with a well-trained and professional military "in a place like" Afghanistan. And so, he asked his audience, rhetorically, "How many more generations of America's daughters and sons would you have me send to fight Afghanistan's civil war when Afghan troops will not? How many more lives, American lives, is it worth, how many endless rows of headstones at Arlington National

Cemetery?"[6] The imperial nation emerges as selfless here—a nation fighting *someone else's war*; it can no longer choose to be a victim of its own largesse.

More American soldiers and Marines were to die before the final boots on the ground were officially withdrawn from Afghanistan on August 30, 2021. Four days earlier, suicide bombers detonated explosives near the gates of Kabul's airport, killing thirteen American troops and an estimated sixty Afghans. "For American forces," the *New York Times*, reported, "the attacks were a gruesome coda to almost twenty years of warfare in Afghanistan—one of their heaviest losses, just days before they are set to leave the country."[7] Had the final image of the war been that of soldiers and Marines blown up while standing on a wall literally lifting children to safety, the figure of the American soldier as selfless victim might have been easier to hold onto. But then came August 29. Anxious about another attack on the airport, the US military made (yet another) fatal mistake. It tracked a car and its driver over the course of the day, convincing itself he was an ISIS bomber en route to the airport. As the car pulled into the driveway of a home, a drone strike was launched: In the minutes between the bomb's release and when it hit the ground, children ran out of the house and gathered around the car. Ten members of one family, seven of them children, were killed. The driver turned out to be Zemari Ahmadi, a longtime worker for a California-based non-governmental organization. Earlier in the day, at a house that turned out to be the home of the American NGO's country director and not an ISIS safe house as military intelligence had concluded, he loaded water canisters, not bombs, into the trunk of his car.[8] Yet another gruesome coda to America's war.

The *New York Times* was the first to report that the killing of Ahmadi and so many members of his family was not a "righteous strike," as previously described by Joint Chiefs Chairman, General Mark Miley.[9] The first in a series of articles over the next several months, this newspaper of record documented multiple American intelligence and military failures over the past two decades of war. In the words of *Times* reporter Azmat Khan,

"The promise was a war waged by all-seeing drones and precision bombs. [And yet] The [Pentagon] documents show flawed intelligence, faulty targeting, years of civilian deaths—and scant responsibility." Syria, 2016: a strike believed to target a "staging area" for ISIS fighters actually flattened "houses far from the front line, where farmers, their families and other local people sought nighttime sanctuary from bombing and gunfire. More than 120 villagers were killed." Iraq, 2017: A strike in western Mosul killed a father, mother, and child stopped in a car at an intersection; assuming the vehicle was carrying a bomb, they were murdered. The family was fleeing fighting nearby. Such "errors" are ubiquitous, Khan reports, ever more so since the "air campaign" was launched by the Obama administration.[10] For its part, the *Washington Post* published articles critical of the war in Afghanistan: ill-defined goals; a neglect of the war once the invasion of Iraq was launched; bad intelligence. The American military and political leadership knew for decades the fight was not going well, and yet, it proceeded to lie to the public, continuously declaring that the US was "making progress" in this seemingly never-ending war.[11]

It would be easy to identify in such reportage—as well as in the turn against the war in Iraq a decade earlier—the birth of a critical, anti-war movement. But that would be a mistake. Talk of failures, mistakes, and mismanagement can just as easily be repurposed and read in the interests of militarism and empire: How might the US fight a more "humane" war? What lessons might be learned for the future? None of this talk, not even the recognition of outright lies, has fostered a widespread and fundamental political critique of American militarism, one that demands political and perhaps even legal accountability for the wars, let alone considers what might be owed in the form of reparations to those whose countries and lives have been destroyed. Indeed, by the mid-aughts there was a growing consensus that the war in Iraq was started on a lie. As the military lost more and more personnel to the Iraqi insurgency, the American public became increasingly disillusioned with the war, wanting an exit to the morass of "sectarian" violence that few recognized was in large part of America's own making. The crucial political judgment, however, is not that Saddam Hussein's possession of weapons of mass destruction or that his connections to Al-Qaeda were lies. If the war was begun on false pretenses, then, following *jus ad bellum,* the war *was a crime.* And one disastrous outcome of that crime, it is worth emphasizing, is the rise of ISIS and the brutal, if short-lived, Islamic State. The ongoing "war" against ISIS—including ISIS-K, responsible for the attack on the Kabul airport in August 2021—is a war of America's own making.

Questions about the invasion of Afghanistan in 2001 have taken far longer to appear and they rarely seem to consider whether the war, even at its start, was legitimate, or at least, whether it was the only available and most reasonable choice. Does one destroy an entire country for the sins of a stateless group of radical militants who have built their base of operations in one corner of the state? *Were there other choices that could have been made,* other ways to hold Al-Qaeda's leadership to account? Should the US have negotiated with the Taliban and accepted their request for amnesty in return for ceding power all the way back in November 2001? For all the criticism that has emerged over the past several years, such questions remain shockingly rare. More common is the argument that while the war began as a righteous fight, it was badly managed, neglected by a Bush administration distracted by Iraq, and that it spun out of control. In the words of *Washington Post* reporter Craig Whitlock, "Unlike the war in Vietnam, or the one that would erupt in Iraq in 2003, the decision to take military action against Afghanistan was grounded in near-unanimous public support." A "just cause" when it commenced, it "deteriorated into a losing one."[12]

If, however, as Whitlock himself documents, *from the very outset,* neither the "enemy" (al-Qaeda? the Taliban?) nor the war's goals (taking out al Qaeda's base of operations? Attacking "the military capability" of the Taliban regime? Regime change?) were clearly identified, can one still say the war began as a just cause?[13] What, precisely, *was the cause?* As Phil Klay, a veteran of the war in Iraq, wrote after the fall of Kabul, in the days and months that followed September 11, 2001, the "national mood" was marked not only by "grief mixed with fear and rage… there was something else. Something dangerously seductive. America had found moral purpose again." "Let's admit it," he says, "those days felt good." "9/11 unified America," Klay continues. "It overcame partisan divides, bound us together, and gave us the sense of common purpose so lacking in today's poisonous politics. And nothing that we have done as a nation since has been so catastrophically destructive as what we did when we were enraptured by the warm glow of victimization and felt like we could do anything, together."[14]

Following the fall of Kabul, perhaps there was an opening—however slight—for an American political reckoning with the reckless nationalism and destructive militarism that has wrought so much damage over the past two decades, and that continues to wreak havoc by deploying special operations forces and drone warfare in many places around the world, including in Iraq and Afghanistan. Perhaps there was an opening for a political conversation that, rather than casting the wars as victims of bad intelligence, poor management, lazy national armies, and impossible (cultural) conditions, would call US militarism and empire to account and demand, at the very least, an end to this temporally unlimited and territorially unbounded military campaign. In September 2021 the House of Representatives finally passed a bill repealing the Authorization of Use of Military Force of 2001 (AUMF), a law that had effectively given carte blanche to every president since 9/11 to conduct and expand the war on terror as each saw fit. The bill, introduced by Barbara Lee, the sole congressperson to have voted against going to war in the aftermath of 9/11, has since stalled in the Senate's Committee of Foreign Relations.[15]

Then Russia invaded Ukraine. On Thursday, February 24, 2022, Putin launched a brazen attack on a sovereign nation. A military not invested in the liberal way of war, cities are being flattened, civilians killed summarily. President Putin's ultranationalist and expansionist agenda is on full display. No doubt inadvertently, he has handed the US a renewed "moral purpose." Even though the Biden administration has declared that the US will not be sending troops to fight the war, it has embraced the defense of Ukraine as a noble cause and positioned itself as the global leader in this latest just war. The very post-war (European) order is at stake, as is the future of liberal democracy and the principle of national sovereignty, US officials explain. Veterans of the American wars in Iraq and Afghanistan have gone off and joined the "foreign legions" fighting in Ukraine, in search of a just war they thought they would find in Iraq and Afghanistan, but, alas, did not. Others are training Ukrainians to defend their own nation, not wanting to squander the skills and expertise they developed at war, this time for what they see as a morally unambiguous war.[16] The US military claims the moral high ground once again. *This is not how "we" fight.* And America's humanitarian largesse is on full display: after decades of cruel indifference to the suffering of displaced Afghans and Iraqis, and to the dangers faced by those who worked with the US military, Biden declared that America would open its borders to Ukrainian refugees.[17]

Let me be clear: I am not suggesting that Ukrainians do not have the right to fight the Russian invasion. Nor am I arguing that Russia's war is legitimate. The Russian invasion is a war crime. But just as history did not begin on that fateful day on September 11, 2001, neither did it begin on February 24, 2022: There is no American innocence here. After the fall of the Soviet Union in 1989, when Francis Fukuyama declared the "end of history"—the victory of western liberal democracy—NATO did not put down its arms.[18] It continued to expand eastward, ever closer to Russia's borders. As the only remaining superpower, the US extended its global power and imperial reach, manifested in many a military venture of its own, seeding the ground for the Russian regime's own turn to renewed authoritarianism and the intensifying of its political imaginary of a Russian (victim) nation under existential threat. But as was the case after 9/11, according to many a pundit, politician, and media report, there is no backstory we need to know here.

The war in Ukraine is engendering yet another "sense of common purpose," to return to Phil Klay's words, even if one not nearly as deeply felt as was September 11. This is *the good fight*. If after two decades of war and the fear of a nuclear confrontation with Russia, the US does not seem to be ready to commit American troops to the fight, it nevertheless positions itself as the moral arbiter, the global leader, in this latest fight of freedom against tyranny. Clearly a tragedy for its own citizens and a grave danger to the stability of Europe, from another perspective the war in Ukraine may be a godsend for the US. Russia's aggression is enabling America to reconstruct its global role as a moral leader of the western world, and to do so without involving American troops in any of the messy and injurious work of violence.[19]

It took well over a decade and a lot of hard work among conservative pundits and politicians to reconstruct US militarism —and to regenerate an American commitment to and belief in its moral, global mission—in the aftermath of the war in Vietnam (chapter 2). The war in Ukraine may make that project a far shorter and simpler endeavor today. A serious political reckoning with the ongoing, if reconfigured forever war, and, more fundamentally, with the depths and dangers of American militarism, may become ever more difficult to mount and sustain. All the while, as the war on terror fades ever more into the background, with fewer and fewer boots on the ground, the figure of the traumatized soldier, hero and victim at one and the same time, remains present—as a ubiquitous figure in popular culture, as the subject of news reports, journal articles, and think tank studies. In American politics and culture, the trauma hero—his virtue, his sacrifices, his pain, and his suffering—might turn out to be the most powerful legacy and the one enduring memory of the post 9/11 wars.[20]

# Acknowledgments

Research for this book was funded by the Presidential Research Award of Barnard College and the Harry Frank Guggenheim Foundation without which it would never have come to pass. I want to acknowledge a few very talented undergraduate research assistants who have helped me over the years and who, by now, have moved on to careers of their own: Elise Guarna, Marina Bea Hanssen, and Naye Idris. In addition, I thank the many colleagues who have engaged in conversations, provided references, and commented on chapters: Gil Anidjar, Brian Boyd, Jean Comaroff, Emma Shaw Crane, Catherine Fennell, Brian Larkin, Claudio Lomnitz, Hélène Quiniou, Joan Scott, Lesley Sharp, Audra Simpson, Naor Ben Yehoyada, Gary Wilder, and Paige West. I am especially thankful for those who generously read the entire manuscript and provided critical insight as this project was coming to a close: Elizabeth Povinelli, who has done this for me more than once before (and whom I will, no doubt, impose upon again); Joseph Masco, for his incisive reading and helpful commentary as I have wandered into a domain of expertise not quite my own; John Comaroff, who read the manuscript with as much attention to the book's overarching analytic and political interventions as to its rather unfortunate and random use of the comma. And finally, I would like to thank Lisa Wedeen who read many a draft of many a chapter and provided invaluable critique. I deeply grateful for her willingness to read again and again, a true testament to our friendship.

Several people were essential to this manuscript coming together in its final form. Joel van De Sande, who put up with the mess that were my references and, against all odds, pulled together the footnotes. Don Reneau for his careful copy-editing and astute, critical reading of the final manuscript before I sent it off to the press. Finally, I would like to thank Jen Harris who copy edited and Dan O'Connor who guided this manuscript through the production process at Verso, and of course, Jessie Kindig, my editor, for her incisive comments on its penultimate draft. They made this a much more legible book.

There are many others to whom I am indebted, from the audiences who asked questions at the many talks I delivered over the years, to those who gave of their time to be interviewed, offer insights and connections, and chat with me at conferences and workshops. And then there are those who put up with me at home, with all the ups and downs that writing entails. Books are collective undertakings in ways not always apparent in their final form.

# Notes

## Introduction

1   Esther Schrader, "These Unseen Wounds Cut Deep," *Los Angeles Times*, November 14, 2004.

2   Schrader, "These Unseen Wounds Cut Deep"; Dana Priest and Anne Hull, "Soldiers Face Neglect, Frustration At Army's Top Medical Facility," *Washington Post*, February 18, 2007. See also Jerry Lembcke, *PTSD: Diagnosis and Identity in Post-Empire America* (New York: Lexington Books, 2013).

3   Schrader, "These Unseen Wounds Cut Deep."

4   I have struggled with the use of pronouns in this book. I use "she" as the generic pronoun, when not referring to soldiers, thereby following a convention that has sought to query the use of "he" as a generic stand-in for all human beings. However, I have chosen to use "he" when referring to the soldier. While there are many women who serve in the military today, it remains dominated by men. And more important still, given the military's hyper-masculinity as an institution, I use the male pronoun to index that masculinity regardless of whether the individual soldier is male or female. Moreover, I realize not all military personnel are soldiers, in the strict sense of enlistees in the Army, but for simplicity's sake, I follow the more colloquial usage of "soldier" to stand in for those in the other branches of the military as well.

5   For but the tip of a very deep iceberg, see: (movies) *The Hurt Locker, American Sniper, The Messenger; Stop-Loss, In the Valley of Elah*; (television) *Grey's Anatomy, Brothers and Sisters,*

*A Million Little Things*. For journalistic accounts and memoirs, see footnote 8.

6   Many scholars and journalists emphasize the image of the damaged and thereby *dangerous* veteran; for example, Jerry Lembcke, *The Spitting Image: Myth, Memory, and the Legacy of Vietnam* (New York: New York University Press, 1998). I maintain that the far more pervasive image in the post-9/11 period construes the soldier as a sympathetic figure who is suffering rather than threatening, and even when they are dangerous, the description of the violence is framed by a call for compassion. He is not comparable to the figure of Kurtz in *Apocalypse Now,* for example. For an interesting discussion of PTSD, "disorderly conduct," and veterans courts, that is, "nonadversarial" treatment courts, see Ken MacLeish, "Care and the Nonhuman Politics of Drunk Driving," *Cultural Anthropology*. 35 (1): 23-30.

7   Karl Marlantes, *What It Is Like to Go to War* (New York: Atlantic Monthly Press, 2011).

8   See, for example: David Finkel, *Thank You for Your Service* (New York: Farrar, Straus and Giroux, 2013); Jennifer Percy, *Demon Camp: A Soldier's Exorcism* (New York: Scribner, 2014); Yochi J. Dreazen, *The Invisible Front: Love and Loss in an Era of Endless War* (New York: Penguin Random House, 2014); David Wood, *What Have We Done: The Moral Injury of Our Longest Wars* (New York: Little, Brown and Company, 2016). See also Erin Finley, *Fields of Combat: Understanding PTSD Among Veterans of Iraq and Afghanistan* (Ithaca, NY: Cornell University Press, 2011); MacLeish, *Making War at Fort Hood*; Zoë Wool, *After War: The Weight of Life at Walter Reed* (Durham, NC: Duke University Press, 2015).

9   Elliott Colla, "The Military-Literary Complex," *Jadaliyya*, July 8, 2014.

10  See especially MacLeish, *Making War at Fort Hood*, and Wool, *After War*.

11  Viet Thanh Nguyen, *Nothing Ever Dies: Vietnam and the Memory of War* (Cambridge, MA: Harvard University Press, 2016), 15.

12  For example, as Zoë Wool writes in the preface to her ethnographic study of soldiers at Walter Reed, "I am also keenly aware of the violence I do not note. I think in particular of the civilians whose worlds and lives these soldiers have invaded in the course of their work and whose deaths have made up an estimated 90 percent of war casualties since the 1990s" (Wool, *After War*, xv). Also worth noting is the lack of any mention of non-American

combatants. An implicit moral equivalence is drawn not between US soldiers and other combatants (as should be the case), but between US soldiers and "other" civilians.

13 As Nguyen shows in his reading of presumably anti-war Hollywood films that grappled with the American war in Vietnam, Vietnamese characters are never subjects in their own right: They are stereotypes, the bodies on which the US military executes its violence. The same is true in the growing film industry on the post-9/11 wars: The woman and child in the opening scene of *American Sniper*, for example, or the Iraqi sniper himself; or the Iraqi woman who is raped in Brian de Palma's *Redacted,* itself a remake of a film he made about the war in Vietnam, *Casualties of War.*

14 See Nguyen, *Nothing Ever Dies.*

15 It is worth emphasizing that even though most soldiers never engage in or see combat, even among those deployed to war zones, this combat-trauma imaginary relies on the figure of the "grunt"—that is, the combat soldier on the front lines.

16 MacLeish, *Making War At Fort Hood*, 90-91.

17 Wool, *After War*, 105.

18 Wool, *After War*, 129 (emphasis added). The reference to the carpenter comes from a conversation with a soldier earlier in the book, during which he related an encounter with a fellow American after his return home: "I said to him, 'You're a carpenter, right? Well, imagine that you went out to a job and built some cabinets and all of a sudden on your way home, everyone is lining up and waving flags and saluting,' and, I mean, that's really what it's like" (Wool, *After War*, 108).

19 See Elaine Scarry, *The Body in Pain: The Making and Unmaking of the World* (New York: Oxford University Press, 1985).

20 For a reading of why films such as *Apocalypse Now* or *The Deer Hunter* are not actually anti-war, see Nguyen, *Nothing Ever Dies.*

21 I encountered such arguments in many fieldwork contexts, including spaces intended for "civil-military" encounters, book readings, and conferences on soldier trauma. See also Nancy Sherman, *Afterwar: Healing the Moral Injuries of Our Soldier* (New York: Oxford University Press, 2015); Wood, *What Have We Done*. Besides my argument that war is quite present via the figure of the soldier, the argument about disengagement also overlooks the material and institutional ways in which war is woven into the everyday lives of all Americans. On this, see Nick Turse, *The Complex: How the Military Invades Our Everyday Lives* (New York: Metropolitan Books, 2008). For an account

of the imbrication of biomedicine and war, see Jennifer Terry, *Attachments to War: Biomedical Logics and Violence in Twenty-First-Century America* (Durham, NC: Duke University Press, 2017).

22  Didier Fassin and Richard Rechtman, *The Empire of Trauma: An Inquiry into the Condition of Victimhood,* trans. Rachel Gomme (Princeton, NJ: Princeton University Press, 2009), 5.

23  For a discussion of TBI, see David Kieran, *Signature Wounds: The Untold Story of the Military's Mental Health Crisis* (New York: New York University Press, 2019).

24  Lembcke, *PTSD,* 15, 11.

25  Wool, *After War,* 149. MacLeish (*Making War at Fort Hood,* 15–16) proposes the concept of "vulnerability" as an alternative to trauma. For a critical ethnography of the work of treating veterans diagnosed with PTSD, see Finley, *Fields of Combat.* For a more sympathetic reading of military efforts to treat soldier trauma, see Kieran, *Signature Wounds.*

26  See Ben Shephard, *A War of Nerves: Soldiers and Psychiatrists in the Twentieth Century* (Cambridge, MA: Harvard University Press, 2001); Allan Young, "The Self-Traumatized Perpetrator as a 'Transient Mental Illness,'" *L'Évolution psychiatrique* 67: 4, 2002. Fassin and Rechtman, *The Empire of Trauma.*

27  Hannah Arendt, *The Human Condition* (Chicago: University of Chicago Press, 1958).

28  Andrew Bacevich, *The New American Militarism: How Americans Are Seduced by War* (New York: Oxford University Press, 2005).

29  Kieran, *Signature Wounds.* Offering an important accounting of PTSD as dealt with by the Army in the post-9/11 era, Kieran demonstrates that treating PTSD is now part of the business of making war. He makes the argument about PTSD and anti-war politics by focusing primarily on politicians who, over time, came to oppose the war in Iraq. But what about the American soldier traumatized by his service in Afghanistan? I also want to point out that even as a few "anti-war" congresspersons invoked the trauma of American soldiers in arguing against the Iraq War, it is worth keeping in mind that this was a *partisan* fight, which I read as rather different than a sustained *political critique* of the war. As I show in this book, focusing on the suffering of traumatized US soldiers does not lead in any obvious or direct way to an anti-war stance. In fact, as *Signature Wounds* itself demonstrates via the military's own focus on PTSD, there is no one-to-one correspondence between concern for combat trauma and anti-war politics.

30 See Stanley Cavell, *Must We Mean What We Say? A Book of Essays* (Cambridge: Cambridge University Press, [1969] 2015). See also Linda M.G. Zerilli, *A Democratic Theory of Judgment* (Chicago: University of Chicago Press, 2016).

31 See Didier Fassin, *Humanitarian Reason: A Moral History of the Present,* trans. Rachel Gomme (Berkeley: University of California Press, 2012); Fassin and Rechtman, *The Empire of Trauma*; Miriam I. Ticktin, *Casualties of Care: Immigration and the Politics of Humanitarianism in France* (Berkeley: University of California Press, 2011).

32 See Fassin, *Humanitarian Reason*; Florence Rush, *The Best Kept Secret: Sexual Abuse of Children* (New York: McGraw-Hill, 1981); Judith Lewis Herman, *Trauma and Recovery: The Aftermath of Violence* (New York: Basic Books, 1992); Ian Hacking, *Rewriting the Soul: Multiple Personality and the Sciences of Memory* (Princeton: Princeton University Press, 1995).

33 Fassin and Rechtman, *The Empire of Trauma*, 1.

34 The mental health advisory team, *Operation Iraqi Freedom 06-08* (Office of the Surgeon Multi-National Force–Iraq and Office of the Surgeon General United States Army Medical Command, Feb. 14, 2008).

35 Underestimation discussed at Strong Star Consortium Combat PTSD Conference, San Antonio, Texas, October 2018 (author's notes). On PTSD and/or TBI controversies, see Rajeev Ramchand et al., "Prevalence of PTSD, Depression, and TBI Among Returning Servicemembers," in *Invisible Wounds of War: Psychological and Cognitive Injuries, Their Consequences, and Services to Assist Recovery*, ed. Terri Tanielian and Lisa H. Jaycox (Santa Monica, CA: RAND Corporation, 2008). See also Finley, *Fields of Combat*.

36 See Kieran, *Signature Wounds*.

37 See Fassin, *Humanitarian Reason*; Fassin and Rechtman, *The Empire of Trauma*; Ticktin, *Casualties of Care*.

38 For an account of MSF and its ties to neoliberal thinkers, see Jessica Whyte, "Powerless Companions or Fellow Travellers?: Human Rights and the Neoliberal Assault on Post-Colonial Economic Justice," *Radical Philosophy* (2018).

39 Ticktin, *Casualties of Care*, 16.

40 Fassin, *Humanitarian Reason*, 211.

41 See Fassin, *Humanitarian Reason*; Eyal Weizman, *The Least of All Possible Evils: Humanitarian Violence From Arendt to Gaza* (New York: Verso Books, 2011).

42 Fassin, *Humanitarian Reason*, 207; Fassin and Rechtman, *The Empire of Trauma*.

43 Fassin, *Humanitarian Reason*, 221.

44 Fassin, *Humanitarian Reason*, 222, 214, 1.

45 See Weizman, *The Least of All Possible Evils*. See also Robert Meister, *After Evil: A Politics of Human Rights* (New York: Columbia University Press, 2011); Ilana Feldman and Miriam Iris Ticktin, *In the Name of Humanity: The Government of Threat and Care* (Durham, NC: Duke University Press, 2010).

46 Meister, *After Evil*, 2, 4.

47 Ticktin, *Casualties of Care*.

48 Meister, *After Evil*, 7. Emphasis in original.

49 Compassion is called upon as well for physical wounds, even if trauma is more ubiquitous as a frame of war. As a consequence of advances in emergency medicine on the battlefield, soldiers have survived devastating injuries, often to face years of medical interventions, unrelenting pain, and uncertain futures (see Wool, *After War*).

50 The new humanitarianism was a baby of neoliberalism. As Eyal Weizman argues, MSF rode the "wave of Thatcherism and Reaganism," emerging in tandem with the retreat of the state and the rise of private actors taking over responsibilities the welfare state had previously assumed (Weizman, *The Least of All Possible Evils*, 41). By the 1990s, "compassionate conservatism" in the US had become the language for outsourcing to "local" private organizations, many of which were religious—which is to say, Christian (Lauren Gail Berlant, *Compassion: The Culture and Politics of an Emotion* (New York: Routledge, 2004, 3, 61–2).

51 As Fassin writes of humanitarian reason, "What counts is not that the event took place, but that it was felt" (Fassin, *Humanitarian Reason*, 208).

52 John W. Dower, *Cultures of War: Pearl Harbor, Hiroshima, 9/11, Iraq* (New York: W.W. Norton, 2010).

53 The literature on the new humanitarianism does not take up this question or historical moment explicitly, making it appear rather seamlessly incorporated into the broader 1970s through the end of the Cold War framework. See, for example, Weizman, *The Least of All Possible Evils*; Meister, *After Evil*; Fassin, *Humanitarian Reason*.

54 The need to develop both precision weapons and remote forms of warfare was one of the central "lessons" taken from the American war in Vietnam, as it became clear that too many American

casualties made wars unsustainable on the domestic front. See Bacevich, *The New American Militarism*; Paul N. Edwards, *The Closed World: Computers and the Politics of Discourse in Cold War America* (Cambridge, MA: MIT Press, 1996).

55  Bacevich, *The New American Militarism*, 160, 162. Emphasis in original.

56  Joseph Masco, *The Theater of Operations: National Security Affect From the Cold War to the War on Terror* (Durham, NC: Duke University Press, 2014), 1 (emphasis added). Masco traces the production of *anticipatory* fear by the post-9/11 anti-terror state, where "terror" points to ever-proliferating and indeterminate risks that can never be fully known or foreseen. To return to Bacevich's description of the new American militarism, "terror" must be stopped *before* actual aggression occurs.

57  See Meister, *After Evil*, ix.

58  Ticktin, *Casualties of Care*, 10.

59  Herman, *Trauma and Recovery*, 8 (emphasis added).

60  Mark Thompson, "The Other 1%," *Time Magazine,* November 21, 2011. See also Thomas Krasnican and Nick Paraiso, "Who Serves: Military Demographics in 2020," *Thank You For Your Service* podcast (February 12, 2020).

61  The one exception to the statistic about the racial makeup of the military holding closely to the racial makeup of the country is that African American women join the military at twice the rate of white women. The officer class, not surprisingly, is far more decidedly white. See Jennie W. Wenger, Caolionn O'Connell and Linda Cottrell, *Examination of Recent Deployment Experience Across the Services and Components* (Santa Monica: RAND Arroyo Center, 2018).

62  A general consensus exists on the left that the military draws disproportionately on impoverished and largely minority communities. The numbers do not bear that out. As Emma Moore explained to the hosts of the podcast *Thank You for Your Service*, the "stereotype of military recruitment coming from exclusively low-income populations" is not right. In part because a high school degree is required to join the military, recruits tend to come from the more middle range of household income. Of course, on the other side, the term "middle class" can muddy the analytic waters, absent recognition of how the middle class has been hollowed out in US society over the past several decades. In other words, it may remain a "class draft," even if it isn't drafting the nation's most impoverished groups. It is also clear, however,

that individuals sign up for complex reasons, finances being but one of them.

63  Thompson, "The Other 1%."

64  In Krasnican and Paraiso, "Who Serves."

65  Krasnican and Paraiso, "Who Serves."

66  David Zucchino and David S. Cloud, "Line of Duty." *Los Angeles Times*, May 24, 2015.

67  Krasnican and Paraiso, "Who Serves."

68  Amy Schafer, *Generations of War: The Rise of the Warrior Caste and the All-Volunteer Force* (Washington, DC: Center for a New American Security, May 2017).

69  Quoted in Thompson, "The Other 1%."

70  Krasnican and Paraiso, "Who Serves."

71  See Wenger, O'Connell and Cottrell, *Examination of Recent Deployment Experience Across the Services and Components*, 5.

72  Krasnican and Paraiso, "Who Serves."

73  Jennifer Mittelstadt, *The Rise of the Military Welfare State* (Cambridge, MA: Harvard University Press, 2015), 5.

74  Mittelstadt, *The Rise of the Military Welfare State*, 5, 8-9.

75  Bacevich, *The New American Militarism*, 108.

76  See Mittelstadt, *The Rise of the Military Welfare State*.

77  Bacevich, *The New American Militarism*, 235. See also MacLeish, *Making War At Fort Hood*; Wool, *After War*.

78  For every US soldier in Afghanistan, there has been about one private contractor. See Thompson, "The Other 1%." See also Peter Warren Singer, *Corporate Warriors: The Rise of the Privatized Military Industry* (Ithaca, NY: Cornell University Press, 2003); Naomi Klein, *The Shock Doctrine: The Rise of Disaster Capitalism* (New York: Metropolitan Books/Henry Holt, 2007); Mateo Taussig-Rubbo, "Outsourcing Sacrifice: The Labor of Private Military Contractors," *Yale Journal of Law & Humanities* 21: 1, 2009. See also, "The Lasting Consequences of America's Shift to Using More Contractors to Fight Wars," *All Things Considered*, NPR, December 2, 2021.

79  See Bacevich, *The New American Militarism*; Mittelstadt, *The Rise of the Military Welfare State*; Thompson, "The Other 1%."

80  Bacevich, *The New American Militarism*, 98.

81  For information on the organization, see wgy6.org.

82  Nick Paraiso and Sarah Claudy, "Supporting the Tropes: Hollywood & Our Military, " *Thank You For Your Service* podcast (April 2, 2019).

83  Annette Wieviorka, *The Era of the Witness,* trans. Jared Stark

(Ithaca, NY: Cornell University Press, 2006), 56, 70. Hannah Arendt was critical of the court's emphasis on first-person accounts, because for her it was an indication that Israeli prime minister David Ben Gurion thought it more important to stage an account of the Nazi genocide than to seek to enact justice. The first-person testimony, she argued, said nothing about Eichmann's guilt. See Hannah Arendt, *Eichmann in Jerusalem: A Report on the Banality of Evil* (New York: Penguin, 2006).

84 Wieviorka, *The Era of the Witness,* 88; see also chapter 3.

85 Weizman, *The Least of All Possible Evils,* 112.

86 See Robert Jay Lifton, *Death in Life: Survivors of Hiroshima* (New York: Random House, 1968); Henry Krystal, ed. *Massive Psychic Trauma* (New York: International Universities Press, 1969).

87 Wieviorka, *The Era of the Witness,* 127, 136. See also Robert Jay Lifton, *Witness to an Extreme Century: A Memoir* (New York: Free Press, 2011).

88 Note that in Hannah Arendt's account of the Eichmann trial, there is no reference to or discourse of trauma. She writes eloquently about survivors recounting their experiences providing a "history lesson," but she in no way assumes either that language is inadequate to express what they had been through or, more generally, that they were traumatized subjects. Nor is there any sense that testifying is therapeutic for the witness, unlike the understanding that would develop in the decades to come about the importance of victims recounting their encounters with violence —extreme or not (see, for example, Herman, *Trauma and Recovery*).

89 See Herman, *Trauma and Recovery*; Fassin and Rechtman, *The Empire of Trauma*. See also Hacking, *Rewriting the Soul.*

90 My concern in this book is with US society, but these tropes are hardly limited to the United States. See Wieviorka, *The Era of the Witness*; Adi Ophir, *The Order of Evils: Toward an Ontology of Morals* (New York: Zone Books, 2005). I also want to note that, interestingly, survivors of 9/11 did not emerge as "witnesses" or truth tellers, perhaps because the US cannot really fathom itself as a victimized nation.

91 See Paul Fussell, *The Great War and Modern Memory* (New York: Oxford University Press, 1975); Roy Scranton, *Total Mobilization: World War II and American Literature* (Chicago: The University of Chicago Press, 2019).

92 Roy Scranton, "The Trauma Hero. From Wilfred Owen to

"Redeployment" and "American Sniper," *the Los Angeles Review of Books,* January 25, 2015.

93  Scranton, *Total Mobilization,* 1–2.

94  See Fassin and Rechtman, *The Empire of Trauma*; Ticktin, *Casualties of Care.* See also Weizman, *The Least of All Possible Evils.*

95  Colla, "The Military-Literary Complex." See also Sinan Antoon, "Embedded Poetry: Iraq; Through a Soldier's Binoculars," *Jadaliyya,* June 11, 2014. Not all combatants enjoy this epistemological privilege, of course. Whether in Phil Klay's short story collection *Redeployment,* in *Yellow Birds* by Kevin Powers, or, for that matter, in television shows such as *Brothers and Sisters* or blockbuster films like *American Sniper* and *The Hurt Locker,* the *American* soldier—his experience, his point of view—is centered and validated.

96  On the politics of injury, see Wendy Brown, *States of Injury: Power and Freedom in Late Modernity* (Princeton, NJ: Princeton University Press, 1995). While many accounts of the civil-military divide focus on stereotypes of the soldier (for example, Wool, *After War*; Got Your 6, at wgy6.org; Ang Lee's film, *Billy Lynn's Long Halftime Walk*), as I show in the final chapter of this book, the American public—that is, those Americans referred to as "civilians"—are also stereotyped. I examine the pernicious political consequences of this second stereotype.

97  Ticktin, *Casualties of Care,* 73.

98  Catherine Lutz, *Homefront: A Military City and the American Twentieth Century* (Boston: Beacon Press, 2001), 238.

99  Certain comments made by Donald Trump, both before and during his presidency, could be argued to signify a decline in respect for soldiers and the military. For example, his purported comment that those who fought in World War II were "suckers" for having done so (Jeffrey Goldberg, "Trump: Americans Who Died in War Are 'Losers' and 'Suckers,'" *The Atlantic,* September 3, 2020). Verbal tantrums aside, however, Trump was enamored by (his own sense of) the military and tried to tether his legitimacy to the military and its might. Moreover, such apparently anti-military outbursts occasioned the rare moments when Democrats and Republicans, liberals and conservatives, agreed in joining together to condemn Trump's words. And the only time Republicans joined Democrats in opposing Trump on a piece of congressional legislation—and overrode his veto—was when Trump refused to sign the military appropriations bill, which included raises for military personnel.

## 1. Psychiatry as Radical Critique

1 Christian G. Appy, *American Reckoning: The Vietnam War and Our National Identity* (New York: Viking, 2015), 494.

2 See Didier Fassin and Richard Rechtman, *The Empire of Trauma: An Inquiry into the Condition of Victimhood,* trans. Rachel Gomme (Princeton, NJ: Princeton University Press, 2009); Allan Young, *The Harmony of Illusions: Inventing Post-Traumatic Stress Disorder* (Princeton, NJ: Princeton University Press, 1995); Ben Shephard, *A War of Nerves: Soldiers and Psychiatrists in the Twentieth Century* (Cambridge, MA: Harvard University Press, 2001); Wilbur J. Scott, *The Politics of Readjustment: Vietnam Veterans Since the War* (New York: Aldine de Gruyter, 1993); Eric T. Dean, *Shook Over Hell: Post-Traumatic Stress, Vietnam, and the Civil War* (Cambridge, MA: Harvard University Press, 1997).

3 Herb Kutchins and Stuart A. Kirk's history of PTSD is much closer to my reading, recognizing a notable shift between its initial articulation in terms of who would subsequently be diagnosed, most commonly, with PTSD. See Herb Kutchins and Stuart A. Kirk, *Making Us Crazy: DSM: The Psychiatric Bible and the Creation of Mental Disorders* (New York: The Free Press, 1997), 116.

4 On the concept of problem space, see David Scott, *Conscripts of Modernity: The Tragedy of Colonial Enlightenment* (Durham, NC: Duke University Press, 2004).

5 Nancy C. Andreasen, "Posttraumatic Stress Disorder: A History and a Critique," *Annals of the New York Academy of Sciences* 1208: 1, 2010, 68.

6 Andreasen, "Posttraumatic Stress Disorder: A History and a Critique," 68.

7 Charles R. Figley, ed. *Stress Disorders Among Vietnam Veterans: Theory, Research, and Treatment* (New York: Brunner/Mazel, 1978), xvi.

8 Abram Kardiner, *The Traumatic Neuroses of War* (Menasha, WI: George Banta Publishing Company, 1941).

9 Launched at the end of January 1968, the Tet Offensive refers to an attack against South Vietnamese troops and their US allies carried out by the Viet Cong and the North Vietnamese People's Army. The offensive marked a turning point for the American war in Vietnam, as, contrary to what the public had been led to believe, it became evident that the US was not winning the war.

10 See Figley, *Stress Disorders Among Vietnam Veterans*; Kutchins

and Kirk, *Making Us Crazy*, 107; Scott, *The Politics of Readjustment*, 297.

11 Fassin and Rechtman, *The Empire of Trauma*, 5, 78.

12 American Psychiatric Association, *DSM-III: Diagnostic and Statistical Manual of Mental Disorders* (Washington, DC: American Psychiatric Association, 1980), 236.

13 Fassin and Rechtman, *The Empire of Trauma*, 91.

14 Fassin and Rechtman, *The Empire of Trauma*, 92.

15 Young, *The Harmony of Illusions*, 114.

16 See especially Young, *The Harmony of Illusions*; Shephard, *A War of Nerves*; Fassin and Rechtman, *The Empire of Trauma*. In contrast to Young and Shephard, Fassin and Rechtman are far more cautious about the claim that Vietnam veterans were cast as victims (88–93). Nevertheless, given the broad genealogical account they develop in the book, in which the American war in Vietnam plays a small if crucial role, their analytical focus falls on what comes next—namely, the emergence of trauma as a condition of victimhood.

17 Harry R. Kormos, "The Nature of Combat Stress," in *Stress Disorders Among Vietnam Veterans: Theory, Research, and Treatment*, ed. Charles R. Figley (New York: Brunner/Mazel, 1978), 16.

18 See Hans Pols and Stephanie Oak, "War & Military Mental Health: The US Psychiatric Response in the 20th Century," *American Journal of Public Health* 97: 12, 2007; see also, Shephard, *A War of Nerves*. Thomas W. Salmon, medical director of the National Committee on Mental Hygiene, was sent to Britain and France in 1917 to study shell shock, after which he advocated for "forward treatment." He had concluded that soldiers suffering shell shock should be treated close to the front as a first line of response, rather than immediately removing them from the battlefields. Only those who did not recover quickly should be removed.

19 Kormos, "The Nature of Combat Stress," 17, 16. Tours of duty in Vietnam were generally limited to twelve months.

20 Figley, *Stress Disorders Among Vietnam Veterans*.

21 Kormos, "The Nature of Combat Stress," 21–2.

22 Patrick Hagopian, *The Vietnam War in American Memory: Veterans, Memorials, and the Politics of Healing* (Amherst: University of Massachusetts Press, 2009), 55.

23 Sarah A. Haley, "When the Patient Reports Atrocities: Specific Treatment Considerations of the Vietnam Veteran," *Archives of General Psychiatry* 30: 2, 1974.

24 Quoted in Wilbur J. Scott, "PTSD in DSM-III: A Case in the

Politics of Diagnosis and Disease," *Social Problems* 37: 3, 1990, 298.

25  Hagopian, *The Vietnam War in American Memory*, 56.

26  Nick Turse, *Kill Anything That Moves: The Real American War in Vietnam* (New York: Metropolitan Books/Henry Holt and Co., 2013).

27  Allan Young, "The Self-Traumatized Perpetrator as a 'Transient Mental Illness,'" *L'Évolution Psychiatrique*. 2002, 67 (4): 630–50, 639.

28  Shephard, *A War of Nerves*, 376.

29  See Hannah Arendt, *Eichmann in Jerusalem: A Report on the Banality of Evil* (New York: Penguin, 2006). On misreading Arendt, see Susan Neiman, *Evil in Modern Thought: An Alternative History of Philosophy* (Princeton, NJ: Princeton University Press, 2002).

30  See Scott, *The Politics of Readjustment*.

31  "Report to the United Presbyterian Church (Special Ministries) and to the Presbytery of New York City on the Status of Stress Disorders in the New APA's Diagnostic Classification," June 23, 1977. Chaim Shatan Papers, NYU Post-Doctoral Psychoanalytic Training Program Archives.

32  Many Vietnam veterans who presented with symptoms of psychological distress were diagnosed with other mental disorders —schizophrenia, personality disorders, depression, alcoholism —rather than with a war-related condition; see Hagopian, *The Vietnam War in American Memory*, 56; see also Sarah A. Haley, "Treatment Implications of Post-Combat Stress Response Syndromes for Mental Health Professionals," in *Stress Disorders Among Vietnam Veterans: Theory, Research, and Treatment*, ed. Charles R. Figley (New York: Routledge, 1978), 257.

33  The American Orthopsychiatric Organization was founded in 1924 by Karl Menninger. See apa.org. The original study group consisted of seven practitioners in addition to Shatan, including Lifton, Haley, Leonard Neff (of the VA in Los Angeles), and Jack Smith (a Marine veteran). See "TASK: A Study Group Has Been Commissioned by the American Orthopsychiatric Association to Research and Draft a Proposed Change in the APA's DSM under the New Major Classification 'XI-Stress Disorders,'" Shatan Papers, Psychoanalytic Archives.

34  See Andreasen, Nancy, A. S. Norris, and C. E. Hartford, "Incidence of Long-Term Psychiatric Complications in Severely Burned Adults," *Annals of Surgery*, 175, 5, 1971.

35  The working group was in conversation with Mardi Horowitz,

an expert on the physiology of stress, who was also a critic of the war (see Scott, *The Politics of Readjustment,* 306); and William G. Niederland, who developed the concept of "survivor syndrome"—an account of the psychological distress suffered by former inmates of Nazi concentration camps. See "TASK: A Study Group Has been Commissioned."

36  "Report to the United Presbyterian Church (Special Ministries) and to the Presbytery of New York City on the Status of Stress Disorders in the New APA Diagnostic Classification," June 23, 1977.

37  Nancy C. Andreasen, "Posttraumatic Stress Disorder: A History and a Critique," *Annals of the New York Academy of Sciences* 1208, no. 1 (2010)," 68–69. According to Andreasen, the other questions most important to the committee were, first, whether the syndrome should be diagnosed only in individuals "who were normal prior to experiencing the stress"; and second, how "the characteristic symptoms [should] be described and defined." Central to the latter was the issue of whether physical as well as psychological symptoms should be included for consideration. Andreasen, "Posttraumatic Stress Disorder: A History and a Critique," 69.

38  See Young, *The Harmony of Illusions*; Shephard, *A War of Nerves*; Fassin and Rechtman, *The Empire of Trauma*; Scott, *The Politics of Readjustment.*

39  See especially Fassin and Rechtman, *The Empire of Trauma.*

40  For example, in a letter to Robert Spitzer, Lawrence C. Kolb noted: "My other concern ... was that in statements as to the etiologic stresses, the most frequently encountered be stated first. Clearly, in modern industrial society, the automobile accidents are first. I would think that experiences such as rape are relatively infrequently encountered against those of the catastrophic reactions surrounding industrial experiences or accidents in the home" (June 3, 1977, APA archives). For many psychiatrists, traumatic stress reaction remained tethered to its origin, namely, the hazards of modern (industrial) life (see Fassin and Rechtman, *The Empire of Trauma*).

41  The books he recommended are Henry Krystal, ed. *Massive Psychic Trauma* (Madison, CT: International Universities Press, 1968); Paul Matussek, *Internment in Concentration Camps and Its Consequences* (New York: Springer-Verlag, 1975); and Terrence Des Prés, *The Survivor: An Anatomy of Life in Death Camps* (New York: Oxford University Press, 1976). See letter from Robert J. Lifton to Robert Spitzer, June 12, 1976 (APA Archives, DSM-III files).

42 "Report to the United Presbyterian Church (Special Ministries) and to the Presbytery of New York City on the Status of Stress Disorders in the New APA Diagnostic Classification," June 23, 1977. Shatan Papers, NYU Psychoanalytic Archives.

43 Vietnam Veterans Working Group, "Further Interim Proposal for Re-Integration of Combat and Other Catastrophic Stress Injuries (Traumatic War Neuroses, "TWN") into DSM-III. Memo #5." June 19, 1976. Shatan Papers, NYU Psychoanalytic Program, 5.

44 Document on DSM-III Proposals/Drafts, untitled (DSM File, Shatan Papers, NYU Psychoanalytic Program Files).

45 Andreasen, "Posttraumatic Stress Disorder: A History and a Critique," 69. Emphasis added.

46 Andreasen, "What is Post-Traumatic Stress Disorder," *Dialogues in Clinical Neuroscience* 13: 3, 2011.

47 "Final Report of VVWG," addressed to Dr. Marion Langer, General Director, American Orthopsychiatric Association, March 27, 1980. Shatan Papers, NYU Psychoanalytic Program.

48 "Preliminary Memorandum, 6/2/75," addressed to Dr. Marion Langer, Executive Director, American Orthopsychiatric Society. Shatan Papers, NYU Psychoanalytic Program.

49 "Further Interim Proposal for the Re-Integration of Combat and Other Catastrophic Stress Disorders ('Traumatic War Neuroses, TWN') into DSM-III," addressed to Dr. Marion Langer and Harold Visotsky, American Orthopsychiatric Association, and Robert J. Spitzer, APA Task Force, May 19, 1976. Shatan Papers, NYU Psychoanalytic Program.

50 In what follows, I engage at length with Lifton's thinking on the trauma of American troops. One of the key figures in defining of PTSD, he was also one of the most public spokespersons for and prolific writers on the phenomenon of post-Vietnam syndrome, initially named as such by Shatan. More broadly, Lifton has been an influential thinker on trauma in the wake of catastrophic violence. He figures prominently in scholarly accounts of the history of PTSD, and of theories of trauma more generally (see Cathy Caruth and Robert Jay Lifton, "Interview with Robert Jay Lifton," *American Imago* 48: 1, 1991; Fassin and Rechtman, *The Empire of Trauma*; Young, "The Self-Traumatized Perpetrator as a 'Transient Mental Illness'"; Ruth Leys, *From Guilt to Shame: Auschwitz and After* (Princeton: Princeton University Press, 2007); Scott, "PTSD in DSM-III: A Case in the Politics of Diagnosis and Disease").

51 Robert Jay Lifton, *Home From the War: Vietnam Veterans:*

*Neither Victims Nor Executioners* (New York: Simon and Schuster, 1973), 16.

52 On the political significance of how "rap groups" were structured, see Robert Jay Lifton, "Advocacy and Corruption in the Healing Profession," in *Stress Disorders Among Vietnam Veterans: Theory, Research, and Treatment*, ed. Charles R. Figley (New York: Brunner/Mazel, 1978).

53 Lifton, *Home from the War*, 40.

54 Casualties among Vietnamese were extraordinarily high. While US forces kept no records of civilian casualties during the war, postwar estimates reasonably reach about 3.8 million. Nick Turse argues in *Kill Anything That Moves* that the number of civilian casualties is only comprehensible if one recognizes that the brutality of the war was built into its very design. The sheer amount of munitions dropped on Vietnam between the Americans' formal entry into the war in 1965 and formal exit in 1973 is astonishing. Between 1965 and 1968, the US military dropped approximately thirty-two tons of bombs per hour on the north, even as, over time, most munitions were dropped on the south, for "the equivalent of 640 Hiroshima sized bombs" (2013: 79). The United States also unleashed an estimated 400,000 tons of napalm on Southeast Asia (2013, 83; see also the thread on the war in Vietnam in Sven Lindqvuist, *A History of Bombing* (New York: The New Press, 2001).

55 Lifton, *Death in Life: Survivors of Hiroshima,* 6, 480. Lifton ascribes this same experience of the grotesque to concentration camp survivors (480).

56 Caruth and Lifton, "Interview with Robert Jay Lifton," 161.

57 Lifton, *Death in Life: Survivors of Hiroshima,* 479, 491.

58 Robert Jay Lifton, "Psychological Effects of the Atomic Bomb in Hiroshima: The Theme of Death," *Daedalus* 92: 3, 1963, 438, 483.

59 Caruth and Lifton, "Interview with Robert Jay Lifton," 165. By the 1990s and early 2000s, Lifton's discourse partakes in a much broader cultural and political imaginary in which the history of memorializing the Holocaust is key. See, for example, Shoshana Felman and Dori Laub, *Testimony: Crises of Witnessing in Literature, Psychoanalysis, and History* (New York: Routledge, 1992). For a critical reading, see Annette Wieviorka, *The Era of the Witness,* trans. Jared Stark (Ithaca, NY: Cornell University Press, 2006).

60 Lifton, *Home from the War*, 43, 36-37.

61 Chaim F. Shatan, "Stress Disorders Among Vietnam Veterans: the

Emotional Content of Combat Continues, " in Charles R. Figley ed., *Stress Disorders Among Vietnam Veterans. Theory, Research, Treatment,* pp. 43-52, 49.

62  Lifton, *Home from the War,* 37.

63  *Home from the War,* 40–1.

64  Jean-Paul Sartre, *On Genocide* (London: Spokesman Books, Publishing House of Bertrand Russel Foundation, 1968), 11, 14, 15.

65  Sartre, *On Genocide,* 21. Emphasis in original.

66  Sartre, *On Genocide,* 11, 15, 21, Emphasis in original.

67  Lifton *Home from the War,* 41, 42.

68  Lifton, *Death in Life,* 5. Lifton was critical of Freud's "historical model," which he considered mythical rather than historical. "If repetition is *the* historical experience, and becomes direct psychological repetition of the individual then there is no history ... And if the individual and the collectivity are indistinguishable and there is no way that historical experience differs from psychological experience ... then in another sense there is no history" (New York Public Library, Robert J. Lifton Papers, Box 770, August 27, 1969).

69  Robert J. Lifton Papers, Box 77.

70  Robert J. Lifton Papers, Box 00765b.

71  Lifton, *Home from the War,* 39.

72  Chaim F. Shatan, "Happiness is a Warm Gun: Militarized Mourning and Ceremonial Vengeance: Toward a Psychological Theory of Combat and Manhood in America," *Studies in Gender and Sexuality* 21: 3, 2020.

73  Frantz Fanon, *The Wretched of the Earth* (New York: Grove Press, 1963).

74  Andrew E. Hunt, *The Turning: A History of Vietnam Veterans Against the War* (New York: New York University Press, 1999), 2, 3.

75  Hunt, *The Turning,* 55, 69, 70.

76  Hagopian, *The Vietnam War in American Memory,* 50, 53.

77  Albert Camus, *Neither Victims nor Executioners* (Eugene, OR: Wipf and Stock Publishers, 2007). (This was a series of essays originally published by *Combat,* the newspaper of the French Resistance, in 1946.) In the aftermath of World War II and at the dawn of the nuclear era, Camus argued that we must all *choose* to be neither victims nor executioners—we must choose to fight for a "relative utopia" rather than risk the destruction of the world.

78  Hagopian, *The Vietnam War in American Memory,* 53. Lifton's position on legal responsibility was not so cut and dried: "These

men are culpable in a moral and legal sense: They did kill people, often civilians. But they are certainly less culpable than their leaders, the generals and the presidents who created ... the atrocity-producing situation in which it is the norm to kill. [The veterans] had to balance themselves between the atrocity-producing situation and their own *struggle for* a sense of responsibility" (Leslie H. Farber and Robert Jay Lifton, "Questions of Guilt," *Partisan Review* 39: 4, 1972, 518. Emphasis added).

79  Hagopian, *The Vietnam War in American Memory*, 53 (emphasis added).

80  Lifton, "Advocacy and Corruption in the Healing Profession," 212; see also Scott, *The Politics of Readjustment*, 17–18.

81  See Hagopian, *The Vietnam War in American Memory*, 55; Hunt, *The Turning*.

82  Hagopian, *The Vietnam War in American Memory*, 55. According to Hagopian, clinicians' and researchers' political positions on the war often mapped directly onto their position on the reality of combat trauma.

83  See Lifton, *Home from the War*.

84  William G. Niederland, "The Survivor Syndrome: Further Observations and Dimensions," *Journal of the American Psychoanalytic Association* 29: 2, 1981.

85  Leys, *From Guilt to Shame*, 5 (emphasis in original).

86  See Krystal, *Massive Psychic Trauma*; see also Leys, *From Guilt to Shame*. By the late 1960s, the concept of survivor guilt had come under attack for its purported implication that survivors were complicit in Nazi crimes. Instead, they were recast in the language of innocence. See Des Prés, *The Survivor*.

87  In addition to Shatan, "Stress Disorders Among Vietnam Veterans," see also Haley, "When the Patient Reports Atrocities."

88  The confrontation with death and what he referred to as "death imagery" (Robert J. Lifton Papers, Box 00765b) is *the* central axis in Lifton's theorization of not just psychic trauma, but trauma of the human psychic economy. For a discussion, see Leys, *From Guilt to Shame*, 49–50.

89  "Responses to VVWG Questionnaire of February 13, 1976." Shatan Papers, NYU Psychoanalytic Program.

90  Martin Buber, "Guilt and Guilt Feeling," *CrossCurrents* 8: 3, 1958, 117.

91  Mardi J. Horowitz and George F. Solomon, "Delayed Stress Response Syndromes in Vietnam Veterans," in *Stress Disorders Among Vietnam Veterans: Theory, Research, and Treatment*, ed. Charles R. Figley (New York: Brunner/Mazel, 1978), 279.

92  Quoted in Haley, "When the Patient Reports Atrocities," 192.

93  Arthur Egendorf, "Vietnam Veteran Rap Groups and Themes of Postwar Life," *Journal of Social Issues* 31, 4, 1975, 120–1. Not everyone was willing to acknowledge their "own complicity." A veteran who stopped by the group insisted, "They had me brainwashed ... I was a machine. A machine can't be guilty." The group seems not to have accepted the man's reasoning, however, and he never returned.

94  Horowitz and Solomon, "Delayed Stress Response Syndromes in Vietnam Veterans," 279.

95  Farber and Lifton, "Questions of Guilt," 517. Lifton also references Karl Jaspers' attempt to sort through the different kinds of guilt that postwar Germans held for the crimes of Nazi Germany. Following Jaspers, Lifton called on all Americans to "recover the idea of guilt as the anxiety of responsibility" (Farber and Lifton, "Questions of Guilt," 519). See Karl Jaspers, *The Question of German Guilt* (New York: Capricorn Books, 1961).

96  Leys, *From Guilt to Shame*, 53.

97  Chaim F. Shatan, "The Grief of Soldiers: Vietnam Combat Veterans' Self-Help Movement," *American Journal of Orthopsychiatry* 43: 4, 1973, 649.

98  "Further Interim Proposal for the Re-Integration of Combat and Other Catastrophic Stress Disorders ('Traumatic War Neuroses, TWN') into DSM-III," addressed to Dr. Marion Langer and Harold Visotsky, American Orthopsychiatric Association, and Robert J. Spitzer, APA Task Force. May 19, 1976. Shatan Papers, NYU Psychoanalytic Program.

99  Buber, "Guilt and Guilt Feeling," 116.

100 Horowitz and Solomon, "Delayed Stress Response Syndromes in Vietnam Veterans," 280.

101 "Final Report of the VVWG." Chaim Shatan Papers.

102 T.M. Luhrmann, *Of Two Minds: An Anthropologist Looks at American Psychiatry* (New York: Vintage Books, 2001), 214.

103 Dagmar Herzog, *Cold War Freud: Psychoanalysis in an Age of Catastrophes* (Cambridge: Cambridge University Press, 2017), 5.

104 Luhrmann, *Of Two Minds*, 225.

105 In the early 1970s, Congress deeply distrusted the National Institute of Mental Health—in 1976 the dollar amount of funding for the institute was lower than it had been in 1969—because there seemed to be no way of distinguishing mental health from mental illness. One of messages from Congress was: "show us that you are doing real research, and we will fund you" (Luhrmann, *Of Two Minds*, 237).

106 See Luhrmann, *Of Two Minds*. See also Kutchins and Kirk, *Making Us Crazy*.

107 Leys, *From Guilt to Shame*, 15.

108 The architects of the DSM-III borrowed from the language of the laboratory sciences, and the replicability of diagnosis was one of the problems they meant to address. Practitioners giving the same patient different diagnoses on a regular basis was no way for a medical profession to behave, they insisted. For a discussion of the work of standardizing PTSD diagnoses, see Young, *The Harmony of Illusions*.

## 2. The Politics of Victimization

1 Ann Wolbert Burgess and Lynda Lytle Holmstrom, "Rape Trauma Syndrome," *American Journal of Psychiatry* 131: 9, 1974, 981.

2 Burgess and Holmstrom, "Rape Trauma Syndrome," 982, 983 (emphasis added).

3 Burgess and Holmstrom drew on the work of psychiatrists such as Elizabeth Kubler-Ross and Daniel A. Hamburg, who studied how individuals face death. See Elizabeth Kubler-Ross, "On Death and Dying," *JAMA*, 1972, 221; Daniel A. Hamburg, "A Perspective on Coping Behavior," *Archives of General Psychiatry*, 1967, 17.

4 Ann Wolbert Burgess, "Rape Trauma Syndrome," *Behavioral Sciences & the Law* 1: 3, 1983, 99.

5 Burgess, "Rape Trauma Syndrome," 99 (emphasis added).

6 See, for example, Menachem Amir, "Victim Precipitated Forcible Rape," *Journal of Criminal Law, Criminology, and Police Science* 58: 4, 1967. For a critical reconsideration of the field, see D. Miers, "Positivist Victimology: a Critique," *International Review of Victimology*, 1989.

7 Miriam Ticktin, "A World Without Innocence," *American Ethnologist*, 44, 4, 2017, 589.

8 Jackie Wang, "Against Innocence: Race, Gender, and the Politics of Safety," *Lies: A Journal of Materialist Feminism* 1, 2012, 153.

9 Georgina Hickey, "From Civility to Self-Defense: Modern Advice to Women on the Privileges and Dangers of Public Space," *Women's Studies Quarterly* 39: 1/2, 2011, 55, 86.

10 Hickey, "From Civility to Self-Defense," 89.

11 See Wendy Brown, *States of Injury: Power and Freedom in Late Modernity* (Princeton, NJ: Princeton University Press, 1995).

12 Susan Brownmiller, *Against Our Will: Men, Women and Rape*

(New York: Bantam Books, 1976), 1, 392-3. See also her Chapter 11.

13 Alice Echols, *Daring to be Bad: Radical Feminism in America, 1967–1975* (Minneapolis: University of Minnesota Press, 1989).

14 Judith Lewis Herman, *Father-Daughter Incest* (Cambridge, MA: Harvard University Press, [1981] 2000), 16, 4.

15 This kind of denial sometimes persisted even in the face of physical evidence, including venereal disease. See Herman, *Father-Daughter Incest*, 11; Florence Rush, *The Best Kept Secret: Sexual Abuse of Children* (New York: McGraw-Hill, 1981); Brownmiller, *Against Our Will*. As is well known, for feminist psychiatrists like Herman, Freud's disavowal of the seduction theory loomed large in any explanation of this disbelief. She also singles out John Henry Wigmore's *Treatise on Evidence* (1934), which established "a doctrine impeaching the credibility of any female, especially a child, who complained of a sex offense," and argued that, although decades old, "his assertions still retain great prestige and influence in the courtroom" (*Father-Daughter Incest*, 11).

16 Herman, *Father-Daughter Incest*; Rush, *The Best Kept Secret: Sexual Abuse of Children*; Eileen Bass, *The Courage to Heal: A Guide for Women Survivors of Child Sexual Abuse* (New York: Harper and Row, 1988).

17 Judith Lewis Herman, "Father-Daughter Incest," in *Post-Traumatic Therapy and Victims of Violence*, ed. Frank Ochberg (New York: Brunner/Mazel, 1988), 185.

18 The genealogy of this ethics to believe "the witness" is rooted in the history of Holocaust and its memorialization. See Annette Wieviorka, *The Era of the Witness*, trans. Jared Stark (Ithaca, NY: Cornell University Press, 2006). On secrets and the need for public witnessing and recognition of the prevalence of sexual assault, see Judith Lewis Herman, *Trauma and Recovery* (New York: Basic Books, 1992).

19 Herman, *Father-Daughter Incest*, 177.

20 Ruth Leys, *Trauma: A Genealogy* (Chicago: University of Chicago Press, 2000), 249.

21 Dagmar Herzog, *Cold War Freud: Psychoanalysis in an Age of Catastrophes* (Cambridge: Cambridge University Press, 2017), 92. Leys, *Trauma*, 110–11.

22 Herman, *Father-Daughter Incest*, 168, 169. See also Rush, *The Best Kept Secret: Sexual Abuse of Children*. I think Leys misreads Judith Herman's early work in significant measure. She incorporates Herman's early writings seamlessly within the ethical

commitments of post-structuralist trauma and post-historicist feminist theorists, such as Cathy Caruth and Eve Sedgwick (see Leys 2000, 2007). As a consequence, Leys collapses a struggle that began in the 1970s, when rape and incest were barely recognized or prosecuted as crimes, into the political and theoretical imaginary of an identity politics better dated to the late 1980s and the decades to come. Feminists in the 1970s did not embrace "victimhood" or identity politics. Nor was "witnessing"—and its relationship to truth—primarily framed as an ethical value or a virtue *in its own right*. Herman certainly comes to articulate that position by her later book, *Trauma and Recovery* (1992), but in her earlier work, as was true of other feminist activists focused on sexual assault in the 1970s and well into the 1980s, the demand that women's and girls' testimonies to having been raped be believed was rooted in a struggle to have crimes acknowledged at a moment when doing so required a radical epistemological turn with profound legal consequences.

23  See Fassin and Rechtman, *The Empire of Trauma*.

24  Alfred C. Kinsey et al., *Sexual Behavior in the Human Female* (Philadelphia: Saunders, 1953).

25  Ian Hacking, *Rewriting the Soul: Multiple Personality and the Sciences of Memory* (Princeton, NJ: Princeton University Press, 1995), 63.

26  Quoted in Brownmiller, *Against Our Will,* 307.

27  Herman, *Father-Daughter Incest,* 23, 26.

28  Herman, *Father-Daughter Incest,* 28, 99, 93, 189. See also Brownmiller, *Against Our Will,* 309.

29  Undated memo, Allan Burstein, MD. APA Archives, DSM-III and DSM-IIIR files.

30  Letter from Richard P. Kluft to Robert Spitzer, August 29, 1985, APA Archives, DSM-III and DSM-IIIR files.

31  For a critical read of the rise MPD and the politics of memory, see Ian Hacking, *Rewriting the Soul.*

32  Robert Spitzer consulted two advisory groups regarding revisions to PTSD, the Advisory Committee on Post-Traumatic Stress Disorder and the Advisory Group on Dissociative Disorders. Like PTSD, MPD, classified as a dissociative disorder, was introduced as a diagnostic category in the DSM-III. For a detailed account of the rise of MPD, and national hysteria over child sexual abuse, see Hacking, *Rewriting the Soul.*

33  Memo: PTSD Definition, R.M. Atkinson, October 1984, APA Archives, DSM-III and DSM-IIIR files.

34  Form Letter from William E. Schlenger, PhD. Call for answers to

questions, October 3, 1984. APA Archives, DSM-III and DSM-IIIR files.

35 Emphasis added.

36 Steven M. Silver letter to Schlenger, no date. APA Archives, DSM-III and DSM-IIIR files.

37 Memo: PTSD Definition, R.M. Atkinson, 10/84.

38 Memo to Ad Hoc Consultants on PTSD, from Mimi Gibbon 11/7/84.

39 See Ruth Leys, *From Guilt to Shame: Auschwitz and After* (Princeton: Princeton University Press, 2007).

40 Letter from David Spiegel to Robert Spitzer, June 6, 1985. APA Archives, DSM-III and DSM-IIIR files.

41 Burgess and Holmstrom, "Rape Trauma Syndrome," 982; Association, *DSM-IV: Diagnostic and Statistical Manual of Mental Disorders*, 116.

42 The other possible causes are sexual or physical assault, transportation crashes in which others were killed, natural disasters, and the death of one's child during childhood or adolescence. Letter from David W. Goy, October 19, 1984. APA Archives, DSM-III and DSM-IIIR files.

43 Ochberg, "Post-Traumatic Therapy and Victims of Violence," in *Post-Traumatic Therapy and Victims of Violence*, ed. Frank M. Ochberg (New York: Brunner/Mazel, 1988), 3, 18..

44 President's Task Force on Victims of Crime, *Final Report*, December 1982.

45 Marlene Young and John Stein, "The History of the Crime Victims' Movement in the United States: A Component of the Office for Victims of Crime Oral History Project" (Dec. 2004), ncjrs.gov.

46 Marlene A. Young, "The Crime Victims' Movement," in *Post-Traumatic Therapy and Victims of Violence*, ed. Frank M. Ochberg (New York: Brunner/Mazel, 1988).

47 See Young and Stein, "The History of the Crime Victims' Movement in the United States." See also Young, "The Crime Victims' Movement."

48 President's Task Force on Victims of Crime (PTF) 1982, vi.

49 Quoted in Loïc Wacquant, "The Great Penal Leap Backward," *The New Punitiveness: Trends, Theories, Perspectives,* ed. John Pratt et al. (Portland, OR: Willen Publications, 2005), 13.

50 Wacquant, "The Great Penal Leap Backward," 13, 12. See also Michelle Alexander, *The New Jim Crow: Mass Incarceration in the Age of Colorblindness* (New York: New Press, 2010); Elizabeth Kai Hinton, *From the War on Poverty to the War on Crime:*

The Making of Mass Incarceration in America (Cambridge, MA: Harvard University Press, 2016).

51  Alexander, *The New Jim Crow*, 40.

52  Hinton, *From the War on Poverty to the War on Crime*, 8, 2, 6.

53  Alexander, *The New Jim Crow*, 40–1.

54  Quoted in Alexander, *The New Jim Crow*, 41.

55  For a critical reading of crime statistics (in the making), see Jean and John C. Comaroff, *The Truth About Crime. Sovereignty, Knowledge, Social Order* (Chicago: the University of Chicago Press, 2016), especially Chapter 2.3.

56  Alexander, *The New Jim Crow*, 42-43.

57  Hinton, *From the War on Poverty to the War on Crime*, 12, 16.

58  Cited in Alexander, *The New Jim Crow*, 46.

59  Alexander, *The New Jim Crow*, 46.

60  Lepore does not grapple with the racial politics of the movement, but she does tease out this second important thread. Jill Lepore, "Sirens in the Night," *New Yorker*, May 21, 2018, 50.

61  Hinton, *From the War on Poverty to the War on Crime*, 308.

62  Alexander, *The New Jim Crow*, 48.

63  Hinton, *From the War on Poverty to the War on Crime*, 308.

64  As Michelle Alexander points out, Reagan's War on Drugs was launched in 1982, which was three years *before* crack cocaine hit the streets of US cities (*The New Jim Crow*, 49).

65  Alexander, *The New Jim Crow*, 49.

66  *Final Report of the President's Task Force on Victims of Crime*, vii.

67  *Final Report of the President's Task Force on Victims of Crime*, 2.

68  *Final Report of the President's Task Force on Victims of Crime*, 2–3.

69  *Final Report of the President's Task Force on Victims of Crime*, 17-18, 58. While not as successful at the federal level, by 1990 a Victims' Bill of Rights had been adopted in all states, and as of 2004 thirty-two states had adopted constitutional amendments (see Young and Stein, "The History of the Crime Victims' Movement in the United States").

70  *Final Report of the President's Task Force on Victims of Crime*, 58.

71  Young and Stein argue that "there is little doubt that the women's movement was central to the development of a victims' movement. Their leaders saw sexual assault and domestic violence —and the poor response of the criminal justice system—as potent illustrations of a woman's lack of status, power, and influence"

(Young and Stein, "The History of the Crime Victims' Movement in the United States"). See also Young, "The Crime Victims' Movement."

72 Young and Stein, "The History of the Crime Victims' Movement in the United States."

73 Young, "The Crime Victims' Movement," 319.

74 Young and Stein, "The History of the Crime Victims' Movement in the United States."

75 Lepore, "Sirens in the Night," 50.

76 Young and Stein, "The History of the Crime Victims' Movement in the United States."

77 Fassin and Rechtman, *The Empire of Trauma*, Chapter 5.

78 Frank M. Ochberg, ed. *Post-Traumatic Therapy and Victims of Violence* (New York: Brunner/Mazel, 1988).

79 Ochberg, "The Victim of War and Atrocity," in *Post Traumatic Therapy and Victims of Violence*, 225–6.

80 John P. Wilson, "Understanding the Vietnam Veteran," in *Post-Traumatic Therapy and Victims of Violence*, 227, 226, 228.

81 Herman, *Trauma and Recovery*, 3. Herman's analytic approach relies on a sharp distinction between victims, perpetrators, and bystanders, and yet she never engages the role of Vietnam veterans as perpetrators; she thus leaves the impression that they too are easily classified as victims. That ambiguity stands in stark contrast to her placing of "militiamen" of other movements/countries definitively in the category of perpetrator and to her mention rape as a "tool of warfare in many parts of the world" (237).

82 See Eric T. Dean, *Shook Over Hell: Post-Traumatic Stress, Vietnam, and the Civil War* (Cambridge, MA: Harvard University Press, 1997), 12, 19.

83 Patrick Hagopian, *The Vietnam War in American Memory: Veterans, Memorials, and the Politics of Healing* (Amherst: University of Massachusetts Press, 2009), 79.

84 Christian G. Appy, *American Reckoning: The Vietnam War and Our National Identity* (New York: Viking, 2015), 27. See also Andrew Bacevich, *The New American Militarism: How Americans Are Seduced by War* (New York: Oxford University Press, 2005), Chapter 3.

85 See Bacevich, *The New American Militarism*; Dean, *Shook Over Hell*; Hagopian, *The Vietnam War in American Memory*.

86 Dean, *Shook Over Hell*, 184. Dean's interest is in making it possible for the United States to use its military power overseas, and he is wary of the ways in which even the conservative 1980s discourse, which tries to reconstruct the war and its veterans, fails.

87 Kathleen Belew, *Bring the War Home: The White Power Movement and Paramilitary America* (Cambridge, MA: Harvard University Press, 2018), 23.

88 Bacevich, *The New American Militarism,* 39. See also Hagopian, *The Vietnam War in American Memory.*

89 Dean, *Shook over Hell,* 20.

90 Richard A. Kulka, et al., "National Vietnam Veterans Readjustment Study" (July 14, 1988), 1–2.

91 Hagopian, *The Vietnam War in American Memory,* 70–71. The Veterans' Outreach program was first proposed in 1970 and signed into law by President Carter in 1979; see Arthur Egendorf, *Healing From the War: Trauma and Transformation After Vietnam* (Boston: Houghton Mifflin, 1985), 31.

92 Hagopian, *The Vietnam War in American Memory,* 71–3.

93 Hagopian, *The Vietnam War in American Memory,* 49.

94 Hagopian, *The Vietnam War in American Memory,* 49.

95 Appy, *American Reckoning,* 28 (emphasis added).

96 Jerry Lembcke, *The Spitting Image: Myth, Memory, and the Legacy of Vietnam* (New York: New York University Press, 1998), 10.

97 Hagopian, *The Vietnam War in American Memory,* 63. Hagopian himself, while critical in almost every other way of the conservative reconstruction of the war, seems to accept that explanation at face value.

98 Seymour Leventman, "Epilogue: Social and Historical Perspectives on the Vietnam Veteran," in *Stress Disorders Among Vietnam Veterans: Theory, Research, and Treatment,* ed. Charles R. Figley (New York: Brunner/Mazel, 1978), 295.

99 Egendorf, *Healing From the War,* 29.

100 On the reconstruction of the US military and the investment in (social service programs for) its personnel, see Bacevich, *The New American Militarism*; Jennifer Mittelstadt, *The Rise of the Military Welfare State* (Cambridge, MA: Harvard University Press, 2015).

## 3. Soldier's Trauma, Revisited

1 The Institute of Medicine, *Treatment for Posttraumatic Stress Disorder in Military and Veteran Populations: Final Assessment* (Washington, DC: National Academies Press, 2014), 1.

2 John W. Dower, *Cultures of War: Pearl Harbor, Hiroshima, 9/11, Iraq* (New York: W.W. Norton, 2010).

3   Strong Star Combat PTSD Conference in San Antonio (October 2018). Conference notes by author.

4   Rajeev Ramchand et al., "Prevalence of PTSD, Depression, and TBI Among Returning Servicemembers," in *Invisible Wounds of War: Psychological and Cognitive Injuries, Their Consequences, and Services to Assist Recovery*, ed. Terri Tanielian and Lisa H. Jaycox (Santa Monica, CA: RAND Corporation, 2008), 42. Since 2003, the MHAT has returned to Iraq and/or Afghanistan and produced an annual report. Initially chartered by the US Army Surgeon General, the early reports focused on the status of Army brigade combat teams in Iraq. The Army carried the heaviest burden in terms of troops deployed. Over time, the role of the Marines increased substantially, and as such, by MHAT's fifth report (2008), it incorporated data on Marines. MHAT VII was a joint project of the various branches of the US military.

5   Terri Tanielian, and Lisa H. Jaycox, eds. *Invisible Wounds of War: Psychological and Cognitive Injuries, Their Consequences, and Services to Assist Recovery* (Santa Monica, CA: RAND Corporation, 2008), iii.

6   The fact that the Army was planning, largely, for a war with the Soviet Union on the European front, and in particular, in imagining future military psychiatric casualties, is striking given the revitalization of counterinsurgency warfare, if often "in secret" in Central America, and the centrality of such warfare to the Reagan era reconstruction of US global power. See, for example, *The New American Militarism: How Americans Are Seduced by War* (New York: Oxford University Press, 2005).

7   David Kieran, *Signature Wounds: The Untold Story of the Military's Mental Health Crisis* (New York: New York University Press, 2019), 21, 23–4.

8   Kieran, *Signature Wounds*, 25, 41, 33–4.

9   The report predicted traumatic brain injury (TBI) would become increasingly common, given that improvised explosive devices (IEDs) were an insurgent weapon of choice. TBI is understood to be an injury to the brain produced by shock waves from large explosions, in some quarters, reviving discussion of the World War I diagnostic category "shell shock." See Erin Finley, *Fields of Combat: Understanding PTSD Among Veterans of Iraq and Afghanistan* (Ithaca: Cornell University Press, 2011), 98.

10  Tanielian and Jaycox, *Invisible Wounds of War*, xix, 3. In Iraq, one fatality occurred for every nine wounded military personnel. In Vietnam, the relationship was 1 to 2.4 and during the Second

World War, 1 to 3; see Jerry M. Sollinger, Gail Fisher, and Karen Metscher, "The Wars in Afghanistan and Iraq—An Overview," in *Invisible Wounds of War: Summary and Recommendations for Addressing Psychological and Cognitive Injuries*, ed. Terri Tanielian, and Lisa H. Jaycox (Santa Monica, CA: RAND Corporation, 2008), 25–6.

11 Tanielian, and Jaycox, *Invisible Wounds of War*, xix. According to Erin Finley, as of 2010, whereas approximately 30,000 American troops had been wounded in action, almost 120,000 had been diagnosed with PTSD (Finley, *Fields of Combat*, 2).

12 Sollinger, Fisher, and Metscher, "The Wars in Afghanistan and Iraq," 21.

13 Niall McCarthy, "2.77 Million Service Members Have Served on 5.4 Million Deployments Since 9/11." *Forbes*, March 20, 2018. During the American war in Vietnam, approximately 3.4 million troops deployed to Southeast Asia, about one-third of them draftees (Sollinger, Fisher, and Metscher, "The Wars in Afghanistan and Iraq," 21).

14 Sollinger, Fisher and Metscher, "The Wars in Afghanistan and Iraq," 22.

15 Acute stress" (or "acute stress disorder") refers to what can be understood as "short-term" PTSD, first introduced in the DSM-IV. A PTSD diagnosis, according to the DSM-IV, calls for symptoms to have been exhibited for over three months. In the DSM-5, the distinction between "acute" and "chronic" is abandoned, with diagnosis requiring PTSD symptoms to have lasted at least one month. See *Diagnostic and Statistical Manual of Mental Disorders V* (Washington DC: American Psychiatric Association, 2013), 271–72.

16 Mental Health Advisory Team, *Operation Iraqi Freedom 06-08* (Office of the Surgeon Multi-National Force-Iraq and Office of The Surgeon General United States Army Medical Command, February 14, 2008), 46. As the American "War on Terror" has extended in time and across space, more of the fighting is being done by special operations troops. By 2018, many of those troops were on as much as their fourteenth deployment. (See Nick Turse, "The Generations Lost to America's Infinite War." *The Nation*, August 6, 2018.) If the reigning assumptions about mental health in relation to increased deployments is correct, there is a serious mental health crisis looming among special-ops troops.

17 Kieran, *Signature Wounds*, 3.

18 Mental Health Advisory Team, *Operation Iraqi Freedom 06-08*, 41, 34, 42. Army deployments increased from twelve months

in 2006 to fifteen months in 2007. The MHAT V report found that 60.8 percent of soldiers reported very high concern about deployment lengths, the second most common concern being separation from family (Mental Health Advisory Team, *Operation Iraqi Freedom 06-08*, 40).

19  Ramchand, "Prevalence of PTSD, Depression, and TBI Among Returning Servicemembers," 51 (emphasis in original).

20  Mental Health Advisory Team, *Operation Iraqi Freedom 06-08*, 14, 4.

21  Charles W. Hoge et al., "Transformation of Mental Health Care for US Soldiers and Families during the Iraq and Afghanistan Wars: Where Science and Politics Intersect," *American Journal of Psychiatry* 173: 4, 2016, 334.

22  Other studies reported somewhat smaller failure rates—for example, 23–40 percent of personnel had not received treatment over the past year (cited in Tanielian, "Introduction," 7). As others have argued, given the financial burden on the federal government from long-term disability entitlements for soldiers diagnosed with PTSD, it perhaps is not surprising that efforts to discourage such diagnoses and even to revoke them have been well documented (see, for example, Hal Bernton, "40% of PTSD Diagnoses At Madigan Were Reversed." *Seattle Times*, March 20, 2012; Mark Benjamin and Michael de Yoanna, "I Am Under a Lot of Pressure to Not Diagnose PTSD." *Salon*, April 8, 2009; Finley, *Fields of Combat*, 128).

23  Tanielian and Jaycox, *Invisible Wounds of War*, xxvii.

24  Finley, *Fields of Combat*, 122.

25  Tanya Luhrmann, *Of Two Minds: An Anthropologist Looks at American Psychiatry* (New York: Vintage Books, 2000), 238.

26  American Psychological Association Presidential Taskforce on Evidence-Based Protocols, "Evidence-Based Practice in Psychology," *American Psychologist* 61: 4, 271, 272.

27  See https://www.ciap.health.nsw.gov.au.

28  Luhrmann, *Of Two Minds*, 207-208.

29  United States Government Accountability Office, *Report to the Ranking Member, Subcommittee on Health, Committee on Veterans' Affairs, House of Representatives: VA Spends Millions on Post-Traumatic Stress Disorder Research and Incorporates Research Outcomes Into Guidelines and Policy for Post-Traumatic Stress Disorder Services* (January 2011), 2.

30  Government Accountability Office, *Report on Veterans' Affairs*, 2.

31  The Management of Post-Traumatic Stress Working Group, *VA/DoD Clinical Practice Guideline for the Management of*

Post-Traumatic Stress (Department of Veterans Affairs and Department of Defense, October 2010), 3.

32  Government Accountability Office, *Report on Veterans' Affairs*, 2–3.

33  Hoge, "Transformation of Mental Health Care for US Soldiers and Families during the Iraq and Afghanistan Wars," 342. See Institute of Medicine, *Treatment for Posttraumatic Stress Disorder in Military and Veteran Populations*, for example; see also Hoge, "Transformation of Mental Health Care" for an account of the efforts the Army has made over the last decade or more to produce a more standardized and organized mental health care system.

34  Finley, *Fields of Combat*, 123.

35  J. Morris, *The Evil Hours: A Biography of Post-Traumatic Stress Disorder* (Boston: Houghton Mifflin Harcourt, 2015), 177.

36  Charles W. Hoge and Kathleen M. Chard, "A Window Into the Evolution of Trauma-Focused Psychotherapies for Posttraumatic Stress Disorder," *JAMA* 319: 4, 2018, 344.

37  Quoted in Morris, *The Evil Hours*, 199.

38  See "PTSD," mentalhealth.va.gov.

39  Morris, *The Evil Hours*, 200.

40  *VA/DoD Clinical Practice Guideline for the Management of Post-Traumatic Stress*, 120. See also Government Accountability Office, *Report on Veterans' Affairs*, 22.

41  *VA/DoD Clinical Practice Guideline for the Management of Post-Traumatic Stress*, 2004: I-21–22. On development of CPT for rape victims, see Patricia A. Resick and Monica Schnicke, *Cognitive Processing Therapy for Rape Victims: A Treatment Manual* (Newbury Park, CA: Sage, 1996).

42  Finley, *Fields of Combat*, 120-121, 120.

43  Finley, *Fields of Combat*, 122.

44  Government Accountability Office, *Report on Veterans' Affairs*, 23. Lest it seem that treatments for PTSD and other mental health disorders among troops and veterans were limited to cognitive behavioral therapies, according to an internal report by the Defense Department's Pharmaco-Economic Center in San Antonio, in 2010 approximately 20 percent of active-duty troops surveyed were taking psychotropic drugs—antidepressants, antipsychotics, sedative hypnotics, or other controlled substances. Estimates of the cost of medicating troops and veterans between 2001 and 2011 were enormous: the VA spent approximately $1.5 billion on just two antipsychotic medications, and the Department of Defense, $90 million. See van der Kolk, *The*

*Body Keeps Score*, 224, 227. Over time, other possible first-line treatments were added: by 2017, VA/DoD clinical guidelines had elevated eye movement desensitization and reprocessing (EMDR) to the list of highly recommended cognitive therapies. See Jessica Hamblin, *The 2017 Revised Clinical Guidelines for PTSD: Guidelines for Psychotherapy* (National Center for PTSD, 2017).

45  See Linda J. Bilmes, "The Long-Term Costs of United States Care for Veterans of the Afghanistan and Iraq Wars," The Watson Institute for International and Public Affairs at Brown University, August 18, 2021.

46  Ramchand, "Prevalence of PTSD, Depression, and TBI Among Returning Servicemembers," 35. In a survey of the literature, the report identified twenty-two independent studies as of 2007 of PTSD, major depression, and/or brain injury among American troops deployed to or deploying to Iraq and Afghanistan (36).

47  *VA/DoD Clinical Practice Guideline for the Management of Post-Traumatic Stress*, 2004: I (emphasis added).

48  On resilience training, including the pre-deployment "psycho-education" project named BATTLEMIND, see Kieran, *Signature Wounds*, 59–64.

49  Finley, *Fields of Combat*, 128.

50  Intramural research refers to research done within the VA system. The VA funds intramural as well as research done in collaboration with those outside the VA. On the new studies, see Government Accountability Office, *Report on Veterans' Affairs*, 10. In August 2013, those departments responded to the call by developing a "national research action plan" focused on "foundational science, epidemiology, etiology, prevention and screening, treatment, follow-up care, and service research" (*Report on Veterans' Affairs*, ii).

51  Institute of Medicine, *Treatment for Posttraumatic Stress Disorder in Military and Veteran Populations*, 176.

52  Diana Dolan, "Staff Perspective: An Interview with Dr. Alan Peterson" (June 11, 2013), deploymentpsych.org/blog.

53  On the basis of her work in developing prolonged exposure therapy and its adoption by the US military and the Department of Veterans Affairs, *Time* magazine named Edna Foa one of the hundred most influential individuals in 2010. Jeffrey Kluger and Edna Foa, *Time Magazine*, April 29, 2010.

54  As we have seen, shorter delivery times are important for active-duty military personnel because the demands of deployment cycles often do not allow for treatments that last even for a few months. The standard PE protocol involves ten ninety-minute

sessions delivered over eight weeks, but it can extend as long as fifteen weeks; see Edna B. Foa et al., "Effect of Prolonged Exposure Therapy Delivered Over 2 Weeks vs 8 Weeks vs Present-Centered Therapy on PTSD Symptom Severity in Military Personnel: A Randomized Clinical Trial," *JAMA* 31: 4, 2018, 355. Foa et al. compared an eight-week protocol of standard PE to a two-week, ten-session protocol, or "massed PE." The study also relied on two control groups: one treated with "present-centered therapy" (PCT), an approach that was not designed specifically for trauma; a second group received "minimal-contact-control," involving brief telephone contact from therapists once a week for four weeks. As summed up by Charles Hoge, "most evidence supporting guideline-recommended trauma focused psychother-apies has been based on studies in civilian populations using very inactive control conditions" (Hoge and Chard, "A Window Into the Evolution of Trauma-Focused Psychotherapies," 343). By focusing on a military population and by using a more active control (PCT), Foa et al.'s study sought to resolve both of those deficiencies.

55   Foa, "Effect of Prolonged Exposure Therapy," 359.
56   Hoge and Chard, "A Window Into the Evolution of Trauma-Focused Psychotherapies," 344.
57   Foa, "Effect of Prolonged Exposure Therapy," 363.
58   See Edna B. Foa et al., "A Comparison of Exposure Therapy, Stress Inoculation Training, and Their Combination for Reducing Posttraumatic Stress Disorder in Female Assault Victims," *Journal of Consulting and Clinical Psychology* 67: 2, 1999.
59   Foa, "Effect of Prolonged Exposure Therapy," 359, See Table 2; 363.
60   Foa, "Effect of Prolonged Exposure Therapy," 359.
61   Annual Meetings of the International Society for the Study of Traumatic Stress, November 7–8, 2013. Field notes.
62   On problems with dropout rates and what therapists describe as the "revolving door" of treatment that these short-term protocols produce, see Michael R. Miller, "'Experiences of VA Therapists Treating OEF/OIF/OND Veterans with Combat PTSD,' A Dissertation Submitted to the Faculty of the Institute for Clinical Social Work in Partial Fulfillment for the Degree of Doctor of Philosophy," issuu.com.
63   Finley, *Fields of Combat*, 125.
64   See also Miller, "Experiences of VA Therapists Treating OEF/OIF/OND Veterans with Combat PTSD."
65   See Chapter 1.

66 Hoge and Chard, "A Window Into the Evolution of Trauma-Focused Psychotherapies," 343, 344.

67 Finley, *Fields of Combat*, 123.

68 Institute of Medicine, *Treatment for Posttraumatic Stress Disorder in Military and Veteran Populations*, 192.

69 According to the IOM, as of 2014, "there were as many mindfulness projects in the NIH report database as there were projects for treating PTSD with a combination of pharmacotherapy and psychotherapy approaches—an indication that research on mindfulness is growing" (Institute of Medicine, *Treatment for Posttraumatic Stress Disorder in Military and Veteran Populations*, 192–3).

70 The DSM-5 was published in 2013, but since studies are often conducted over multiyear periods, we are just beginning to see some using DSM-5 criteria. I discuss the shifts in the diagnosis later in the chapter.

71 Brett T. Litz and Susan M. Orsillo, "The Returning Veteran of the Iraq War: Background Issues and Assessment Guidelines," in *Iraq War Clinician Guide* (National Center for Post-Traumatic Stress Disorder, Washington, DC, June 2004), 21. The idea that *war,* and not just a career in the military, might be a growth experience strikes me as particularly pernicious. But insofar as the military is presented as just another a "job," the slide into war itself being a growth experience seems to be pulled along in tow.

72 Litz and Orsillo, "The Returning Veteran of the Iraq War," 21, 24 (emphasis in original).

73 Litz and Orsillo, "The Returning Veteran of the Iraq War," 25.

74 Litz and Orsillo, "The Returning Veteran of the Iraq War," 25, 31.

75 See Miller, "Experiences of VA Therapists Treating OEF/OIF/OND Veterans with Combat PTSD," 7.

76 For a discussion of Shatan, see Chapter 1.

77 Tyler Boudreau, "The Morally Injured," *Massachusetts Review* 52: 3/4, 2011, 747.

78 Lt. Col. Douglas A. Pryer, Moral Injury and the American Service Member: What Leaders Don't Talk About When They Talk About War," Association of the United States Army, August 14,2014, ausa.org.

79 Boudreau, "The Morally Injured," 752.

80 Boudreau, "The Morally Injured," 752.

81 Institute of Medicine, *Treatment for Posttraumatic Stress Disorder in Military and Veteran Populations*, 32. The DSM-5 also recategorized PTSD. Now no longer considered a form of "anxiety disorder," it is classified under "trauma- and stressor-related

disorders" (see *Treatment for Posttraumatic Stress Disorder in Military and Veteran Populations*, 29).

82 The Defense Authorization Act of 2010 mandated that the Secretary of the Department of Defense, in consultation with the Secretary of Veterans Affairs, commission an Institute of Medicine study to evaluate PTSD treatment programs and services in both the DoD and the VA (see *Treatment for Posttraumatic Stress Disorder in Military and Veteran Populations*).

83 Institute of Medicine, *Treatment for Posttraumatic Stress Disorder in Military and Veteran Populations*, 13–14 (emphasis added).

84 With respect to the cumulatively traumatic effects of living in poverty, see Bessel van der Kolk, *The Body Keeps the Score: Brain, Mind, and Body in the Healing of Trauma.* New York, NY: Penguin Books, 2015.

85 Morris, *The Evil Hours*, 204–5.


## 4. The Politics of Moral Injury

1 For an interesting, if different critical reading of moral injury than the one I develop here, see Kenneth MacLeish, "Moral Injury and the Psyche of Counterinsurgency," *Theory, Culture, Society*, o (o), 2021.

2 Brett T. Litz et al., "Moral Injury and Moral Repair in War Veterans: A Preliminary Model and Intervention Strategy," *Clinical Psychology Review* 29: 8, 2009, 696.

3 Brett, Litz et al., "A Randomized Controlled Trial of Adaptive Disclosure for Moral Injury Project Narrative," 1.

4 Litz et al., "Moral Injury and Moral Repair in War Veterans," 697.

5 Litz et al., "A Randomized Control Trial of Adaptive Disclosure for Moral Injury," 1.

6 For example, see "Moral Injury," Sonya B. Norman and Shira Maguen, ptsd.va.gov.

7 Jonathan Shay, *Achilles in Vietnam: Combat Trauma and the Undoing of Character* (New York: Schribner, 1994), 3.

8 Shay, *Achilles in Vietnam*, xx–xxi.

9 Shay, *Achilles in Vietnam*, xiii.

10 Jonathan Shay, *Odysseus in America: Combat Trauma and the Trials of Homecoming* (New York: Scribner, 2002), 151. He borrows the concept of "complex PTSD" from Judith Herman's book *Trauma and Recovery*. For Herman, complex PTSD is

caused by repeated abuse lived and endured over time. She developed the concept when working with incest survivors.

11 Shay, *Achilles in Vietnam*, 5, 6.

12 Shay, *Achilles in Vietnam*, 12–13.

13 Shay, *Odysseus in America*, 66–7.

14 Jonathan Shay, "Casualties," in *The Modern American Military*, ed. David M. Kennedy (New York: Oxford University Press, 2013), 304–5.

15 Shay, "Casualties," 304.

16 Shay, *Odysseus in America*, 160.

17 Shay, *Odysseus in America*, 150–1.

18 Shay, *Achilles in Vietnam*, 4, 5.

19 Shay, *Odysseus in America*, 166.

20 See Chapter 3.

21 Shay, *Odysseus in America*, 168, 174, 153.

22 Shay, *Odysseus in America*, 176 (emphasis in original).

23 Shay, *Odysseus in America*, 177.

24 Joseph Masco, *The Theater of Operations: National Security Affect From the Cold War to the War on Terror* (Durham: Duke University Press, 2014).

25 Bebinger, Martha, "'Moral Injury': Gaining Traction, But Still Controversial," *WBUR*, June 25, 2013.

26 Shay, "Casualties," 304. While I quote here from a chapter by Shay, the same story is narrated in slightly different form in the WBUR program.

27 Bebinger, "'Moral Injury': Gaining Traction, But Still Controversial."

28 Litz et al., "Moral Injury and Moral Repair in War Veterans." Shay sums up this latest iteration of moral injury: "when someone 'betrays what's right,' and the violator is the self, in a high stakes situation." He argues, "moral injury in my meaning can lead to moral injury in the above clinicians/researchers' meaning" (183).

29 In reading through Shay's two books, one gets the sense that his explicit emphasis on commanders betraying "what's right" belies the complexity of his own descriptions of moral injury. "[T]he soldier inflicts lifelong injuries on himself when he makes rape or rape-murder part of his war. Much of the sex practiced upon prostitutes in Vietnam was extremely violent. Many of the women were murdered, but since their lives meant nothing to the South Vietnamese civilian authorities, these cases came to the attention of the American military only under unusual circumstances" (Shay, *Odysseus in America*, 134–5). For many of his patients, sex had become a trauma-triggering event; they could

not separate sex from violence. The commission of rape and rape-murder are, in Litz's terms, a violation of "what's right" *by the self*; such acts are not easily, or seamlessly, reduced to a badly functioning command structure.

30  See Chapter 1.

31  Litz et al., "Moral Injury and Moral Repair in War Veterans," 697.

32  Litz et al., "Moral Injury and Moral Repair in War Veterans," 697. See also Brett T. Litz et al., *Adaptive Disclosure: A New Treatment for Military Trauma, Loss, and Moral Injury* (New York: The Guilford Press, 2016).

33  Michael Dillon and Julian Reid, *The Liberal Way of War: Killing to Make Life Live* (New York: Routledge, 2009). On the guilt of liberal subject as soldier, see Talal Asad, *On Suicide Bombing* (New York: Columbia University Press, 2007), especially chapters 1 and 2.

34  Listening to Trauma, Washington, DC. October 20–22, 2016. Notes by author.

35  Of course, his account ignores the brutality of aerial bombing during the Second World War, most horrendously in the fire-bombing of German cities and the nuclear bombs dropped on Hiroshima and Nagasaki. See Sven Lindqvist, *A History of Bombing,* trans. Linda Haverty Rugg (New York: The New Press, 2001).

36  Shira Maguen and Brett Litz, "Moral Injury in Veterans of War," *PTSD Research Quarterly* 23: 1, 2012, 1.

37  Litz et al., "Moral Injury and Moral Repair in War Veterans," 696.

38  AnnaBelle O. Bryan et al., "Moral Injury, Suicidal Ideation, and Suicide Attempts in a Military Sample," *Traumatology* 20: 3, 2014. See also Bebinger, "'Moral Injury': Gaining Traction, But Still Controversial." According to Douglas A. Pryer, a retired lieutenant colonel and an advocate for the concept: "The US military has a growing suicide problem. The evidence for the existence of moral injury is overwhelming and, in the wake of two wars there is no reasonable doubt that this condition is contributing to the military's growing suicide rate." See Douglas A. Pryer, "Moral Injury and the American Service Member: What Leaders Don't Talk About When They Talk About War," *Fort Leavenworth Ethics Symposium* (May 2014, 43). The link between moral injury and suicide should not be taken at face value, however. Suicide is also linked to PTSD diagnoses more generally; and to complicate matters further, studies have found no one-to-one

correlation between deployment to the war zone and suicidality. For example, see Gary Sheftick, "Army STARRS Study Busting Myths on Suicide," September 17, 2013.

39 Shira Maguen et al., "The Impact of Reported Direct and Indirect Killing on Mental Health Symptoms in Iraq War Veterans," *Journal of Traumatic Stress* 23: 1, 2010, 89 (emphasis added).

40 S.L.A. Marshall, *Men Against Fire: The Problem of Battle Command in Future War* (Norman: University of Oklahoma Press, [1947] 2000), 53–4.

41 Marshall, *Men Against Fire*, 50. This book had long been received as a classic of military history. It turns out, however, that Marshall's evidence may have been concocted. Decades later, Harold R. Linbaugh, a rifle commander in World War II, was deeply suspicious of the fire-ratio claims. He concluded, among other things, that Marshall did not have the evidence he claimed to. (Linbaugh also accused Marshall of "maligning" the memory of men who had fought hard to win World War II.) See Fredric Smoler, "The Secret of the Soldiers Who Didn't Shoot," *American Heritage* 40: 2, 1989.

42 Marshall, *Men Against Fire*, 77–8.

43 Marshall, *Men Against Fire*, 78.

44 Marshall, *Men Against Fire*, 79. Marshall claims to have drawn on his own experiences of combat. According to military records, however, he never saw combat during WWII. See Smoler, "The Secret of the Soldiers Who Didn't Shoot."

45 Grossman, *On Killing*, 252, xxxi. According to Grossman, after 9/11 *On Killing* was put on the required reading list at a variety of military and police training schools: the FBI Academy, the DEA Academy; the United States Marine Corps put the book on the commanders' required reading list; it is also required reading at the US Air Force NCO Academy and at West Point.

46 Grossman, *On Killing*, 54. Grossman asserts that "at least 98 percent of all soldiers in close combat will ultimately become psychiatric casualties" (Grossman, *On Killing*, 84).

47 Grossman, *On Killing*, 50, 51, 52, 78, 53, 201.

48 See Adam Carey, "Seminar on Training Police to Kill Without Hesitation Coming to Kansas City This December," *Pitch*, June 2, 2020.

49 Maguen, "The Impact of Reported Direct and Indirect Killing," 89.

50 Shira Maguen et al., "The Impact of Killing in War on Mental Health Symptoms and Related Functioning," *Journal of Traumatic Stress* 22: 5, 2009, 435.

51 Maguen, "The Impact of Reported Direct and Indirect Killing," 86. Starting in 2003, post-deployment health assessments included questions about depression, PTSD, and safety (thoughts about suicide and homicide). In March 2005, a second mental health assessment conducted three to six months post-deployment was added; see Charles W. Hoge et al., "Transformation of Mental Health Care for US Soldiers and Families During the Iraq and Afghanistan Wars: Where Science and Politics Intersect," *American Journal of Psychiatry* 173: 4, 2016, 355.

52 See also Sarah A. Haley, "When the Patient Reports Atrocities: Specific Treatment Considerations of the Vietnam Veteran," *Archives of General Psychiatry* 30: 2, 1974; Naomi Breslau and Glen C. Davis, "Post Traumatic Stress Disorder: The Etiologic Specificity of Wartime Stressors," *The American Journal of Psychiatry,* 144, 5, 1977.

53 Alan Fontana and Robert Rosenheck, "A Model of War Zone Stressors and Posttraumatic Stress Disorder," *Journal of Traumatic Stress* 12: 1, 1999, 111 (emphasis added). This paper relies on data from the National Vietnam Veterans Readjustment Study (see Chapter 2). The NVVRS included a "combat exposure measure" that assessed "a myriad of war-related experiences and situations," but included only one item "related to killing"— namely, veterans were asked whether they fired a weapon. (See the discussion in Maguen et al. 2009; see also my discussion of the NVVRS in Chapter 2.) Relying on NVVRS data to assess the psychological effects of killing isn't straightforward because the question of whether the veteran had actually killed was never posed explicitly.

54 Fontana and Rosenheck, "A Model of War Zone Stressors," 112, 121, 113.

55 Fontana and Rosenheck, "A Model of War Zone Stressors," 114.

56 Maguen, "The Impact of Reported Direct and Indirect Killing," 87. Other questions include: "During combat operations did you become wounded or injured?" "During combat operations, did you personally witness anyone being killed?"

57 Quoted in Natalie Purcell et al., "Veterans' Perspectives on the Psychosocial Impact of Killing in War," *The Counseling Psychologist* 44: 7, 2016, 1071.

58 Purcell, "Veterans' Perspectives," 1074.

59 Quoted in Purcell, "Veterans' Perspectives," 1074.

60 Purcell, "Veterans' Perspectives," 1074-1075.

61 "Notably, several veterans in the group reported not feeling any conflict, guilt, or shame associated with killing ... For them,

the logic that justified killing on the battlefield remained sound and solid once they returned home. 'I don't think about it and it didn't bother me when I was in that situation ... For us it's kill or be killed—your friends were getting killed, so it wasn't that hard to kill somebody ... If you're going to kill me, I'm going to kill you. So, for me it was easy. I don't have any guilt about it, really'" (Purcell, "Veterans' Perspectives," 1077–8). Whether or not particular individuals experienced guilt or shame, however, Purcel reports that many experienced "a persistent, generalized emotional numbness in the aftermath of prolonged exposure to killing and death" (1078). One VA psychologist, however, warned me against assuming that killing is "necessarily injurious. We abhor killing and we assume killing is harmful, that it shatters everything about humanity. But that is naïve—it is biased." He cautioned that "civilian" attitudes toward killing don't necessarily coincide with how professional soldiers experience the act. For a discussion of complex responses to killing not captured in moral injury frameworks, see MacLeish, "Moral Injury and the Psyche of Counterinsurgency."

62  Purcell, "Veterans' Perspectives," 1076.

63  Purcell, "Veterans' Perspectives," 1080, 1088.

64  Nathan R. Stein et al., "A Scheme for Categorizing Traumatic Military Events," *Behavior Modification* 36: 6, 2012, 791. The study relied on categories from three inventories: the Deployment Risk and Resilience Inventory (DRRI) Combat Experiences Scale; the DRRI Aftermath of Battle Scale; and the Life Events Checklist; see Lynda A. King et al., "Deployment Risk and Resilience Inventory: A Collection of Measures for Studying Deployment-Related Experiences of Military Personnel and Veterans," *Military Psychology* 18: 2, 2006; Matt J. Gray et al., "Psychometric Properties of the Life Events Checklist," *Assessment* 11: 4, 2004. I discuss the DDRI scale in more detail later in the chapter.

65  Stein, "A Scheme for Categorizing Traumatic Military Events," 798–9. See also Maguen, "The Impact of Killing in War"; Maguen, "The Impact of Reported Direct and Indirect Killing." A subsequent publication goes further than the Stein study in that it specifies the particular affective correlates of these different kinds of war-zone traumas; see Carmen P. McLean et al., "Trauma-Related Cognitions and Cognitive Emotion Regulation as Mediators of PTSD Change among Treatment-Seeking Active-Duty Military Personnel With PTSD," *Behavior Therapy* 50: 6, 2019, 1054.

66  King et al., "Deployment Risk and Resilience Inventory," 90,
    90–1. They also note that existing combat exposure measures
    were "largely developed in the context of the Vietnam War," and
    yet it is safe to assume that combat experiences differ war to war,
    which must be taken into account in future research.

67  King et al., "Deployment Risk and Resilience Inventory," 91,
    97–8.

68  In its latest iteration (DSM-5, APA 2013), Criterion A for a
    PTSD diagnosis specifies "Exposure to actual or threatened
    death, serious injury, or sexual violence in one (or more) of the
    following ways: 1. Directly experiencing the traumatic event(s).
    2. Witnessing, in person, the event(s) as it occurred to others. 3.
    Learning that the traumatic event(s) occurred to a close family
    member or close friend. In cases of actual or threatened death of
    a family member or friend, the event(s) must have been violent
    or accidental. 4. Experiencing repeated or extreme exposure to
    aversive details of the traumatic event(s) (e.g., first responders
    collecting human remains: police officers repeatedly exposed to
    details of child abuse)." The American Psychiatric Association,
    "DSM-5: Diagnostic and Statistical Manual of Mental Disor-
    ders," 2013, 271.

69  Bessel van der Kolk, *The Body Keeps the Score: Brain, Mind, and
    Body in the Healing of Trauma* (New York: Viking, 2014), 10, 16.

70  King, "Deployment Risk and Resilience Inventory," 97, 109. The
    highest correlations with PTSD, depression, and anxiety were
    the following six categories: difficult living and working envi-
    ronment; concerns about life and family disruptions; perceived
    threat; fear of NBC [nuclear, biological, chemical] exposures;
    post-deployment stressors. And the strongest "resilience factor"
    was post-deployment social support. (The results are derived
    from focus group and survey data of veterans of the 1991 Gulf
    War.)

71  Elizabeth A. Povinelli, *Economies of Abandonment: Social
    Belonging and Endurance in Late Liberalism* (Durham: Duke
    University Press, 2011), 13; see also Ruth Leys, *From Guilt to
    Shame: Auschwitz and After* (Princeton: Princeton University
    Press, 2007), 9.

72  Litz et al., *Adaptive Disclosure*, 20.

73  Quoted in Litz et al., *Adaptive Disclosure*, 30.

74  Litz et al., *Adaptive Disclosure*, 7 (emphasis in original), 9–10.

75  Litz et al., *Adaptive Disclosure*, 29, 30.

76  Litz et al., *Adaptive Disclosure*, 33.

77  Litz et al., *Adaptive Disclosure*, 37–41.

78 Litz et al., *Adaptive Disclosure*, 42.
79 Laurence J. Kirmayer and Harry Minas, "The Future of Cultural Psychiatry: An International Perspective," *Canadian Journal of Psychiatry* 45: 5, 2000, 438, 440. Also of fundamental importance to the field were "cross-cultural comparative studies of psychiatric disorders and traditional healing" and a reflexive engagement with psychiatry as a discipline, now reframed in terms of being "the product of a specific cultural history."
80 Litz et al., *Adaptive Disclosure*, 3.
81 Litz et al., *Adaptive Disclosure*, 3, 4.
82 Litz et al., *Adaptive Disclosure*, 94.
83 Litz et al., *Adaptive Disclosure*, 98.
84 Litz et al., *Adaptive Disclosure*, 78.
85 Litz et al., *Adaptive Disclosure*, 102, 104, 107 (emphasis in original).
86 Litz et al., *Adaptive Disclosure*, 107,109.
87 Litz et al., *Adaptive Disclosure*, 117, 119, 91.
88 Asad, *On Suicide Bombing*. See also Didier Fassin and Richard Rechtman, *The Empire of Trauma: An Inquiry Into the Condition of Victimhood,* trans. Rachel Gomme (Princeton, NJ: Princeton University Press, 2009).
89 Litz et al., *Adaptive Disclosure*, 61.
90 Litz et al., *Adaptive Disclosure*, 127, 128, 124 (emphasis in original).
91 Litz et al., *Adaptive Disclosure*, 125.
92 Michel Foucault, *The History of Sexuality: Volume 1: An Introduction,* trans. Robert Hurley (New York: Vintage Books, 1990), 58, 68.
93 Leys, *From Guilt to Shame*, 11.
94 See Chapter 2.
95 Brett Litz et al., "A Randomized Controlled Trial of Adaptive Disclosure for Moral Injury Project Narrative."
96 The Institute of Medicine, *Treatment for Posttraumatic Stress Disorder in Military and Veteran Populations: Final Assessment* (Washington, DC: National Academies Press, 2014), 14, 182. In their review of the literature, the authors describe a clinical study of adaptive disclosure therapy, albeit not identified as such: "One study investigates the potential to augment any evidence-based-treatment with an additive CBT module designed specifically to address issues related to killing in a war zone" (274).
97 Brett T. Litz, "Resilience in the Aftermath of War Trauma: A Critical Review and Commentary," *Interface Focus* 4: 5, 2014, 7.

98  Van der Kolk, *The Body Keeps the Score*, 21.

99  Diana Dolan, "Staff Perspective: An Interview with Dr. Alan Peterson" (June 11, 2013), deploymentpsych.org.

100  The Institute of Medicine, *Treatment for Posttraumatic Stress Disorder*, 19, 185.

101  See Kira Peikoff, "The Mind-Blowing Promise of Neural Implants," (Sept. 13, 2018), leaps.org.

102  Povinelli, *Economies of Abandonment*, 13.

103  Brett Litz et al., "A Randomized Controlled Trial of Adaptive Disclosure for Moral Injury Project Narrative," n.p., 10.

104  William P. Nash et al., "Psychometric Evaluation of the Moral Injury Events Scale," *Military Medicine* 178: 6, 2013, 650.

105  Craig Jones, *The War Lawyers: The United States, Israel, and Judicial Warfare* (Oxford, UK: Oxford University Press, 2021).

106  Asad, *On Suicide Bombing*, 36.

107  Litz et al., *Adaptive Disclosure*, 125.

108  Litz et al., *Adaptive Disclosure*, 19.

109  Zoë Wool, *After War: The Weight of Life at Walter Reed* (Durham: Duke University Press, 2015), 105.

## 5.  Caring for Militarism

1  There is a large scholarly literature on the question of secularism and the ways in which contemporary Christianity, and "faith" more broadly, is configured within its grammar. That is not my concern here, however, and as such, I do not unpack the discourse of "faith-based organizations," chaplains, or others who position their interpretation of combat trauma as religious in contrast to a "secular" psychiatric one. For a foundational text in this scholarly field, see Talal Asad, *Formations of the Secular: Christianity, Islam, Modernity* (Stanford, CA: Stanford University Press, 2003).

2  Didier Fassin, *Humanitarian Reason: A Moral History of the Present,* trans. Rachel Gomme (Berkeley, CA: University of California Press, 2012); Miriam I. Ticktin, *Casualties of Care: Immigration and the Politics of Humanitarianism in France* (Berkeley, CA: University of California Press, 2011). See also Robert Meister, *After Evil: A Politics of Human Rights* (New York: Columbia University Press, 2011). See the introduction for a discussion of the new humanitarianism.

3  Slavoj Žižek, *Six Sideways Reflections on Violence* (New York: Picador, 2008).

4  Ticktin, *Casualties of Care*, 62–3.
5  Rita Nakashima Brock and Gabriella Lettini, *Soul Repair: Recovering from Moral Injury after War* (Boston: Beacon Press, 2016), xxv.
6  January 1971; see Chapter 1.
7  Brock and Lettini, *Soul Repair*, xxv. The Commission was held at Riverside Church in New York City in March 2010. See warresisters.org.
8  Since 2017, Rita Brock has been senior vice president for the Shay Moral Injury Center at Volunteers of America, a nonprofit that offers services to both low-income Americans and veterans.
9  Shira Maguen and Brett Litz, "Moral Injury in Veterans of War," *PTSD Research Quarterly* 23: 1, 2012, 3.
10  Brock and Lettini, *Soul Repair*, xi, 51.
11  Beth A. Stallinga, "What Spills Blood Wounds Spirit: Chaplains, Spiritual Care, and Operational Stress Injury," *Reflective Practice: Formation and Supervision in Ministry* 33: 1, 2013, 14, 15.
12  Paul D. Fritts, "Adaptive Disclosure: Critique of A descriptive Intervention Modified for the Normative Problem of Moral Injury in Combat Veterans," cgscfoundation.org.
13  Stallinga, "What Spills Blood Wounds Spirit," 15.
14  Quoted in Stallinga, "What Spills Blood Wounds Spirit," 16. Stallinga was quoting from a manual on pastoral care: John Sippola et al., *Welcome Them Home, Help Them Heal: Pastoral Care and Ministry with Service Members Returning From War* (Duluth, MN: Whole Person Associates, 2009).
15  Stallinga, "What Spills Blood Wounds Spirit," 16.
16  Winnifred Fallers Sullivan, *A Ministry of Presence: Chaplaincy, Spiritual Care, and the Law* (Chicago: University of Chicago Press, 2014), 9.
17  Quoted in Sullivan, *A Ministry of Presence*, 27.
18  Sullivan, *A Ministry of Presence*, 11. On the past and present of the military chaplaincy, see Sullivan, *A Ministry of Presence*; Kim Philip Hansen, *Military Chaplains and Religious Diversity* (New York: Palgrave Macmillan, 2012); Anne C. Loveland, *American Evangelicals and the US Military, 1942–1993* (Baton Rouge: Louisiana State University Press, 1996).
19  Sullivan, *A Ministry of Presence*, 22, 27.
20  Quoted in Sullivan, *A Ministry of Presence*, 27. Spiritual fitness is part of the Army's Comprehensive Fitness Program, launched in 2010. For a discussion of the project, see Sullivan, *A Ministry of Presence*, 23–3.
21  Chad E. Cooper, "Spiritual Fitness is One of Several Components

Aimed at Promoting Health and Well-Being in the Army" (April 17, 2018), army.mil.

22   Sullivan, *A Ministry of Presence*, 25.

23   See armyhistory.org.

24   Sullivan, *A Ministry of Presence*, 69; see also Hansen, *Military Chaplains and Religious Diversity*.

25   Sullivan, *A Ministry of Presence*, 181-2, 181, 175, 182.

26   Stallinga, "What Spills Blood Wounds Spirit," 17. The reality is actually somewhat more complex. Military chaplains, many argue, answer to two authorities, the church that ordained them and the military in which they serve. Their ultimate responsibility is to get soldiers back out into the fight. As a consequence, some have argued that to avoid these kinds of conflicts of interest, military chaplains should not be paid by the military (field notes, 2017 UTS conference).

27   Laura Werber, Kathryn Piktin Derose et. al. *Faith-Based Organizations and Veteran Reintegration. Echoing the Web of Support*. Santa Monica, CA: RAND Corporation, 2015. 8, 7, 1. The RAND report is based on interviews with care providers, not veterans.

28   Wollom A. Jensen and James M. Childs, *Moral Warriors, Moral Wounds: The Ministry of the Christian Ethic* (Eugene, OR: Cascade Books, 2016), 4.

29   Timothy Mallard, "The (Twin) Wounds of War." *Providence*, February 13, 2017.

30   Emphasis added.

31   Stallinga, "What Spills Blood Wounds Spirit," 17, 19.

32   See Ticktin, *Casualties of Care*; Fassin, *Humanitarian Reason*. See also the introduction to this book.

33   Lifton Papers, NYPL, BOX 00765b; see Chapter 2.

34   Jensen and Childs, *Moral Warriors, Moral Wounds*, 101.

35   Mallard, "The (Twin) Wounds of War."

36   Sullivan, *A Ministry of Presence*, 174.

37   Susan Neiman, *Evil in Modern Thought: An Alternative History of Philosophy* (Princeton, NJ: Princeton University Press, 2002), 9, 303. See Hannah Arendt, *Eichmann in Jerusalem: A Report on the Banality of Evil* (New York: Penguin, 2006).

38   Adi Ophir, *The Order of Evils: Toward an Ontology of Morals* (New York: Zone Books, 2005), 11. Ophir's goal is to move the philosophical discussion of evil off the metaphysical terrain and onto what he refers to as an ontological one. He asks: What are the evils that exist in the world, how are they made, and how might we work towards countering or reducing "superfluous evils"?

39   Neiman, *Evil in Modern Thought*, 297.

40  Jensen and Childs, *Moral Warriors, Moral Wounds*, 43, 72.

41  Sullivan, *A Ministry of Presence*, 25. For a discussion of the role of evangelical Christians (including chaplains), in transforming the US military in the aftermath of the American war in Vietnam, see Jennifer Mittelstadt, *The Rise of the Military Welfare State* (Cambridge, MA: Harvard University Press, 2015).

42  Jensen and Childs, *Moral Warriors, Moral Wounds*, 144, 72, 26, 27 (emphasis added).

43  Hannah Arendt, *Responsibility and Judgment* (New York: Schocken Books, 2003). It could be argued that what is being called a "moral code" here is more aptly described as a political one, in the sense that "[t]he political order does not require moral integrity but only law-abiding citizens" (68).

44  Fritts, Adaptive Disclosure, 2.

45  See Tomaž Mastnak, *Crusading Peace: Christendom, the Muslim World, and Western Political Order* (Berkeley, CA: University of California Press, 2002). Although many note that the prohibition against killing is not limited to Christianity, this discourse tends to rotate around the biblical commandment "Thou Shalt not Kill," which is often referred to in the context of having been raised in the church.

46  Field notes.

47  Jensen and Childs, *Moral Warriors, Moral Wounds*, 35.

48  Fritts, Adaptive Disclosure, 5-6.

49  Neiman, *Evil in Modern Thought*, 275.

50  Joseph M. Palmer, *They Don't Receive Purple Hearts: A Guide to an Understanding and Resolution of the Invisible Wound of War Known as Moral Injury* (Northbrook, IL: Military Outreach USA, 2015), 71. Military Outreach USA describes itself on its website as a "faith-based, Judeo-Christian organization," whose work is "focused on Veterans and First-Responder Communities, regardless of their denomination or beliefs, demonstrating the compassion, love and healing of Christ our Lord." See military outreachusa.org.

51  Notes taken by author.

52  Tyler Boudreau, "The Morally Injured," *Massachusetts Review* 52: 3/4, 2011.

53  Fritts, "Adaptive Disclosure," 4.

54  Arendt, *Responsibility and Judgment*, 67, 90.

55  In *Soul Repair*, Brock and Lettini do engage political questions of war, empire, and racism when revisiting the war in Vietnam at the end of the book, as well as projects among American veterans of that war to return to Vietnam and engage in reparatory

projects in Vietnamese communities. Interestingly, however, such critique appears nowhere in Brock's subsequent writings or public engagements, as far as I have found, a point to which I return below (see foonote 87).

56  Palmer, *They Don't Receive Purple Hearts,* 25. Emphasis in original.

57  Sullivan, *A Ministry of Presence,* 174–5.

58  Arendt, *Responsibility and Judgment,* 51. The majority of those involved in conversations about PTSD and moral injury who engage critically with the question of whether or not the wars in Iraq and/or Afghanistan are just are military or ex-military personnel. In Chapter 6, I focus on the civil-military divide and who is and is not authorized to judge war.

59  Powers, "Moral Injury and Original Sin," 326, 327.

60  Powers, "Moral Injury and Original Sin," 330–1.

61  Powers, "Moral Injury and Original Sin," 331-2, 333.

62  Warren Kinghorn, "Combat Trauma and Moral Fragmentation: A Theological Account of Moral Injury," *Journal of the Society of Christian Ethics* 32: 2, 2012, 59.

63  Kinghorn, "Combat Trauma and Moral Fragmentation," 64, 60. For a discussion of Lifton and Haley, see Chapter 2.

64  Kinghorn, "Combat Trauma and Moral Fragmentation," 63, 63–4.

65  Kinghorn, "Combat Trauma and Moral Fragmentation," 66-7, 67, 68.

66  Emphasis added.

67  Werber, *Faith-Based Organizations and Veteran Reintegration,* 3.

68  Melinda Cooper, *Family Values: Between Neoliberalism and the New Social Conservatism* (New York: Zone Books, 2017), 266, 267. Cooper traces the origins of this shift further back to Lyndon Johnson's War on Poverty of the 1960s. In contrast to the provisions that structured the New Deal, Johnson's initiative allowed "partnerships between government and charitable organizations," and religious groups became some of the main beneficiaries of the shift. Nevertheless, as Cooper puts it, if under Johnson's project religious nonprofits were "included within the reach of an ever-expanding welfare state," by the 1980s, they began to be seen as a "substitute for services that were being eroded or starved of funding" under Ronald Reagan's economic reforms.

69  Cooper, *Family Values,* 269-70, 25, 271, 299–300.

70  Mittelstadt, *The Rise of the Military Welfare State,* 6–7.

71  Mittelstadt, *The Rise of the Military Welfare State,* 190, 191, 222.

72 Werber, *Faith-Based Organizations and Veteran Reintegration*, 3.
73 M. David Rudd, scientific director of the National Center for Veteran Studies at the University of Utah, argued that the two most important points for intervention in mental health needs of veterans were colleges and universities, on the one hand, and "communities of faith," on the other. In his words, "There is empirical evidence indicating a significant need, along with data to suggest these two domains offer unique opportunities and promise to help ease the transition to civilian life."
74 According to Chaplain Michael McCoy Sr. (associate director at the National Chaplain Center in the Veterans Health Administration of VA), "In 2007, the VA National Chaplain Center started the VCOI [Veterans' Community Outreach Initiative] to educate community clergy about the spiritual and emotional needs of our returning Veterans and their families. Nationwide, VA chaplains have conducted over 200 training events and provided education to approximately 10,000 clergy through this effort."
75 Werber, *Faith-Based Organizations and Veteran Reintegration*, 6.
76 Palmer, *They Don't Receive Purple Hearts*, iii, 85, 20; see also Kinghorn, "Combat Trauma and Moral Fragmentation," 65.
77 See also Jensen and Childs, *Moral Warriors, Moral Wounds*, 101–0.
78 Kinghorn, "Combat Trauma and Moral Fragmentation," 69.
79 Edward Tick, *War and the Soul: Healing our Veterans from Post-Traumatic Stress Disorder,* Wheaton, IL: Quest Books, 2005; see also the PBS documentary, *Almost Sunrise* (Premiered November 13, 2017).
80 David Wood, *What Have We Done: The Moral Injury of Our Longest Wars* (New York: Little, Brown and Company, 2016), 5, 4, 3–4.
81 Fritts, "Adaptive Disclosure," 23.
82 Kinghorn, "Combat Trauma and Moral Fragmentation," 64.
83 Jensen and Childs, *Moral Warriors, Moral Wounds,* 144.
84 Jensen and Childs, *Moral Warriors, Moral Wounds,* 145.
85 He draws on an argument made by Edward Farley in *Good and Evil: Interpreting a Human Condition* (Minneapolis, MN: Fortress Press, 1990).
86 There are a few parallels, of course. See, for example, the Islah Reparations Project, founded by Ross Caputo, a Marine veteran of the war in Iraq who fought in the second siege of Fallujah, and Kali Rubai, an Iraqi-American anthropologist; see reparations.org/. See also the "People's History of Fallujah Digital Archive," still under development, and put together by Caputo and Hajer Zead

Nowaf, an Iraqi activist from Anbar province, ncph.org. Others have returned in different ways, as journalists, for example, or for humanitarian work. On humanitarian work, see, for example, tylerboudreau.com/public-activity.

87 Fritts, "Adaptive Disclosure," 29. See Brock and Lettini, *Soul Repair*. It is a curious and perhaps telling fact that, while Brock and Lettini discuss such efforts and the inherent contradictions they raised following the American war in Vietnam, as Brock became a prominent public spokesperson for recognizing the moral injury of American soldiers in the post-9/11 wars, she seemed to back away from any such explicitly political engagement or critique. That is testament, I think, to the power of the moralist anti-politics of the combat trauma imaginary of the new millennium.

88 Ibid. Recognizing the limitations posed for "non-Christian" soldiers, he clarifies: "In the same way non-Christian Soldiers may not regard a Christian chaplain as a religious or oral authority, non-Christian Soldiers may not regard the Christian church as an accessible community of the face. Presumably those Soldiers are able to find comparable communities of the face in their own religious traditions. One could argue, in fact, that communities of the face should essentially and necessarily be non-sectarian" (ibid).

89 See, for example, Palmer, *They Don't Receive Purple* Hearts, 89–90. The Outreach USA guide draws on reconciliation efforts in South Africa as one model, without any acknowledgement that such a process would necessarily involve being in relation to Iraqis and Afghans who suffered and continue to suffer the effects of US military violence.

90 Jensen and Childs, *Moral Warriors, Moral Wounds*, 113. *Jus post bellum* "refers to the criteria for ending a war justly ... It seeks to be sure that the conflict has ended with justice having been done. It seeks to ensure that those guilty of war crimes receive appropriate punishment and that the innocent are spared ... Ending the war justly may also involve aid to the innocent victims of the defeated country and assistance in rebuilding." It is worth emphasizing that these broader elements of *jus post bellum* receive no more attention that their mere mention in the book.

91 Jensen and Childs, *Moral Warriors, Moral Wounds*, 139, 142.

92 See warriorwriters.org. Founded in 2004, Operation Homecoming was established as a partnership between the National Endowment for the Humanities and the Department of Defense, and it was funded by Boeing. It was, to quote Elliott Colla, "a

massive writing, publishing and archiving project dedicated to fostering the writing talents of soldiers and their families." For a critical reading of the project, and the larger phenomenon of what he calls the "military-literary complex" born of the post-9/11 wars, see Elliott Colla, "The Military-Literary Complex." *Jadaliyya*, July 8, 2014; and Sinan Antoon, "Embedded Poetry: Iraq; Through a Soldier's Binoculars," *Jadaliyya*, June 11, 2014.

93 Judith Lewis Herman, *Trauma and Recovery* (New York: Basic Books, 1992).

94 Bryan Doerries, *The Theater of War: What Ancient Tragedies Can Teach Us Today* (New York: Vintage Books, 2016), 35, 36.

95 Doerries, *The Theater of War*, 37.

96 Doerries, *The Theater of War*, 59, 62. On the Walter Reed "scandal" see, Dana Priest and Anne Hull, "Soldiers Face Neglect, Frustration At Army's Top Medical Facility," *Washington Post*, February 18, 2007.

97 Doerries, *The Theater of War*, 65, 65-6, 66.

98 See theaterofwar.com.

99 Doerries, *The Theater of War*, 72, 109–10.

100 Doerries, *The Theater of War*, 76, 77.

101 "Roughly 95 percent of the injured service members who lived long enough to receive medical treatment would survive their injuries and return to the States to begin the long road to recovery." As important an achievement as that is, Doerries continues, "by saving so many lives, we had also refined our ability to prolong the agony and isolation of wounded soldiers … We created a vast subclass of profoundly injured veterans who would be dependent on the care of others for decades to come." He also notes that "the suicide of a combat veteran, one of the most graphic and iconic depictions of suicide in western literature," stands at the core of the story. Doerries, *The Theater of War*, 65–65, 96.

102 For example, David Straithern, Paul Giamatti, Adam Driver, Diane Wiest, Francis McDormand, and James Earl Jones. For a complete list, see "Cast" on the "About Us" page at theaterofwar.com.

103 Doerries, *The Theater of War*, 83.

104 Doerries, *The Theater of War*, 83, 74.

105 Doerries, *The Theater of War*, 4.

106 Doerries, *The Theater of War*, 85.

107 Doerries, *The Theater of War*, 85.

108 Doerries explains the current "skyrocketing" rates of soldier suicide in reference to betrayal. He points out that while the rate

has risen among all active-duty personnel, it doubled among soldiers who had seen combat but *tripled* among those never deployed. How can that possibly be, he asks? *Ajax,* he writes, may "shed light on the underlying reasons behind some military suicides. While the play describes the unraveling of a combat veteran, the trigger … is related not to combat but to the internal politics of the Greek army. It is the feeling that those above him in the chain of command have devalued and betrayed him, both as a warrior and as a man, that ultimately sends him to his death" (Doerries, *The Theater of War,* 97). Someone who identified himself as active duty and a Columbia student, intervened: "One of things we've noticed within the force, a lot of those committing suicide have never been to combat. Some of our youngest members, one or two years in, [have] never been in war. It is larger than that—not just about war"; it's "a larger societal issue."

109 Quoted in Doerries, *The Theater of War,* 108.
110 This was a very particular audience. It included Columbia faculty and students—and some of the latter were veterans—as well as veterans from a local vet center. The performance had been organized as part of the university's core curriculum. It was thus the case that many of those in the audience had read Sophocles in preparation for the event.
111 My emphasis.
112 Weil and James P. Holoka, *Simone Weil's the Iliad, or the Poem of Force: A Critical Edition,* trans. James P. Holoka (New York: Peter Lang, 2003), 18, 6.
113 Weil and Holoka, *Simone Weil's the Iliad, or the Poem of Force,* 11, 13.
114 Weil and Holoka, *Simone Weil's the Iliad, or the Poem of Force,* 26–7.

## 6. The (American) Civilian

1 "Gold Star" references those who have lost a family member in military service.
2 "Full Transcript and Video: Kelly Defends Trump's Handling of Soldier's Death and Call to Widow," *New York Times,* October 19, 2017.
3 Helen M. Kinsella, *The Image Before the Weapon: A Critical History of the Distinction between Combatant and Civilian* (Ithaca, NY: Cornell University Press, 2011), 29,7.

4   As I noted in the Introduction (footnote 4), I use "she" as the generic pronoun when not referring to soldiers, following a convention that has sought to query the use of "he" as a stand-in for all human beings. Having said that, in thinking about the distinction between citizens who "serve" and those who don't, "she" functions as more than a mere disruption of a grammatical norm. Insofar as the military promotes and is saturated by hypermasculinity—as Kelly puts it, those who step up to "protect" the country—the Other citizen is feminized. Her very safety and form of life is ensured by a military that stands guard. Recall the climactic scene from the Rob Reiner film *A Few Good Men*: In his confrontation with a JAG lawyer during the course of a trial for abuse and murder at the Guantanamo Bay Naval Base, the commander (played by Jack Nicholson) yells, in almost uncontrollable rage: "You *want* me on that wall! You *need* me on that wall!" On gender politics and the military, see, for example, Cynthia Enloe, *Bananas, Beaches, and Bases. Making Feminist Sense of International Politics.* (Berkeley, CA: University of California Press, 2000); Jennifer Mittelstadt, *The Rise of the Military Welfare State* (Cambridge, MA: Harvard University Press, 2015); Zoë Wool, *After War: The Weight of Life At Walter Reed* (Durham, NC: Duke University Press, 2015). (I thank Naor Ben Yehoyada for reminding me of that scene in *A Few Good Men*.)

5   This is not to suggest there is no discussion of Iraqi or Afghan civilians at all, or for that matter, of civilians killed in other places by the US military. When those civilians are being referred to, however, they are often either qualified—"Iraqi" or "Afghan" civilian, for example—or it is evident from the context that the civilian is a noncombatant in a war zone (for example, in newspaper accounts of civilians killed in US military operations in Kabul). Nevertheless, as most commonly invoked in domestic discourse about the post 9/11 war, and when used as an *unmarked term*, "civilian" tends to refer to American citizens who have no experience of war.

6   Andrew Bacevich, *The New American Militarism: How Americans are Seduced by War* (New York: Oxford University Press, 2005). On the concept of acknowledgement, see Stanley Cavell, *Must We Mean What We Say? A Book of Essays* (Cambridge: Cambridge University Press, [1969] 2015); see also, Linda M.G. Zerilli, *A Democratic Theory of Judgment* (Chicago: University of Chicago Press, 2016).

7   David Finkel, *The Good Soldiers* (New York: Farrar, Straus and Giroux, 2009), 205.

8  Finkel, *The Good Soldiers*, 206.

9  For an account of David Wood's work as an American journalist in Afghanistan, see David Wood, *What Have We Done: The Moral Injury of Our Longest Wars* (New York: Little, Brown and Company, 2016), 12–13. In this chapter, I do not draw a sharp distinction between moral injury and PTSD as iterations of war trauma. The journalists, philosophers, and others who write about moral injury are less interested in the distinction than in getting across the point that *this is what combat trauma looks like today*—that is, during the post-9/11 era of counterinsurgency warfare.

10  David Wood, "The Grunts: Damned If They Kill, Damned If They Don't," *Huffington Post*, March 18, 2014, huffingtonpost. com.

11  According to Wood, "These new wars ... threw young troops into legal and moral swamps that GIs of past [twentieth-century] wars could hardly imagine ... [I]n the alien world of combat in Iraq and Afghanistan, the enemy used the tactics of atrocity at will ... At ground level in these wars, the insistence of Higher headquarters that American troops play by those old rules seemed quaint and irrelevant, even dangerous" (*What Have We Done*, 83–4).

12  Wood, "The Grunts: Damned If They Kill, Damned If They Don't."

13  See also Joseph Goldstein, "US Soldiers Told to Ignore Sexual Abuse of Boys by Afghan Allies," *New York Times*, September 20, 2015. The article begins with a quote from the final phone call home made by an American soldier before he was killed. As recalled by his father, the soldier had said, "At night we can hear them screaming, but we're not allowed to do anything about it." He urged his son to tell his superiors, but his son "said that his officers told him to look the other way because it's their culture." As the article continues, however, the very framing of this as a "cultural" problem—by the US military and in the article—is belied by local Afghans: "The reason we were here is because we heard the terrible things the Taliban were doing to people, how they were taking away human rights," said Dan Quinn, a former Special Forces captain who once beat up an American-backed militia commander for keeping a boy chained to his bed as a sex slave. "But we were putting people into power who would do things that were worse than the Taliban did—*that was something village elders voiced to me*" (emphasis added). See also Bill Edmonds' article "God Is Not Here" (2018), in which he talks

about the different "rules" and "culture" informing Iraqi military attitudes toward torture, presumably in contrast to his own.

14  See Chapter 5.

15  See Tyler E. Boudreau, "The Morally Injured," in *War and Moral Injury: A Reader*, ed. Robert Emmet Meagher and Douglas A. Pryer (Eugene: Cascade Books, 2018). See also, Boudreau, *Packing Inferno: The Unmaking of a Marine* (Port Townsend, WA: Feral House, 2008).

16  See James Fallows, "An Important Book on Moral Injuries, *Afterwar*," *Atlantic*, November 23, 2015. See also Nancy Sherman, *Afterwar: Healing the Moral Injuries of Our Soldier* (New York: Oxford University Press, 2015), for an account of the moral injury of an American Marine resulting from his failure to retrieve a body from Iraqi authorities for proper burial and return it to the family; it was the body of the father killed by another Marine at a checkpoint when he turned a corner unaware. For a robust, critical reading of the practice of shooting at checkpoints, see Gregory Thomas, "Dangerous Feelings: Checkpoints and the Perception of Hostile Intent," *Security Dialogue* 50: 2, 2019.

17  David Finkel essentially re-embeds himself with veterans from the Army unit he was with in Iraq once they are back home in order to tell their story of return. Nancy Sherman, a professor of philosophy at Georgetown University, describes her book on moral injury as the product of someone who "embedded within" the communities of service members back home.

18  American soldiers and veterans are often described as mere kids: "many of them, barely out of their teens, are insufficiently prepared for high-stress, critical decision-making because adolescents' brains are not fully developed. Not until teens reach their mid-twenties do their brains reach full maturity. Until then, as parents of teenagers are well aware, they tend to be excitable, easily swayed by peer pressure, and not so good at anticipating the consequences of their actions" (Wood, *What Have We Done*, 28; see also Sherman, *Afterwar*). No such adolescent innocence, however, is ever ascribed to the insurgents they fight against.

19  Wood, *What Have We Done*, 39, 41, 43.

20  Ashley Gilbertson and Michelle Paley, "The Life and Lonely Death of Noah Pierce," *Virginia Quarterly Review* 84: 4, 2008, 32, 37.

21  Quoted in Gilbertson and Paley, "The Life and Lonely Death of Noah Pierce," p. 38.

22  Quoted in Gilbertson and Paley, "The Life and Lonely Death of Noah Pierce," 41.

23  Sherman, *Afterwar*, xiii–xiv.

24  Phil Klay, "American Purpose After the Fall of Kabul," *New Yorker,* August 25, 2021. The essay is a critical reengagement with the "noble purpose" that Americans found in the aftermath of the 9/11 attacks.

25  *Listening to Trauma*, Washington, DC, October 20–22, 2016; notes by author.

26  Wood, "The Grunts: Damned If They Kill, Damned If They Don't."

27  Timothy Kudo, "On War and Redemption," in *War and Moral Injury: A Reader*, ed. Robert Emmet Meagher and Douglas A. Pryer (Eugene, OR: Cascade Books, 2018), 79.

28  Elizabeth D. Samet, *No Man's Land: Preparing for War and Peace in Post-9/11 America* (New York: Farrar, Straus and Giroux, 2014), 78–9.

29  Samet, *No Man's Land*, 79.

30  Matt Richtel, "Please Don't Thank Me for My Service," *New York Times*, February 21, 2015.

31  Richtel notes, "The issue has been percolating for a few years, elucidated memorably in 'Billy Lynn's Long Halftime Walk,' a 2012 National Book Award Finalist [and, subsequently, Hollywood film] about a group of soldiers being feted at halftime of a Dallas Cowboys game. The soldiers express dread over people rushing to offer thanks, pregnant with obligation and blood lust and 'their voices throbbing like lovers'" (Richtel, "Please Don't Thank Me for My Service").

32  Sherman, *Afterwar*, 39.

33  Sherman, *Afterwar*, 39, 44, 19.

34  Sherman, *Afterwar*, 1.

35  This trope and/as accusation also appears in Ben Fountain's *Billy Lynn's Long Halftime Walk* (2012).

36  Sherman, *Afterwar*, 1.

37  Sherman, *Afterwar*, 32.

38  Wood, *What Have We Done*, 260.

39  Boudreau, "The Morally Injured," 55.

40  Wood, *What Have We Done*, 264, 265 (my emphasis).

41  Sherman, *Afterwar*, 3. Elizabeth Samet is not quite as sure that the distinction can be maintained: "There are contradictions inherent in being, as many Americans claim to be, for the troops but against the war," although she does not elaborate on those contradictions (see Samet, *No Man's Land: Preparing for War and Peace in Post-9/11 America*).

42  Bill Edmonds, "God is Not Here," in *War and Moral Injury:*

*A Reader*, ed. Robert Emmet Meagher and Douglas A. Pryer (Eugene: Cascade Books, 2018), 49-50 (emphasis in original).

43 Wood, *What Have We Done*, 267, 268 (emphasis added).

44 See Brett T. Litz et al., *Adaptive Disclosure: A New Treatment for Military Trauma, Loss, and Moral Injury* (New York: The Guilford Press, 2016).

45 See Laura Werber et al., *Faith-Based Organizations and Veteran Reintegration: Enriching the Web of Support* (RAND Corporation, 2015).

46 Zoë Wool, *After War,* 192. Wool positions herself squarely within that difference: "But, of course, I can only know and write *about* this knowledge, grasping at the periphery of its experiential core. I cannot *have* this knowledge or live *in* it. That I live an ordinary life, as much as anyone can, puts me in a distant relationship to the extra/ordinary lives and pain of the soldiers I worked with." Surely, we can never actually "live in" *anyone else's* experiences; her compulsion to make that explicit vis-à-vis the lives of soldiers echoes the grammar of American militarism I trace in this book. As Wool notes in the book's final paragraph, she hopes that one of "the more specific implications of" her "exploration" is that "it is only through a particularly privileged position of civilian safety that we are able to make claims about the appropriateness or veracity of soldiers' knowledge about the world" (193–4, emphasis in original).

47 Roy Scranton, "The Trauma Hero: From Wilfred Owen to 'Redeployment' and 'American Sniper.'" *Los Angeles Review of Books*, January 15, 2015.

48 Yuval Noah Harari, *The Ultimate Experience: Battlefield Revelations and the Making of Modern War Culture, 1450–2000* (New York: Palgrave Macmillan, 2008), 1, 299, 20.

49 Harari, *The Ultimate Experience*, 7, 231.

50 Harari, *The Ultimate Experience*, 7 (emphasis in original).

51 Even though the specifics of the war experience are often spoken of as beyond comprehension for those who have not gone to war, there is a second, paradoxical foundation on which many who lead workshops on combat trauma ground the possibility for empathy: that we all have some experience of trauma in our lives. In the words of this particular workshop leader, "Now I've never been in the military, and I've never been in combat, so superficially you would think my life experience hasn't really provided me with a lot of basis for being able to have a conversation with veterans about their traumatic or moral injury experiences. But as I'm sure you all know in your own lives and in your own

work, the thing that makes it possible for me to do this with any kind of credibility and empathy is the fact that trauma touches everybody in one way or another."

52  Joan W. Scott, "The Evidence of Experience," *Critical Inquiry* 17: 4, 1991, 776, 777, 778.

53  Walter Benn Michaels, "'You Who Never Was There': Slavery and the New Historicism, Deconstruction and the Holocaust," *Narrative* 4: 1, 1996.

54  In addition to Harari, see Patrick Hagopian, *The Vietnam War in American Memory: Veterans, Memorials, and the Politics of Healing* (Amherst: University of Massachusetts Press, 2009), and Paul Fussell, *The Great War and Modern Memory*. New York, NY: Oxford University Press, (1997) 2013. See also Roy Scranton, *Total Mobilization: World War II and American Literature*. Chicago, IL: University of Chicago Press, 2019.

55  Didier Fassin and Richard Rechtman, *The Empire of Trauma: An Inquiry Into the Condition of Victimhood,* trans. Rachel Gomme (Princeton, NJ: Princeton University Press, 2009).

56  See Didier Fassin, *Humanitarian Reason: A Moral History of the Present,* trans. Rachel Gomme (Berkeley: University of California Press, 2012).

57  See Didier Fassin and Richard Rechtman, *The Empire of Trauma*; Fassin, *Humanitarian Reason*; Miriam I. Ticktin, *Casualties of Care: Immigration and the Politics of Humanitarianism in France* (Berkeley: University of California Press, 2011).

58  Catherine Lutz, "The Wars Less Known," *The South Atlantic Quarterly,* 101: 2, 2002, 286.

59  Wood, *What Have We Done*, 63.

60  To take but the most obvious example, in November 2001, the Taliban offered to surrender to the US military if the United States would grant them amnesty. "The United States is not inclined to negotiate surrenders," said Secretary of Defense Donald H. Rumsfeld during a news conference at the time. (Alissa J. Rubin, "Did the War in Afghanistan Have to Happen?" *New York Times,* August 23, 2021.) Twenty years hence, the US was forced into its own unconditional surrender and to hand the country back over to the Taliban. As for profits made by defense contractors, see William D. Hartung, "Profits of War: Corporate Beneficiaries of the Post 9/11 Pentagon Spending Surge" The Watson Institute for International and Public Affairs at Brown University, September 13, 2021.

61  Wood, *What Have We Done*, 149–50.

62  I was cautioned by one clinical psychologist at the VA not to

assume everyone is harmed by the act of killing; that is a "civilian" misconception, he told me. Many take pleasure in the kill.

63  Hannah Arendt, *Responsibility and Judgment* (New York: Schocken Books, 2003), 59.

64  Zerilli, *A Democratic Theory of Judgment*, 1. See Hannah Arendt, *The Human Condition* (Chicago: University of Chicago Press, [1958] 1998).

65  She argued that even though the torture that went on at Abu Ghraib was sanctioned by those up the chain of command, the only people who were punished were those of enlisted ranks.

66  Wood, *What Have We Done*, 35, 113, 78–9.

67  Roy Scranton, "Choosing War," *Dissent* 63: 1, 2016, 151.

68  See Chapter 1.

69  Anti-war organizations do exist, but they have never had the size or reach of their Vietnam War–era counterparts. See ivaw.org; aboutfaceveterans.org. Moreover, as mentioned by a participant in the Theater of War discussion at Columbia University discussed in Chapter 5, in contrast to the war in Vietnam, there has been no remarkable dissent or resistance within the ranks of active-duty troops. Common Defense is a veteran organization launched more recently, in opposition to Trump, that is devoted to ending the Forever War and challenging American militarism, and it is a growing voice in the progressive wing of the Democratic Party; see commondefense.us. Nevertheless, this organization emerged rather late in the game and does not match—or even aspire to match—the public and often quite radical oppositional politics in which anti-war Vietnam veterans engaged.

70  "Poll Finds Strong Support for Bush in US Military," *New York Times*, October 16, 2004; Jeffrey M. Jones, "Veterans and the 2008 Election," August 23, 2007, news.gallup.com; Jeffrey M. Jones, "Veterans Solidly Back McCain," August 19, 2008, news.gallup.com.

71  As Wood himself writes, "By 2006, the year Stephen Canty was itching to join the marines, fighting in Iraq had increased in intensity and savagery." Most Americans "back home" had turned against the war, and yet he was "itching" to go (Wood, *What Have We Done*, 78).

72  See also Patrick Hagopian, *The Vietnam War in American Memory*.

73  Bacevich, *The New American Militarism*.

74  Sherman, *Afterwar*, 3 (emphasis added).

75  Scranton, "Choosing War," 154–5.

76  A member of an audience responded when I spoke of the American ritual of thanking the troops, by saying that as an Italian

he finds it shocking. It would be considered fascist in an Italian context.

77  Wendy Brown, *States of Injury: Power and Freedom in Late Modernity* (Princeton, NJ: Princeton University Press, 1995), 96.

78  Brown, *States of Injury*, 70, 75.

79  Sherman, *Afterwar*, 49 (my emphasis).

80  "The Germans saw themselves absolutely as victims, since, after all, they had been compelled to survive not only the winter battles of Leningrad and Stalingrad, not only the bombardments of their cities, not only the judgment of Nuremberg, but also the dismemberment of their country"; see Jean Améry, *At the Mind's Limits,* trans. Sidney and Stella Rosenfeld (Bloomington: Indiana University Press, [1964] 1980), 66.

81  Améry, *At the Mind's Limits*, 77.

82  J.M. Bernstein, *Torture and Dignity: An Essay on Moral Injury* (Chicago: University of Chicago Press, 2015), 76 (my emphasis). In writing about moral injury, Bernstein draws not from the discourse about trauma and war that I have been mapping, but from an essay by Jean Hampton that rereads Kantian ethics through the concept of moral injury to explore the harm of rape (see Bernstein, *Torture and Dignity*).

83  Scranton, "Choosing War," 152.

84  Bernstein, *Torture and Dignity*, 4.

85  Boudreau, "The Morally Injured," 56.

86  In his recent book, *Humane. How the United States Abandoned Peace and Reinvented War,* Samuel Moyn argues that focusing on the *conduct* of war has allowed fundamental questions about the post 9/11 wars to be set aside. The desire to make war more "humane" enables endless war, he writes. Rather than asking questions about whether or not the wars are legitimate, and what they are/were *for,* military lawyers and human rights organizations alike parse and argue about, the proper conduct of warfare according to international law, thereby sidelining fundamental *political* questions about the legitimacy and even legality (in the case of Iraq, in particular) of the wars themselves. I don't disagree with him. Nevertheless, if one also looks at this question from the perspective of the combat trauma imaginary, it becomes clear that even questions about *how the wars have been fought,* that is, the brutality of the US military, can also be set side. See Samuel Moyn, *Humane. How the United States Abandoned Peace and Reinvented War.* (New York, NY: Farrar, Strauss, Giroux, 2021); for a history of the role of lawyers in war-making, see Craig Jones, *The War Lawyers: The United States, Israel, and*

*Judicial Warfare* (Oxford, UK: Oxford University Press, 2021). For an analysis of the overlap between the work and expertise of human rights groups on the one hand, and militaries on the other, see also Eyal Weizman, *The Least of All Possible Evils: Humanitarian Violence From Arendt to Gaza* (New York: Verso Books, 2011).

87  See, for example, Brianna Keiler, "The Moral Injury of Abandoning Allies," CNN, August 18, 2021. Patricia Kime, "'We've Abandoned the People Who Helped Us': Vets Grapple with Emotions over the Fall of Afghanistan," *Military News*, August 17, 2021. "The Veterans Struggling to Save Afghan Allies," *New Yorker,* August 30, 2021. It is worth noting that veterans were involved in efforts to evacuate those who had helped them on the ground, using personal and institutional ties to evacuate former translators, fixers, and others who worked with them on the ground. That the responsibility for evacuating such allies fell to veterans is itself a source of much criticism and controversy. See Elliot Ackerman, "It Shouldn't Fall to Veterans to Clean Up Biden's Mess," Opinion, Guest Essay, *The New York Times,* 8/28/2021.

88  As of June 2021, according to the Costs of War Project at the Watson Institute at Brown University, "Over 801,000 people have died due to direct war violence, and several times as many indirectly; "the war has produced 37 million war refugees and displaced persons; and, the US is carrying out counterterror missions in 80 countries; see watson.brown.edu/costsofwar/. The Costs of War's tabulation of civilian deaths is an important counterpoint to Samuel Moyn's argument about humane war, that is, that as fewer and fewer civilians are killed in warzones, the easier it is to carry out endless war. While certainly true that civilians are, in general, not slaughtered as randomly as they were in earlier American wars, for example, during the war in Vietnam in which free fire zones were a formal operating procedure, it is also true that *how* one counts civilian deaths resulting from the US invasions and occupations matters immensely. Does one have to be the actual shooter, to return to Rita Brock's words cited in Chapter 5, to have killed someone? What about the "civil war" that the US occupation of Iraq brought about and participated in? The rise of ISIS and its consequences not just for Iraq, but also, for Syria? What about the long-term health consequences of the wars, say, from the fall-out and environmental destruction brought on by the use of uranium depleted weapons or burn pits? Not to include such deaths (and future deaths) when discussing

the reduction in harm that is "humane" war is to remain entirely inside the epistemic project of American militarism and war. The disappearing of those effects are crucial to maintaining the image of "humane" warfare, after all. (For a very different critique of "humane" war and the myriad forms of violence that have characterized US warfare, see Omar Dewachi," Blurred Lines: Warfare and Health Care," *MAT. Medicine, Anthropology, Theory*, 2:2, 2015.)

89  Cavell, *Must We Mean What We Say?*

90  Scranton, "Choosing War," 152.

91  Arendt, *Responsibility and Judgment*, 154.

92  Arendt, *Responsibility and Judgment*, 97, 67.

93  I am mapping here the grammar of a prevalent and powerful discourse, but I do not mean to imply there are no exceptions (see, for example, footnote 86). What's more, the US military does pay reparations, on occasion, to individuals/family members of those they deem to have wrongly injured or killed. The final drone strike in Kabul upon the US withdrawal of its troops is the most recent example of killing an innocent man and members of his family and offering monetary compensation in response (see Eric Schmitt, "A Botched Drone Strike in Kabul Started with the Wrong Car," *New York Times*, September 21, 2021). That genre of monetary compensation, however rare it is, is fundamentally distinct from *political* reparations: It is based on an understanding of a particular lethal strike having been an error of information or judgment, not a matter of taking responsibility for the war itself and for the damage and destruction it has, of design and necessity, inflicted on entire populations.

94  Note that Wood's description makes the common move of drawing an implicit moral equivalence between US military personnel, on the one hand, and Iraqi and Afghan *civilians* on the other. This is crucial to maintaining the virtue of the American soldier in contrast to combatants on the other side.

95  Adi Ophir, *The Order of Evils: Toward an Ontology of Morals* (New York: Zone Books, 2005), 26.

96  Arendt insists on the distinction between "guilt" and "responsibility." She argues that one can be responsible for things one has not done but that "there is no such thing as being or feeling guilty for things that happened without oneself actively participating in them." "Guilt, unlike responsibility, always singles out; it is strictly personal. It refers to an act, not to intentions or potentialities"; "'We are all guilty' is actually a declaration of solidarity with the wrongdoers" (*Responsibility and Judgment*, 147–8).

97  Arendt, *Responsibility and Judgment*, 149.

98  Arendt, *Responsibility and Judgment*, 158–9.

99  Arendt, *Responsibility and Judgment*, 146.

100  Ticktin, *Casualties of Care*.

101  Arendt, *The Human Condition*.

102  Wood, *What Have We Done*, 272.

103  "Is it Okay to Commemorate One of Iraq's Bloodiest Battles in a Video Game?" *All Things Considered*, National Public Radio, June 23, 2021. The story then devolves into a description of a video game—*Six Days in Fallujah*—designed and intended to teach the American public about the battle of Fallujah, on the basis of interviews with Marines who fought the battles, and part of the game is to be played from the perspective of an Iraqi family trying to escape the city. Needless to say, the idea of a video game as a lesson in the complexity of war is rather controversial. As one woman who lost her son in Iraq said, "Ken never got the chance to put another quarter in and play another game." The organization Muslim Advocates responded that "it's entertainment made from a battle where Americans killed many Iraqi civilians"; "it's simply irredeemable." Ackerman, for his part, has no problem with it: "one of the huge problems we have right now is that so many Americans are just totally disconnected from our wars and our military." He continued, "so if you can get people paying attention and engaging with the subject matter through a video game, great. Like, I'm all for it."

104  Richtel, "Please Don't Thank Me for My Service."

105  Judith Butler, *Frames of War: When is Life Grievable?* (New York: Verso, 2009).

106  Viet Thanh Nguyen, "I Can't Forget the Lessons of Vietnam. Neither Should You." Opinion, *New York Times*, August 19, 2021.

107  Quoted in Richtel, "Please Don't Thank Me for My Service."

## Epilogue

1  See, for example, James Gordon Meek, "US Special Operations Vets Carry Out Daring Mission to Save Afghan Allies," ABC News, August 21, 2021; Amy McKinnon, "A 'Digital Dunkirk' to Evacuate Afghan Allies," *Foreign Policy*, August 20, 2021; Donovan Slack, "Veterans Wanted out of Afghanistan, but sudden collapse brings mental health to light," *USA Today*, August 17, 2021; Jaweed Kaleem & Kurtis Lee, "For Many U.S.

Veterans, the fall of Afghanistan to the Taliban stirs confusion, disappointment, and anger," *The Los Angeles Times,* August 14, 2021; Kristen Fontenrose, "PTSD Is an endless war for Veterans. The news from Afghanistan is making it Worse," *The Atlantic Council,* August 25, 2021; Brianna Keilar, "The Moral Injury of Abandoning Afghan Allies," CNN, August 18, 2021; Chuck Goudie, Barb Markoff, et. al., "Afghan Exit leaves behind hurting families, angry vets, pointed questions," ABC7, Chicago, August 31, 2021. See also, Chakrabarti and Annie Sinsabaugh, "Operation North Star: The Military Veterans Working to Protect Afghan Allies from the Taliban," *On Point,* WBUR, January 31, 2022.

2    "Read the Full Transcript of President Biden's Remarks on Afghanistan," *The New York Times,* August 16, 2021.

3    "Read the Full Transcript of President Biden's Remarks on Afghanistan."

4    Ellen Knickmeyer, "Costs of the Afghanistan war, in lives and dollars," AP News, August 17, 2021.

5    See "Human Cost," at Costs of War, watson.brown.edu/costsofwar/figures.

6    "Read the Full Transcript of President Biden's Remarks on Afghanistan."

7    Matthieu Aikins, Sharif Hassan, Thomas Gibbons-Neff, Eric Schmitt, and Richard Pérez-Pena, "Suicide Bombers in Kabul Kill Dozens, Including 13 Troops," *The New York Times,* August 26, 2021.

8    "Times Investigation: In U.S. Drone Strike, Evidence Suggests no ISIS Bomb," *The New York Times,* September 10, 2021 (updated, January 5, 2022).

9    Sophie Reardon, "Afghanistan drone strike the Pentagon previously described as 'righteous' killed as many as 10 civilians, officials say," CBS News, September 17, 2021.

10   Azmat Khan, "Hidden Pentagon Papers Reveal Patterns of Failure in Deadly Airstrikes," The Civilian Casualty Files, *The New York Times*, December 18, 2021.

11   Craig Whitlock and the Washington Post, *The Afghanistan Papers. A Secret History of the War.* New York, NY: Simon and Schuster, 2021.

12   Craig Whitlock and the Washington Post, *The Afghanistan Papers,* 6.

13   Craig Whitlock and the Washington Post, *The Afghanistan Papers,* 6, 8.

14   Phil Klay, "American Purpose after the Fall of Kabul," *The New Yorker,* August 25, 2021.

15 The law (Public Law 107-40), effectively became a blank check for the president after president in authorizing "anti-terror" operations anywhere around the globe. It declares: "That the President is authorized to use all necessary and appropriate force against those nations, organizations, or persons he determines planned, authorized, committed, or aided the terrorist attacks that occurred on September 11, 2001, or harbored such organizations or persons, in order to prevent any future acts of international terrorism against the United States by such nations, organizations or persons." On the repeal, see H.R.1274, 116th Congress.

16 Patrick J. McDonnel, "U.S. military veterans answer Zelensky's call to fight, but not all are chosen," *The Los Angeles Times,* March 31, 2022; Matt Gallagher, "My Advice to Veterans who want to get on a plane to Ukraine," *The New York Times,* April 10, 2022; Mac William Bishop, "U.S. Veterans start a 'Resistance Academy' in Ukraine. Will it Backfire?" *Rolling Stone*, March 12, 2022.

17 Julia Ainsley and Alexandra Bacallao, "Biden announced 'streamlined' program to bring Ukrainian refugees to the U.S.," NBC News, April 21, 2022.

18 Francis Fukuyama, *The End of History and the Last Man.* (New York, NY: Simon and Schuster, 2006).

19 This war is, of course, extremely lucrative for the American arms industry. See William T. Hartung and Julia Gledhill, "The Pentagon is Cashing in on the Ukraine Crisis," *The Nation*, April 19, 2022.

20 See, for example, Jennifer Steinhauer, "Veterans Struggle with issues that are often invisible to others," *The New York Times,* September 7, 2021; Stephanie O'Neil, "More veterans who struggle with PTSD will soon get help from service dogs. Thank the 'Paws' Act," *National Public Radio,* November 26, 2021; Dave Phillips, "The Unseen Scars of Those who kill via Remote Control," *The New York Times,* April 15, 2022.

# Index

Index

as a growth experience, 293n71
humane war, 319–20n88
*jus ad bellum*, 254
*jus in bello*, 180, 190
*jus post bellum*, 201, 245,
    308n90
Just War Doctrine, 186, 201
as ordinary job, 164
preventive war, doctrine of, 20
specifics of the experience,
    315–6n51
stories of, 201–12
trauma of, 81, 216–21
war, imperial, 8, 10, 15–9, 43,
    53–4, 97, 125, 200
warfare, remote forms of,
    266–7n54
War on Drugs, 87
War on Poverty, 84
War on Terror, 7–8, 20, 21, 215,
    241, 288n16
warrior code, 186
Warrior Writers, 201–2
war zones
    civilians in, 189
    reactions to stressors in, 141
    traumatic injuries in, 190
Weil, Simone, 210–2
Weizman, Eyal, 266n50

Wellfleet Psychohistory Group, 53
Werber, Laura, 194
*What Have We Done: The Moral
    Injury of Our Longest Wars*
    (Wood), 198, 218, 226, 244
White House Office of Faith-Based
    and Community Initiatives,
    193–4
Whitlock, Craig, 254
Wieviorka, Annette, 27–8
Wilson, John P., 91–2, 97
Winter Soldier Investigation, 55,
    170
Wohlstetter, Albert, 20
Wood, David, 219–20, 222–3,
    227, 229–30, 233–5, 237, 245
    *What Have We Done: The
    Moral Injury of Our Longest
    Wars*, 198, 218, 226, 244
Wool, Zoë, 5, 164, 229, 262–
    3n12, 315n46

yoga, 119–20
Young, Allan, 9, 36, 42, 64, 89,
    241, 284–5n71
Young, Marlene, 83

Žižek, Slavoj, 169

337